P9-CCU-394

Praise for
WILL *Write* FOR *Food*

"*Will Write for Food* is a concise, illustrative and eminently useful guide to
the nuts and bolts of professional food writing. Dianne Jacob gets right to the
heart of what it takes not just to write—but to write well—about food.
And she's managed to wrangle a remarkable group of veterans to share
their experiences and examples."
—Anthony Bourdain, author of the
New York Times bestseller *Kitchen Confidential*

"Considering today's food-writing labyrinth, *Will Write for Food* leads writers to
success, step by step. It's a must on my can't-do-without bookshelf and a
resource I always recommend to food writers."
—Antonia Allegra, Director of the Symposium for Professional Food Writers
at The Greenbrier, and Food Writing Coach

"Dianne has saved me so much trouble about what to tell would-be food writers
who might someday have my job: Buy Dianne's book!"
—Nancy Leson, *Seattle Times* food and restaurant writer

"Required reading for everyone interested in learning how to translate their
passion for food into words. Dianne Jacob offers up a smorgasbord of practical
advice for anyone who has ever aspired to write about food, and she shows how
to make writing a tasty and lucrative pastime."
—Darra Goldstein, Editor-in-Chief,
Gastronomica: The Journal of Food and Culture

"You'll find everything you need to know about becoming a food writer in this
indispensable information-packed book. And if you're already a food writer, this
book will help you become a better one. Dianne Jacob takes you by the hand
through every step of the process from hatching an idea to getting published.
Useful writing exercises concluding each chapter help sharpen your skills.
Dozens of quotes from successful food writers tell how they got started and
what their working lives are really like. If food writing is your passion,
then grab a copy of *Will Write for Food* and get busy!"
—Greg Patent, author of *Baking in America*

"*Will Write for Food* is a great gift, not just for those who are new to food writing, but for those already ensconced in the business. Dianne's clarity, kind suggestions, and nudges and admonitions to work well are truly inspiring."
—Deborah Madison, author of
Vegetarian Cooking for Everyone

"Dianne Jacob has done a masterful job in this book of amassing everything a fledgling food writer needs to know. Whether one yearns to review restaurants for a local newspaper or turn a passion for food into magazine articles, or even a cookbook, *Will Write for Food* offers invaluable practical advice along every step of the way."
—Fran Gage, author of *Bread and Chocolate*

"This book does a great job of covering the nuts and bolts of food writing, for sure, but Jacob delivers much more than the usual advice: She shoots straight about the realities of the business, provides loads of insider insights and practical exercises, and radiates enough genuine enthusiasm to get both beginning writers and seasoned pros up and at 'em."
—Martha Holmberg, former publisher, *Fine Cooking* magazine

"Dianne Jacob has presented budding food writers with a clear blueprint on how to get started in the business."
—Michael Bauer, Executive Food and Wine Editor, *San Francisco Chronicle*

"My only complaint about *Will Write for Food*—and it's a big one— is that it wasn't around when I started my career. If you're serious about becoming a food writer, save yourself years of banging your head against the wall in frustration and run to the checkout with this book now."
—David Leite, food writer, and publisher
and editor of *Leite's Culinaria*

"In *Will Write for Food*, Dianne Jacob combines all the right ingredients for a delectable read."
—Joanne Fluke, author of the Hannah Swensen Mysteries series

WILL

Write

FOR *Food*

The Complete Guide to Writing
Cookbooks, Blogs, Reviews,
Memoir, and More

Dianne Jacob

Da Capo
∞
LIFE
LONG

A MEMBER OF THE PERSEUS BOOKS GROUP

Many of the designations used by manufacturers and sellers to distinguish their products are claimed as trademarks. Where those designations appear in this book and Da Capo Press was aware of a trademark claim, the designations have been printed in initial capital letters.

Copyright © 2005, 2010 by Dianne Jacob

All rights reserved. No part of this publication may be reproduced, stored in a retrieval system, or transmitted, in any form or by any means, electronic, mechanical, photocopying, recording, or otherwise, without the prior written permission of the publisher. Printed in the United States of America. For information, address Da Capo Press, 11 Cambridge Center, Cambridge, MA 02142.

Set in 10.5 point Caslon by the Perseus Books Group

Library of Congress Cataloging-in-Publication Data

Jacob, Dianne, 1955–
  Will write for food : the complete guide to writing cookbooks, blogs, reviews, memoir, and more / by Dianne Jacob. — 2nd ed.
    p. cm.
  First published: New York : Marlowe and Co, c2005.
  Includes bibliographical references and index.
  ISBN 978-0-7382-1404-7 (alk. paper)
  1. Food writing. I. Title.
  TX644.J33 2010
  808'.066641—dc22

                                                2010014224

Published by Da Capo Press
A member of the Perseus Books Group
www.dacapopress.com

Da Capo Press books are available at special discounts for bulk purchases in the U.S. by corporations, institutions, and other organizations. For more information, please contact the Special Markets Department at the Perseus Books Group, 2300 Chestnut Street, Suite 200, Philadelphia, PA, 19103, or call (800) 810-4145, extension 5000, or e-mail special.markets@perseusbooks.com.

10 9 8 7 6 5 4 3

*To my parents, who taught me to appreciate food
as a vehicle for memory and identity; and who loved
a good story, whether they told it themselves or read it*

Contents

Contents

WILL

Write

FOR *Food*

Foreword
by David Lebovitz

The pleasure of sitting down to a good meal is not limited to just eating what's set in front of you. It can also be about the sensations or memories associated with it. Perhaps it's sitting at a linen-topped table, gnawing on a delicate morsel of stuffed quail while sipping a glass of crisp, clear Sancerre, or standing in a dusty parking lot, slugging down a beer, waiting your turn in front of a taco truck, watching the steaming clouds wafting off the carne asada. Or perhaps you're charring a steak over a glowing fire with your best friends after a long day on the beach, or mixing up a darkly rich chocolate batter by yourself in the kitchen, pouring it into a well-buttered mold, then licking the beaters clean (when no one is looking, of course) before you pop the cake in the oven.

Maybe it's flying over an ocean just to slurp down a boiling bowl of handmade noodles while you're squeezed on a firm wooden bench between fixated Japanese businessmen, or you find yourself miserably lost in a train station in rural France, but you've found consolation littering the station floor with irregular flakes from the warm pain au chocolat your nose detected that the baker next door was just taking out of the oven. Or perhaps you watched the scruffy pizza maker in Naples effortlessly toss and spin his dough into near-perfect circles for your pizza while checking out the near-perfect backsides of a group of Swedish tourists.

Food writing is one of the richest, most evocative forms of writing. From recounts of butter-soaked meals in Paris to a dinner of crickets (hopefully not still chirping) in Oaxaca, everything we put in our mouths evokes a response and an emotion. And for many of us, we feel compelled to share these experiences by writing about them. Good food writers are able to recount those meals and feelings not necessarily with precision and perfect prose, but to draw the reader in and make them feel as though they were sitting at the table—or standing at the kitchen counter—right alongside us.

Traditionally, food writing was the provenance of glossy magazines and newspapers, which will always be valuable and trusted resources for restaurant reviews and travel pieces. But as the online world has expanded, the line has blurred between professional and non-professional, and literally hundreds of thousands of people with nothing but a keyboard and a screen have become food writers. Within a short amount of time, anyone, anywhere in the world, can sit down in front of a computer or touchpad, write a story or a recipe, and quickly have it reach literally millions of people. Some of these writers get snapped up by the print media and others prefer to keep writing for their own domains. And although there were initially plenty of pessimists, the success stories have surprised even hard-core naysayers who felt that restaurant criticism was only for those with years of writing experience, and recipe writing was only the domain of chefs and cookbook authors. There's no doubt about it, food writing has changed quite a bit since the first edition of *Will Write for Food* was published in 2005.

When this book was first released, I couldn't be happier to find that Dianne Jacob, a seasoned editor, had compiled all the information anyone might need to know who wants to explore a career writing about food, in one informative book. Interviews with top food writers and chefs made the book especially helpful, and it was refreshing to find subjects that are often not discussed, such as *How much can I make writing about food?* and *How do I find an agent or editor to publish my book?* or *Should I write for free?* openly written about with candor. And more importantly, Dianne provided checklists for beginning food writers on how to make it happen.

With this updated edition, Dianne added interviews with prolific food bloggers, and digs deep beyond the cliché of people writing about "What I had for dinner last night" to learning how successful and popular food bloggers have been able to grab readers, and more importantly, keep them coming back for more. And earn a living from doing so. She answers questions about ethics and monetization honestly. Those who've never written a restaurant review or been faced with getting products for review will certainly benefit from her tips on when it's okay to accept, and when it's better to decline.

When Dianne asked me to write the foreword to this updated edition of this book, midway through, the irony of the situation hit me: When *Will Write for Food* was originally published, I immediately bought a copy, learning all I could to embark on my own writing career as I transitioned completely from chef to cookbook author and blogger. And her advice worked, because within a few years after I read it (and re-read it), I expanded my repertoire from writing cookbooks, to authoring a memoir, and starting a blog that's now read around the world.

While I should say no one was more surprised than me, in retrospect, I mostly followed Dianne's advice in this book, which gave me the knowledge and courage necessary to push my own career to the next level. And following her wisdom and advice, I hope aspiring writers will find it as much of an invaluable resource as I did.

—David Lebovitz, author of *The Sweet Life in Paris* and *Ready for Dessert*; www.davidlebovitz.com

Introduction

Wabhen I began teaching classes on food writing, I wanted to recommend a book to help students. Not finding one, I decided to write it myself, packing it with sound guidance and wisdom from experts on all kinds of food writing, from memoir to blogging to cookbooks.

Within these pages I'd like to be your friendly guide, encouraging you with practical and realistic advice no matter what stage of development you're at:

- If you hope to support yourself full-time, you're in for a challenge, but some people do it, and you'll learn how.
- If you are already a food writer, this book builds on your skills and shows you how to branch out to other types of food writing.
- If you'd like to blog as a hobby or write articles for fun, you're in good shape. "A day job and a rich husband helps," one agent advised me. You'll find plenty of useful advice about honing your writing skills and how to approach editors.
- If you want to self-publish, you'll find detailed information about how to write recipes and advice on self-publishing.

If you come to this book without any desire to be published, but with curiosity about how to express your passion for food, this book will answer questions you've always wanted to ask, and will provide the tools to move you forward. At the very least, it will help you appreciate the effort that goes into writing, selling, and publishing food writing.

Will Write for Food takes you inside the heads of some of America's most powerful food writers, bloggers, editors, and agents. Their wisdom, recommendations, and experiences appear in every chapter, along with stories of how successful food writers broke into the business. I've also packed the book with nitty-gritty tools, resources, and exercises designed to enrich your knowledge and skill level. Understanding the process behind food writing, the characteristics of those who succeed, and which tools are necessary will help lessen any anxieties you're bound to endure.

My own adventure with food writing began after graduating from journalism school, when I became the editor of a city restaurant magazine, writing features about restaurants in Vancouver, Canada. Later in my career in California, I became a full-time magazine editor and freelance food writer, writing restaurant and cookbook reviews, recipe columns, cover stories, profiles, feature articles, advice-based essays, and opinion pieces for magazines and websites. In 2008 I co-authored the cookbook *Grilled Pizzas & Piadinas* with Chicago chef Craig Priebe. In 2009 I started a blog on food writing, also called Will Write for Food, at www.diannej.com/blog. My career as an editor and writer for newspapers, magazines, books, and Web sites has spanned more than thirty years, giving me a valuable well of experience from which to draw.

For more than a dozen years I've coached writers in the US, Canada, and Europe on how to freelance or get a book published. I've edited manuscripts for both individuals and book publishers, and I've judged cookbook awards for both the James Beard Foundation and the International Association of Culinary Professionals (IACP).

Teaching is a particular passion. I teach food-writing workshops for the Writing Salon in San Francisco and Berkeley; for Book Passage in Corte Madera, California; and online for Leite's Culinaria. I have also taught at the Smithsonian and at the University of California Extension in Los Angeles and the Silicon Valley. I've been a guest speaker at many conferences, including the International Association of Culinary Professionals, BlogHer Food, and the Food Blogger Camp at Club Med.

The material in this book comes from my own experience, my research, and from interviews with established food writers, editors, and agents. Almost every quote in this book was the result of a personal interview. Occasionally I quote from previously published material, indicated by past tense, such as "said." I've also quoted a few times from speakers at conferences or on a radio program. To help you keep track of who's who, the Appendix in the back lists interviewees.

How to Use This Book

Writing specifically about food, as opposed to writing in general, is the focus of *Will Write for Food*. This is not a basic book on writing. Sections such as memoir and fiction focus on the use of food as a vehicle, and do not address the entire subject of how to write in that form. Many excellent books will give you comprehensive information in those areas. You will find them listed within the chapters.

I prefer that you read the chapters consecutively, but you may also open to any chapter. Each is designed to be as complete in itself as possible, but sometimes you will want information that lurks in other sections. I've provided page numbers to enable you to flip back and forth quickly.

Each chapter ends with writing suggestions designed to put what you have learned to immediate use. The usefulness of any one exercise may not seem apparent, but if you complete at least one in each chapter, you will find new points of entry into your head. You'll uncover new material, open vaults of memory, and access your passion. If you already write, these exercises will expand the way you find and process material and test whether your current skills are still producing satisfactory results.

It's normal to have resistance to writing suggestions and to turn the page. Find it in yourself to examine your reasons not to write. The exercises are short, fun, and not very time consuming. The goal is to write, so why not get started? I hope that's why you bought this book in the first place. Trust yourself.

Food writing is a tough field with fierce competition, and it's extremely difficult to make a living at it. I aim not to frighten you to the point of discouragement but to inspire you to act on a lifelong dream or to move forward as a writer. You deserve inside information, resources, and support. It's so much easier than moving forward all alone.

Don't stop with my book. Find others who will guide you by joining industry groups or volunteering. And most importantly, make time every day to write. Don't give up. Persistence is half the battle. Besides, you need written work to show the editors who are actively looking for you. Give them something to read.

Please let me know if this book has helped you. Write to me at dj@diannej.com, or comment on my blog, Will Write for Food, at www.diannej.com/blog. I look forward to hearing from you.

1

What, Exactly, is Food Writing?

A recipe for fettuccine with prosciutto, cream, and nutmeg. The history of tea. A blog post about eating in Chinatown. Where to get the best deli sandwiches. A guide to sustainable cooking. Food writing wanders over dozens of subjects; the storytellers and their craft are what bring it together. Hundreds of people publish books and articles on food, some writing for the first time. One of them could be you. It's easier to choose what to write about if you understand why you want to write about food in the first place. Says freelancer David Leite, "People get this warm glow when they say, 'I want to become a food writer.' It becomes this romanticized overarching career." What's your reason to write about food?

- You'd like to tell your life story and pass down recipes to family members.
- You're a caterer, chef, or restaurateur whose customers have asked for recipes.
- You're fascinated by the history of a certain food and want to research it.
- You want to write a cookbook based on expertise you've developed.

- You can't find a cookbook that deals with your child's allergies, and you know other parents could use one.
- You want to capture the cuisine of a country and people you love.

Whatever motivates you, food writing has a requirement that makes it irresistible: you like food, and you get to eat and write about it. What's better than that?

If you have the desire, perseverance, and writing skills, you can join the ranks. This book shows you how. It explores food writing in all its sensuous and practical glory, with insights from the best writers in the business, practical information on how to succeed, and most of all, what tools you need to pursue your passion.

Today is a great time to be a food writer, full of opportunities. While at its most basic, food writing covers recipes and restaurant reviews, just about any topic and form can be about food, including:

- blogging
- essays and memoir
- fiction writing
- historical analysis
- political writing
- reporting and news stories
- travel writing
- science writing

This first chapter explores writing in blogs, newspapers, magazines, and books as a starting point to define food writing. I asked some of the most creative minds in the field to tell me what good food writing means to them. Is it simply good writing? Or is the most important element that it makes readers hungry, helps them experience pleasure, activates their senses, and evokes images of a certain place and time?

Good Writing Is the Essence

I believe good writing is the main determining factor of good food writing, and I set out to see what others had to say. *Saveur* magazine co-founder Colman Andrews put it bluntly: "If you're not capable of being a good writer, you can't be a good food writer. It's about clarity of expression, style, voice, accuracy, knowledge of structure and rhythm of language. The idea that food writing is a separate discipline is false."

Ruth Reichl, former editor of *Gourmet* magazine and author of several memoirs, is even more adamant. She told me the term "food writer" is pejorative, like "woman writer." She's a writer, she says. That's it.

I'm a big admirer of author Calvin Trillin, who has written about food for decades in the *New Yorker* magazine. He adamantly refuses to describe his work as food writing. He calls it "writing about eating," and doesn't distinguish it from any other nonfiction. He insists he is not a cook, has no culinary knowledge, and does not rate food. "It's probably fair to call me an amateur," he cracks.

To further make his case, Trillin told me he does not describe food in anything he writes. I found it hard to believe. How could someone write about food without adjectives? I dashed to my bookshelf and reviewed several of his essays. Here's the furthest he will go, from his 1974 book, *American Fried: Adventures of a Happy Eater:* "Being in a traveling trade myself, I know the problem of asking someone in a strange city for the best restaurant in town and being led to some purple palace that serves 'Continental cuisine' and has as its chief creative employee a menu-writer rather than a chef. I have sat in those places, an innocent wayfarer, reading a three-paragraph description of what the trout is wrapped in, how long it has been sautéed, what province its sauce comes from, and what it is likely to sound like sizzling on my platter—a description lacking only the information that before the poor beast went through that process it had been frozen for eight and a half months."

For Trillin, the most important part of the craft is "careful writing, making sure every word is the right word." He says he learned from A. J. Liebling, a *New Yorker* writer and author of *Between Meals: An Appetite for Paris,* an acclaimed 1959 account of eating well in Paris.

Well then, if you're a writer whose subject is food, what constitutes that form? David Leite of Leite's Culinaria (www.leitesculinaria .com) explains: "While the best food writing is evocative, has an unmistakable voice and an immutable sense of place, it does all the things good writing can do. Some people can write about changing motor oil with as much sensuality as eating a peach. It's how you use the language, how you communicate."

"Food writing is a wonderful, weird passion," adds blogger Shauna James Ahern of Gluten-Free Girl and the Chef, (http://glutenfree girl.blog spot.com). "You can drop artifice and pretensions and just start to write about what you love, even if it's what you had for breakfast. If you have a strong, distinctive voice and you've honed it well, readers will feel like they know you. You know you've succeeded when people will want to meet you."

As in other fine writing, there's lots of room for creativity, say two award-winning freelancers. *Vogue* magazine columnist and author Jeffrey Steingarten says his work takes the form of "flashbacks and flash forwards." *GQ* magazine columnist and contributing editor Alan Richman says food writing provides more opportunity for free expression than most other forms of journalism. "When it's a review or critique of food, the experience is subjective, so you can say whatever you want. You can be mean, funny, or profound," he explains. "When it's a piece about a head of lettuce or a new shop or a restaurant opening, you're writing about a subject that's been covered thousands of times, and you have the opportunity to seek out a new angle. The repetitive nature of food writing should encourage creativity, not stifle it."

What All Food Writing Has in Common

Some say there's something specific about food writing, that it must, at minimum, stimulate the senses and make you hungry. "You get to make a primal appeal to an appetite that is neither intellectual nor social. It's the 'amphibian brain,'" says freelance writer and author Molly O'Neill. "Writers need to leverage the seduction of the senses in a clever, controlled, highly conscious way." Antonia Allegra, founder of the Symposium for Professional Food Writers at the Greenbrier, in West Virginia, says food writing spurs her to action. "It's writing that makes me want to either taste, cook, or look at food. It drives me food crazy and gets all those senses going."

Some believe food writing is all about consumption. "The primary requisite for writing well about food is a good appetite," writes A. J. Liebling. "Without this, it is impossible to accumulate, within the allotted span, enough experience of eating to have anything worth setting down. Each day brings only two opportunities for fieldwork, and they are not to be wasted minimizing the intake of cholesterol."

And then there's the factor of overall pleasure and enjoyment. Says Darra Goldstein, editor of *Gastronomica,* "Some food writing is almost utopian. Communicating pleasure and enjoyment is a part of that."

Food writing often evokes a place or memory, or the immediacy of a moment. Judith Jones, a vice president and senior editor at Knopf who has edited such legends as Julia Child and James Beard, says food writing "describes taste, textures, flavors, and smells, and gives a food experience a larger context by writing about a more common experience, drawing on something universal that speaks to everyone." She points to an essay by M. F. K. Fisher, whom she also edited, titled "P is for Peas," where the author and her family pick peas in the vineyards of Switzerland. Here's a sentence:

> I dashed up and down the steep terraces with the baskets, and my mother would groan and then hum happily when another one appeared, and below I could hear my father and our friends cursing just as happily at their wry backs and their aching thighs, while the peas came off their stems and into the baskets with a small sound audible in that still high air, so many hundred feet above the distant and completely silent Leman.

Yes, this is food writing, because peas are the subject. But there's so much more: a scene, a terrain, ambiance, and relationships, all vividly drawn. You are there with her on the hillside, watching the scene.

James Villas, another classic food writer, excels at capturing the moment. Here's the opening line of his essay titled "The Unsung Sardine," from *Villas at Table: A Passion for Food and Drink:* "At the fashionable Brasserie Lipp on the Boulevard St.-Germain in Paris, a svelte young French socialite sits in the front room chatting with her companion, sipping a *vin blanc cassis,* and checking out the crowd. When the black-tie waiter approaches to take orders, she doesn't hesitate. '*Les sardines beurre,*' she directs, '*suivies par la sole meunière.*' Sardines and sautéed sole, simple and uncomplicated, perfect for a light dinner." Villas takes a fly-on-the-wall approach. He puts you in the restaurant with him, gives you a chair at his table, and lets you take in the scene. Many travel-writing pieces use this style to draw readers in.

AN EDITOR WHO CULTIVATES
BRILLIANT FOOD WRITERS

Judith Jones, vice president and senior editor of Knopf, has influenced American culinary culture for decades by publishing gifted food writers, including Julia Child, M. F. K. Fisher, Edna Lewis, and Laurie Colwin. When I asked Jones how she came to work with them, she said modestly, "You follow your instincts, the things that you love. If you feel strongly about a book, the rationalization is that there must be others like you who want it. I thought if I wanted to know that much about food, there were others like me."

Here's more about these writers and how Jones became involved with them:

Julia Child: In 1960, Jones received a manuscript for what would become *Mastering the Art of French Cooking*. "The first choice had been Houghton Mifflin, but when the editor there reviewed the manuscript, her reaction was: Why would any American want to know this much about French cooking?" Jones had recently returned from living in Paris for three-and-a-half years, and had been hired at Knopf as a French editor to deal with translations. She lobbied to become the editor of Child's book and Alfred Knopf gave her a chance. The rest is history.

M. F. K. Fisher: Jones became friends with Fisher over years of mailing her galleys of Knopf books. Fisher was already known, and Jones wanted her to endorse Knopf books. In the 1960s, Jones visited California with her husband Evan, a distinguished food writer in his own right. Fisher invited them to her home in St. Helena for lunch. "It was so hot we ate in the cellar," recalls Jones. Fisher made a "Provençal lunch, cold salads and other things. She owed one more book to her current publisher, then we did a book together." *Among Friends* came first in 1971, followed by *A Considerable Town* in 1978, *Sister Age* in 1983, and *As They Were* in 1982.

W. H. Auden once said he could not think of anyone in the United States who wrote better prose than Fisher, but because she chose food as her subject, her audience was extremely limited. Perhaps, but she is probably America's best-known food writer, with a continuing fan base that enjoys her sensuous, humorous, and beautifully sad voice.

Fisher's most quoted essay is the foreword to *The Gastronomical Me*, which begins: "People ask me: Why do you write about food, and eating and drinking? Why don't you write about the struggle for power and security, and about love, the way others do? . . . The easiest answer is to say that, like most other humans, I am hungry."

"I tell about myself, and how I ate bread on a lasting hillside, or drank red wine in a room now blown to bits, and it happens without my willing it that I am telling too much about the people with me then, and their other deeper needs for love and happiness."

Edna Lewis: In the 1970s, Lewis had a restaurant in New York frequented by the likes of Truman Capote and Tennessee Williams. Jones was intrigued. "I could see right away that she had a story about her whole relationship with food, her family, that she was part of the American experience," Jones remembers. "She had a beautiful way of talking about food. She was an instinctive cook. I said, 'Write your own book, your own experience, and let's do it together.'"

The result was the classic *The Taste of Country Cooking*, published in 1976. You'd never know Lewis owned a New York restaurant. This book goes back to her roots and celebrates how her family prepared and enjoyed American food in a rural Virginia town founded by freed slaves. Dignified and knowledgeable, she expresses her joy of fresh, natural tastes, capturing a simpler time of living off the land, where vegetables came from a garden, meat from a smokehouse, fruit from orchards, and canned jams and condiments from the previous summer.

In her foreword, Lewis explains why she wrote *The Taste of Country Cooking:* "Whenever I go back to visit my sisters and brothers, we relive old times, remembering the past. And when we share again in gathering wild strawberries, canning, rendering lard, finding walnuts, picking persimmons, making fruitcake, I realize how much the bond that held us had to do with food. Since we are the last of the original families, with no children to remember and carry on, I decided that I wanted to write down just exactly how we did things when I was growing up in Freetown that seemed to make life so rewarding."

Laurie Colwin: Primarily a fiction writer whose themes were love and family, Colwin attracted an ardent following by word of mouth. In her novels, her characters are domestic sensualists who like to cook humble but deeply satisfying dishes. She wrote two simple and unpretentious books about cooking and food, *Home Cooking: A Writer in the Kitchen* and *More Home Cooking: A Writer Returns to the Kitchen.* Reading her makes you feel as though she is your favorite bighearted, funny friend, instructing you with love on how to entertain, and confiding about how much it delights her to cook and eat with friends and family.

Jones was a fan. Over lunch with the editor of *Gourmet*, Jones suggested that Laurie Colwin would be a strong new voice for the magazine, writing about food. "I had read all her stories, and they always had food in them, so I said, 'I bet she would be good.'"

Colwin wrote *Home Cooking* and *More Home Cooking* with Jones as her editor. In *Home Cooking*, she writes about her cozy home in New York, where she fed people plain, old-fashioned food such as roast chicken, string beans, lemon cake, and coffee. "One of the delights of life is eating with friends; second to that is talking about eating," starts a passage in *Home Cooking*'s foreword. "And for an unsurpassed double whammy, there is talking about eating while you are eating with friends." Colwin died prematurely of heart failure in 1992. All her books remain in print.

Other award-winning authors Jones has edited are Lidia Bastianich, James Beard, Marion Cunningham, Marcella Hazan, Ken Horn, Madhur Jaffrey, Irene Kuo, Joan Nathan, Claudia Roden, and Nina Simonds.

Writing about the Senses

As you've read in some of the examples I've provided, food writing is often all about the senses: touch, smell, sound, appearance, and taste. Many newcomers to the form focus on how food tastes and skimp on the other senses. When I hand out a list of adjectives (see page 161) to students in my classes, it always thrills them. Seasoned food writers work many senses into a single paragraph, while putting them in context. Here's an erotic passage from Ruth Reichl in *Comfort Me with Apples:* "He kissed me and said, 'Close your eyes and open your mouth.' I sniffed the air; it smelled like a cross between violets and berries, with just a touch of citrus [smell]. My mouth closed around something very small and quite soft [touch], the size of a little grape but with a scratchy surface [appearance]. 'Do you like it?' he asked anxiously. I tasted spring [taste]. 'They're fraises de bois from France!' He slipped another one in my mouth."

Smell is the most important sense, because most of what you taste comes from smelling it first. That's why you can't taste food when you have a cold. Jean-Anthelme Brillat-Savarin, a lawyer and gastronome, figured it out in his 1825 book, *The Physiology of Taste.* "For my part I am not only convinced that without the cooperation of smell there can be no complete degustation, but I am also tempted to believe that smell and taste are in fact but a single sense, whose laboratory is the mouth and whose chimney is the nose; or to be more precise, in which the mouth performs the degustation of tactile bodies, and the nose the degustation of gases." (Brillat-Savarin was the author of the famous comment, "Tell me what you eat and I will tell you what you are.")

Smell can also induce emotions, feelings of nostalgia, and involuntary memories, known as the Proustian Effect. You've probably experienced it when a smell triggers a childhood taste memory, and a wave of emotion hits as hard as a punch to the gut.

Identifying odors and tastes is elusive, and writing about them is just as difficult. Writes Diane Ackerman, in *A Natural History of the Senses,* "Smells coat us, swirl around us, enter our bodies, emanate from us. We live in a constant wash of them. Still, when we try to describe a smell, words fail us like the fabrications they are." Most writers convey a flavor or aroma by using analogy, where something is "like" something else. But it's tricky. "You could say basil tastes a little like mint," proposes Colman Andrews. "What if you've never tasted mint?"

It's easy to get carried away with adjectives when writing about the senses because adjectives are a perfect way to describe them. Too many will weaken writing, making you sound sentimental. Darra Goldstein suggests reading M. F. K. Fisher, who uses "one perfect adjective that somehow manages to encompass a whole range of sensation, or something atmospheric that allows you to understand what the sensation was." She gives this example from a *New Yorker* magazine essay: "It was reward enough to sit in the almost empty room, chaste rococo in the slanting June sunlight, with the generous tub of pure delight between us, Mother purring there, the vodka seeping slyly through our veins, and real wood strawberries to come, to make us feel like children again and not near-gods." Rococo is anything but chaste, says Goldstein. "It's over the top, but Fisher manages to convey the sense of childlike innocence she goes on to describe in the sentence by means of this single adjective."

While taste and smell are critical to food writing, so is touch. Touch informs the reader about the ripeness of a cantaloupe, or how to judge a steak's doneness. Steingarten believes we should monitor other physical sensations as well, such as the sense of locomotion in stirring, where you detect physical changes and sensitivity to temperature as a sauce thickens. Chef and author Anthony Bourdain explores touch in *A Cook's Tour: In Search of the Perfect Meal:* "I had to learn to use bits of bread, pinching the food between the two—and only two—fingers and the thumb of the right hand, the digits protected by a layer of folded bread . . . Abdul (was) tearing the white centers from each little triangle of bread, creating an ersatz pocket . . . I called him on it, accused him playfully of cheating while I struggled with the thick, not easily folded hunks."

Then there's the visual aspect. Some writers excel at writing about the physical features of food using similes and metaphor rather than adjectives. Similes compare, using "like" and "as." Metaphor calls it something else. In *An Omelette and a Glass of Wine*, Elizabeth David describes sugar-coated coriander and caraway seeds, "bright as shiny tiddlywinks (simile)." In *Between Meals*, Liebling wrote that the haricot verts he was served "resembled decomposed whiskers from a theatrical-costume beard (metaphor)." While these examples instantly bring images to mind, note that one sounds delectable while one does not. Food writing is not always about rhapsodizing.

David, a British writer who educated first England and then the world on Mediterranean food, writes in a sensuous, stimulating, and intellectual style. Here she focuses on sight, scent, and taste: "Now there are signs of autumn on the leaves of some of the almond trees. They have turned a frail, transparent auburn, and this morning when I awoke I devoured two of the very first tangerines of the season. In the dawn their scent was piercing and their taste was sharp."

Writers Jane and Michael Stern provide an elegant example combining touch and visual writing in *Gourmet*, where they describe the ultimate apple pie. You can see their minds going into slow motion to describe the experience: "The crust is as crunchy as a butter cookie, so brittle that it cracks audibly when you press it with your fork; grains of cinnamon sugar bounce off the surface as it shatters. The bottom crust is softer than the top, but browned and still breakable. Where the top and bottom meet, there's a knotty cord of dough that becomes impregnated with enough fruit filling to make it chewy. Inside is a dense apple pack of firm Ida Red crescents bound in syrupy juice." The specificity of the words, combined with active verbs such as bounce, crack, and shatter, makes this description evocative. Note the use of simile as well, in "crunchy as a butter cookie," and metaphor in "knotty cord."

Some writers think the least important sense is sound. But consider how it enlivens the experience in Alan Richman's colorful *Bon Appétit* essay, "The Great Texas Barbecue Secret": "Because the meat is seldom pricked during cooking, the fat accumulates, sizzling and bubbling. Slice, and the drama unfolds. Think of a bursting water pipe. Better yet, imagine a Brahman bull exploding from the gate at a rodeo."

Describing your perceptions is difficult to get right. Most beginning writers tend to overdo it. In the worst case, says *Los Angeles Times* food section editor Russ Parsons, descriptions can be cloying, gratuitous, and prurient. "The idea is not to be flashy but elegant. You want to use enough sensual language that you get across your pleasure and your involvement with the topic, but don't want to come across as overblown, which reads as cheap and unconvincing. Write it and keep going over it, taking out as much as you possibly can and leaving the essence."

So how do you become skilled in describing the senses? Molly O'Neill advises beginning writers to live by their senses for a while. She kept a taste journal for ten years. "Every time I tasted something I wrote about it. Now I have a large anthology of the experience of taste," she explains. She uses the journal to feed an "unconscious kind of database that exists beneath the realm of consciousness, looking for what will trigger it to come to the surface."

Perhaps the best way to access the senses is not to take them for granted. I like the way Richman and the Sterns slow down to describe each moment as it unfolds. Editor Judith Jones advises writers to use the senses as a starting point, the evocative element, and then go on to the larger theme or context.

Getting Passion Across

Just like the senses, passion is an essential part of food writing but difficult to get across. Strong feelings can mislead. It's easier to tell readers about your enthusiasm by stating it outright than by revealing it through the words you choose. The classic writing rule of "show, don't tell" applies here, where your job is to show your devotion rather than to tell the reader about it. It's challenging. When you turn a camera on people to get to their passion, says Andrews, they freeze up, use big words, and become stilted, especially when they're very emotional about a subject. "You can't just open a vein and let it flow out. If you're very passionate about some wonderful dish, you have to tame your passion to write about it, [or] it will probably come across sounding stupid."

Passion is what makes writing come alive, says O'Neill. "The writing says, 'I really have something to tell you.' It's an act of will versus a compulsiveness to share, to examine, and to tell a story. It has fresh language and accuracy. It propels the writer like a life force. It's not a commodity, but a state of mind. With enough practice one learns to work with it."

When you're in the midst of feeling this kind of fervor as you write, it's a beautiful thing. Goldstein says passion overtakes her and won't ever let her go. Even when she was writing her dissertation and working as a professor, she had to write about food because she was thinking about it all the time. That's because passion is really a compulsion, explains Jones, conveyed in a sense of urgency.

Intensity during writing comes and goes, like being in and out of love, says Leite. "At times I'm on a holy tear," he admits. "It's just coming out. I'm channeling something. As quickly as it came, one day I wake up and it's gone. I have to accept that. The only way to get it back on a regular basis is to sit down and write every day." Sometimes he writes for six hours and it's only the last sentence of the day that delights him, he says. But when that happens, "It's enough to float me, to give me energy to pick up and start writing again tomorrow." The bottom line about passion, he says, is to take advantage of it when it's there, because there's no regular way to get it.

Obsession can be a by-product, and in that case, "Jeffrey Steingarten is the king of obsession, the ultimate foodie in the history of the world," says Richman. He means that as a compliment. Many of the people interviewed for this chapter admire the obsessive way Steingarten takes on a subject. Here's an example from Steingarten's first book, *The Man Who Ate Everything,* in his essay on choucroutes:

"Whenever I travel to France, I like to hit the ground eating, but my urgency on this trip was even more intense than usual—a brief week in Alsace was barely long enough to sample the fourteen authentic choucroutes. I had passed a sleepless night and morning on the trip to Strasbourg—two plane flights and an endless wait for airport connections—while my wife slumbered beside me like a puppy. Anticipating that I would lose consciousness as soon as we rented our car, my instructions to her had been the model of clarity: Drive directly from the airport to Itternheim on the forlorn outskirts of Strasbourg, avoid the twofold snare of ineffable scenery and Medieval churches. Park at the Hotel-Restaurant au Boeuf and make a reservation for lunch. Enjoy yourself very quietly for the next two hours. Wake me at 1:00 P.M. for our first steaming plate of true choucroute."

Jones, editor of *The Man Who Ate Everything,* says Steingarten is equally at home whether tasting baguettes at a contest or fishing for tuna, as he "becomes the average man who has passion but makes the same gaffes and laughs at his own compulsiveness." When I asked him about humor, Steingarten says it's not necessary to be funny all the time. "Some writers aren't funny in every sentence but you know you're going to end up laughing," he says.

Obsessiveness can lead to being in love with your subject, which occasionally means including too much information in a piece. Even Steingarten admits he needs editing. "I'm not about to chastise Anna Wintour (editor in chief of *Vogue*) about not finding something interesting," he says. "I will change it a little and she'll read it over. People don't realize she reads every word twice." For more on how to edit your own work, see page 135 in chapter 5.

The Role of Voice

Great writers, including food writers, spend years perfecting their voice. Voice combines writing style and point of view. It is also called style. *The Elements of Style,* an essential handbook for writers, refers to voice simply as "the sound a writer's words make on paper." It's what makes you authentic. It conveys your personality, flair, and originality. "Voice exists to make the piece more readable, to make it more enjoyable, to explain or illuminate difficult concepts without seeming dry," explains Andrews. "People can explain a difficult subject and because they write conversationally, it comes across better."

You can't invent a voice, most say. I once asked Don Fry, a writing coach at The Symposium for Professional Food Writers at the Greenbrier, how I could write in a voice as lyrical as Molly O'Neill's. He suggested an exercise where I copy O'Neill's style by parodying it, which would give me insight into how she pulls it off. Ten years later, I was back at the Greenbrier as a speaker, and did the exercise again by analyzing a piece by Ruth Reichl. I found it sensuous, visual, evocative, poetic, and reflective. I also noticed her use of personification, alliteration, and even violence, as Fry pointed out. Then I did a writing exercise by employing some of her techniques, and found the exercise liberating.

But editor Judith Jones disagrees. "Woe unto a writer who tries to imitate another writer's voice," she cautions. "It's not something borrowed or imitated, it is you. It describes how you actually feel. It's what makes the writer individual."

Certainly, however, reading other writers can influence your work. When Molly Wizenberg started Orangette, (www.orangette.blog spot.com) she was reading Steingarten, Trillin, and M. F. K. Fisher. "I didn't actually do an imitation, but I noticed certain things, like Trillin had a plain sentence structure. He wasn't getting all flowery and poetic with it. Someone more lyrical tapped into emotions, like MFK. She wrote about some philosophical things, like about the way we link food with love. All of these things have come through in my writing."

Trillin, she says, does an incredible job of "noticing the nuances that are often universal in our lives," such as his obsession with Kansas City Barbeque. "Something in us becomes obsessed too. I love his sense of humor, his ability to create his own pathological enthusiasm. He puts us immediately in his shoes. His details are vivid, visual, and play on the senses."

As for the role of voice, O'Neill says, "Voice is a guide in a landscape, the guide in a journey. Voice holds a reader's hand and says,

'Come on, this is going to be fun, it's okay to do, we've got a lot of serious things to look at here and I'm going to help you.' As long as voice is clear and consistent, the reader will respond. The reader has to know where you're coming from and how it's going to affect them."

Voice helps readers form an image of the writer. To put it in modern business parlance, it's as though you were creating a brand. It's possible to write a story without using much voice, particularly in newspapers, where news stories are more likely to be straightforward. When I wrote my first essay after years of news writing, I was startled by my own voice. I wondered if I was revealing too much of my personality.

But for readers to get the most out of a story, they should understand who you are, perhaps even trusting you more than liking you. Your voice gives the narrative unity and strength, says Goldstein. "Writers starting out are afraid to put their voice in there. They think, 'What if people criticize it or don't like it?' Without it, your writing can be a little pallid, and sounds like everyone else's writing. Voice makes you sound sure of yourself." So don't worry about being "writerly," because it makes your work more serious and boring. Write the way you speak.

Your writing expresses your uniqueness. "Voice is the sound, rhythm, and point-of-view that unequivocally evokes the writer," wrote David Leite on Egullet (www.egullet.org). "You know it when you read it." He suggests reading passages by Jeffery Steingarten, Calvin Trillin, Tony Bourdain, M. F. K. Fischer, and Ruth Reichl. You can hear each author's voice in your head as you read. "And more importantly, you can never confuse or interchange them. Bourdain is not Steingarten, who is not Trillin, who is not Reichl."

"Voice is often misunderstood," explains Russ Parsons. People usually think they must reveal their inner secrets and it's a deeply personal matter. But voice is not about you. "It's the rhythm of language, writerly tricks, the choice of words."

Maybe the way to use the writing coach's advice is to find your own voice by exaggerating it. Amanda Hesser, author of the memoir *Looking for Mr. Latte: A Food Lover's Courtship, With Recipes,* said she exaggerated both her own characteristics and her boyfriend's to make their voices more clear, and she did so without worrying that the story was becoming fictional. "She was the bumbling, snobby food person who needed to be put in her place; he was muse and hero," she explained in an interview.

The best food writers capture the authentic emotion of the moment, the tone of what's going on at the time, and what they feel physically. If you have trouble finding your voice, consult your list of descriptions as a starting point (see page 18). Ask a few friends to describe your voice to you. Often they're better at it than you are, because you might think of your voice as "just you," and therefore not describable.

Other ways to make your voice stronger in writing include your choice of language and cultural references. Examine your word choices and play with them. Do you use big words, for example, or reference movies or music? Your voice can show age, geographic location, gender, or even your religious persuasion. Here's how restaurant critic Jonathan Gold opens a review: "If you grew up eating hot dogs in the swinging San Fernando Valley '70s, your family probably had allegiances to the Hot Dog Show or Flooky's or the Wiener Factory, which were as inarguable, as inevitable, as the question of Orthodox, Conservative or Reform." Without his ever explicitly saying so, you can assume he's Jewish, grew up in Los Angeles, and probably is in his forties now. Without a strong voice, you risk becoming a superficial narrator.

~~~~~~

WRITERS DESCRIBE THEIR OWN VOICES

Alan Richman, editor-at-large of *GQ* magazine: I'm a diffident, cranky, New York guy who walks into a restaurant and waits to see how he's going to be abused. I'm a passive-aggressive guy who gets the last word. I am someone to whom things happen. Writers should take a passive role so readers feel represented.

Clotilde Dusoulier, author and blogger, Chocolate & Zucchini: At first my voice was clear enthusiasm and joy for my subject. Those feelings have not left me, but I'm probably a little calmer now. You can't be emphatic all the time. After a while, if I kept being that bubbly, people were going to think I'm on something. I became a little understated. I feel more mature now. My way of writing is friendly, approachable, and relatable.

Darra Goldstein, author and editor of *Gastronomica*: *The Journal of Food and Culture*: My voice changes when I write for different publications. For an essay in *Gourmet*, I had a kind of cheerful, playful voice that underlies subject. For my editor letter in *Gastronomica*, I feel compelled to sound intellectual. Now I'm working on a scholarly article. I have to restrain the impetuous voice. It's not appropriate for the audience.

David Lebovitz, author, freelance writer, and blogger: Friendly, funny, approachable.

David Leite, freelance writer, author, and publisher of the Leite's Culinaria Web site: I write the way I speak, influenced through a lifetime of hearing my mother's humor. I can be a little wicked at times. I turned to humor in adolescence. I developed that person and it came out on the page.

Jeffrey Steingarten, author and *Vogue* magazine food critic: Obsessive, possibilities to humor.

Calvin Trillin, book author, freelance writer, and columnist: Genial glutton.

Judith Jones, author and Knopf vice president and senior editor: I focus on how I feel, how I think. That's what makes it individual.

Molly O'Neill, author and freelance writer: Poetic writing has to be balanced by precision, clarity, [and the] tension between humor and gravity. You only have one voice but it has many different expressions. My piece for the *New Yorker* is different than a news story for the *New York Times* or a memoir about my family. All are particular parts of my voice. I have more range in longer form.

Molly Wizenberg, author and blogger: I like to think of my voice as somewhat playful or whimsical. It's very important to me to be honest.

Michael Ruhlman, author and blogger: Authoritative, as in I've studied this, I've been in culinary schools, I've worked with the best chefs in the country. I have opinions.

Russ Parsons, food editor, the *Los Angeles Times*: By nature I'm kind of a smart-ass. I try to score as many points off myself as other people when I'm writing in the first person. It's important to be self-deprecating, not self-aggrandizing. I pay a lot of attention to rhythm, sentence length, and structure.

Ruth Reichl, author and editor: Forthright.

DESCRIBE YOUR OWN VOICE

Writing becomes stronger when you know who you are. If you decide you are sarcastic, for example, then you have a tool with which to assess your writing to ensure your voice comes across that way. Go through the following list and pick the top five adjectives that you think describe you and your voice. If you have trouble, ask friends to select some adjectives for you.

- Reassuring
- Humble
- Vulnerable
- Believable
- Mysterious
- Funny

- Knowledgeable
- Approachable
- Relaxed
- Competent
- Knowing
- Authoritative

Writing Exercises

1. This exercise will make your writing livelier. It shows you how to use simile and metaphor instead of adjectives, how to substitute generic nouns, and how to use varying sentence length to your advantage. Write a long paragraph about eating a favorite piece of fruit, using all the senses. Use a simile and a metaphor in your paragraph. (A simile tells the reader what something is like, such as "The grapes were like a string of tiny black pearls." A metaphor directly compares one thing to another, as in "I tossed one of the sticky puffs into my mouth.") When you're done, go back over the paragraph, and look for generic nouns, substituting concrete ones for them. For example, if you're writing about a farm, you might re-

place the word "people" with the word "farmhands." Once you've made some replacements, go over your work once more and look at your sentence structure. Are you in a rut, with sentences all of one length? Adjust them to make some short and some long. Right away, you'll see a stronger, more distinct voice emerge in your writing. Elizabeth Lyon, author of *A Writer's Guide to Nonfiction*, led a class on this practical exercise at a writer's conference seminar I attended.

2. More ways to use simile and metaphor: Fill in the blanks by comparing the following foods to non-edible objects such as wet newspaper or diesel oil. Write a long sentence. Instead of "The cheese was as ripe as a locker room," write, "The cheese was as ripe as a locker room of thirty sweaty soccer players disrobing after a game." The cheese was as ripe as . . . The donut smelled stale, like a . . . The roast beef sandwich tasted as though . . .

3. David Leite told me about an exercise for the senses he learned when he studied acting. Every day for a week, the actor holds an imaginary familiar object in his or her hands—in David's case, an ordinary coffee mug. Each day he smelled, looked at, and tasted imaginary coffee. He did this exercise for five minutes a day for one week. It's a great way to slow down, study one thing, and capture its essence. Record your observations to see whether you are stuck using one particular descriptive device, such as adjectives. Mix it up by using cultural references one day or similes the next.

4. Develop your writing ability to show rather than tell. Choose a favorite food. Write two paragraphs explaining why you love it. Get your passion across without sentences starting with "I just can't get enough of. . . ." If you love licorice, show your devotion by writing about the lengths to which you will go to procure it, for example, or how often you consume it.

2

Characteristics of a Food Writer

If you want to be a food writer, you're probably already passionate about food and eating, and perhaps cooking as well. That's where it begins. Almost all the writers interviewed for this book talked about passion, or else exuded passion, no matter how many years they had been on the job. If your friends think you're odd because you love to talk about food, take heart. You're on the right path.

Knopf vice president and senior editor Judith Jones, who has edited such superstars as Julia Child and James Beard, says she's "absolutely convinced" people love food because they are born with a food-loving gene. "I saw that in my own family, I was always curious and asked questions, loved food, whereas my sister couldn't care less," she recalls. "You can develop taste, but passion is certainly a genetic thing, like a good ear for music."

Many food writers I've met are enthusiastic, intense, and energetic in an obsessive kind of way, and love nothing more than immersing themselves in research. And who can blame them? After all, if you get paid to write about a day in the life of a Bing cherry farmer, the history of *tres leches* cakes, or a restaurant roundup in Rome, it's hard not to throw yourself into the task.

Based on interviews with food writers and editors, I've made a list of characteristics. Some play off each other. For example, it's easy to be a fastidious researcher when you're passionate about your subject. It's easy to be knowledgeable about your subject if you've done your research. It's easy to be energetic if you're passionate. See how these traits come together?

Some characteristics can be learned. When I studied newspaper reporting in journalism school, I learned how to research anything and how to persist until I got the interviews I needed for stories. Those skills have served me well all through my career. Few writers have all the traits I've listed below. You don't need every single one to succeed. Certain characteristics may predispose you to be good at certain types of food writing. Researchers like historical writing and longer stories. Skeptics make good restaurant reviewers. Attention to detail, persistence, and curiosity are terrific characteristics for any kind of food writing, but particularly for recipe developers. In chapter 5, you'll learn why developing recipes requires making and testing them repeatedly. You've got to be persistent and curious about why your braised lamb turns out different each time.

Here's my list of characteristics. As you read, consider how many of these describe you. (If you don't mind marking up book pages, check them off.) You need to see if you are suited to the task, just as some people become firemen because it suits their personality, values, and interests. Some of these identifications may be no-brainers, but others will deserve more thought. Many are interrelated. There's no magic number to tick off. Only you can decide whether you have the skills and determination to write about food.

Passionate: People who love food are an eager, enthusiastic bunch, and it carries over when they write. A huge appetite for joy and appreciation fuels food writers, says freelance writer and cookbook author Molly O'Neill. It pushes them to communicate pleasurable and enjoyable experiences their readers have never had.

"Passion is really a compulsion, conveyed in a sense of urgency," says Jones. "This is what makes writing come alive." Passion usually involves the pleasure experienced by writers and readers, but not always. I felt passionate about being a board member of a food bank, which led to a long essay on feeding the hungry in *Gastronomica* magazine. I wanted my readers to feel outrage, compassion for the less fortunate, and compunction to act, even if it was just to donate food or money.

I felt intensely dedicated to my goal of communicating how our country feeds hungry people. My job was to get emotion onto the page, so readers would want to jump into the story and continue all the way through.

Some of the best writers remain passionate despite years on the job. Alan Richman, contributing writer for *GQ* magazine, says when on an assignment to find and eat food, he becomes "crazy with happiness when things taste so good," perhaps in part because it's not that common. You'll learn more about restaurant reviewing in chapter 5.

Enthusiastic researcher: You can never have too much information on a subject before you begin writing about it. Food writers are always asking questions. As fastidious readers and researchers, it's common to have an obsessive personality, and think every aspect of, say, a goat cheese producer's life, is fascinating. By the time they have done enough work on the subject to justify writing about it, they burst with information. *Los Angeles Times* food section editor Russ Parsons admits, "When I'm researching a story, I go completely berserk. I may have 300 pages of research and photocopies for a 1,500-word article. I want to know everything, to have total saturation in every aspect of the subject."

Saturation is a starting point for the article. Your next job is to sift through the information and decide what's compelling and necessary. That depends on the angle of the story, who your readers are and what they want to read, your word count, and your structure. More about this a bit later, when we get to the importance of focus (page 24).

Research doesn't necessarily mean spending hours in a dingy library poring over dusty tomes. It can be much more exotic. Food writers are constantly on the go—traveling, finding familiar foods in new and unusual places, tasting the way people in another country prepare a familiar food, and bringing new flavors to readers, says Toni Allegra, head of the Symposium for Professional Food Writers at the Greenbrier.

Cooking is another part of research. It's easier to write well about some subjects if you cook, advises *Gastronomica* editor Darra Goldstein, as it helps you understand your subject. If your research involves historical cooking methods or recipes, for example, try the methods or make the recipes. Describing it is not enough, because cooking is an important part of your understanding of the food and how the context of cooking works into your story. You must be willing to make or eat whatever is necessary in the name of research.

In recipe writing, research might mean looking up the origin of a dish, understanding the chemistry of how it works, or comparing recipes to see how others made the dish.

Enthusiasm keeps you interested, keeps you asking questions, keeps you engaged and challenged. It's the same in any competitive industry.

Energetic: You can't be running around the world, transcribing notes, endlessly looking up information, and interviewing without being energetic. O'Neill, for example, says she often works seven days per week, twelve hours per day. Not everyone works that hard, and it's not like you won't succeed if you don't. But O'Neill's seemingly boundless energy might be one of the reasons for her success.

And as I mentioned earlier, passion is the best fuel for working long hours or pushing yourself to get the story, chapter, or recipe done. On days where you're so immersed in your work that the hours fly by, you know you've chosen a great profession.

Focused: When you find a topic endlessly fascinating, it gets hard to decide what to leave in and what to leave out. You need focus. I have this problem occasionally. While researching a story on table etiquette, for example, I ended up on the floor in a bookstore, enthralled by outdated books on how to supervise servants doing meal preparation. I liked the quaint notions so much that I mentioned some to my editor, who reminded me that I was writing about today's social graces and asked if I had the right sources for the story. Oops. Fortunately, word counts will rein you in. Outlines are a good tool as well. The thing to understand is that people don't have to know everything, just what's most important. The more you add, the larger the subject becomes, and soon it's about everything and not something in particular.

Skeptical: Research often includes the ability to approach information with healthy skepticism. Ernest Hemingway, who often wrote about food in his novels, said in a 1958 interview in the *Paris Review,* "The

most essential gift for a good writer is a built-in, shockproof, shit de-
tector. This is the writer's radar and all great writers have it." It's not that
you have to spend months trying to verify information and sources,
but you shouldn't just rely on what other people have written unless you
know that they themselves are good sources or experts. Origins of customs or events are particularly suspect in food writing, says Goldstein,
because even when wrong, they become myths perpetuated as common
knowledge.

I just read in the food section of a daily paper that Julia Child
dropped a chicken on the floor during a television show, picked it up,
and said it's fine to serve because no one will know. I've seen that
episode. She was transferring a potato-based dish from the stove onto
a plate and dropped some of it on the stovetop. No chickens were involved, but the writer of the newspaper story just took what she read
somewhere and ran with it. In a perfect situation, she would have been
suspicious of that outrageous-sounding story, and she would have
found a way to check it out.

Editors and writers can tell when others don't do their homework.
Parsons, the editor of the *Los Angeles Times*' food section, says there's lots
of writing that wouldn't be regarded as research, such as the passing
along of secondhand information, as in the chicken story above. But
you can't pull off something accurate without testing it yourself. Or
without researching it yourself. An author I worked with spent hours
in the library verifying assertions some famous people had made about
themselves, such as "I was the first to" or "I won an award for." Most of
the time, she discovered, these people had exaggerated.

Fearless: Research requires fearlessness. It's easier to be fearless if,
once again, you're so enthusiastic that you plunge into things. Food
writers must "taste things they don't want to taste, talk to someone
they don't want to talk to, and get themselves wedged into a situation
to get the information, to learn," says author and freelance writer David
Leite. Author and television host Anthony Bourdain is the king of
fearlessness. He traveled around the world for his book *A Cook's Tour*
and for a television show, doing extreme eating, a term he disavows. "It's
really important to be a good guest, because the table is the best re-
flection of a nation and fastest way into that culture," he counsels. "You

have to be willing to put yourself in a situation and let things happen. You can't be squeamish or hesitant. It might require that you match your hosts shot for shot with vodka laced with bear bile. Now is not the time to say 'I'm a vegetarian' or 'I'm lactose intolerant.'"

"It's a common flaw to be contemptuous of the subject or afraid of the nasty bits like dirt, strange food, unfamiliar experiences, or to feel jaded," he continues. "Fear of the other makes a lot of food and travel writers bad writers. Get people to talk about eating in Mexico—they complain about the water, think they might get sick, and they don't want to eat raw vegetables." You have to be the kind of person who wants whatever it is so badly that you go for it. Bourdain knew there would be consequences to his extreme eating around the globe, and if you've read *A Cook's Tour*, you know that he was quite ill sometimes. But it didn't keep him from eating a still-beating snake heart, or downing street food in Southeast Asia.

Sometimes fearlessness is about getting up the nerve to contact people you hold in high esteem. I had that challenge writing this book, and I'm here to tell you that two authors I worshipped from afar and feared calling turned out to be polite, accessible, prompt, and interested in helping me. What would have happened if I never got up the nerve to contact them? Not only would the book be the poorer for it, but I wouldn't have the rosy glow I have right now from remembering our interactions.

Here are three ways to get difficult tasks done. If you have to make a phone call, do it first thing in the morning, as soon as you get to your desk. That way you won't stew over it all day long and keep procrastinating. Act "as if." That means behaving as though you are a super confident, warm, witty person who would be fun to talk with, even if you're nervous as hell and don't believe it. Ask yourself, "What's the worst that could happen?" Often, fear of what will happen is blown out of proportion compared to the consequences.

Inquisitive: Food writers share endless curiosity and culinary adventurism. They like to wander around hoping to stumble upon something curious or magnificent, such as finding four new kinds of melon at a French street market or meeting a master bread baker at a party and talking for hours. Richman says he has been called a culinary anthropologist because of the amount of research he unearths while working on his stories. If you're not curious enough, says Leite, "You're not going to get to the next sentence, and you're not going to discover the next thing to write about."

Persistent: Hand-in-hand with curiosity is the ability to be relentless. Former *New York Times* restaurant critic Mimi Sheraton writes in her memoir, *Eating My Words,* that she went to a restaurant twelve times until she was sure how she felt about it. Luckily, the *Times* picked up the bill. Even if the work seems tedious, such as pouring through tons of information to find a few facts, or asking so many questions you run the risk of sounding thick, the best food writers keep going until they get what they want.

Knowledgeable about the subject: When they're ready to write, the best food writers know the subject matter inside out. This strategy increases confidence and helps provide credibility if you're not an expert on a certain food or ingredient. If you're not an expert, suggests Colman Andrews, co-founder of *Saveur,* "The next best thing is to learn about it and take the reader along with you as you go." This takes guts, because you must sound like you know what you're talking about. People have done it. Laura Werlin took this approach with her first book about cheese (see pages 183–184).

I've done it myself. I pitched a story to a national magazine about how to serve cheese plates at a dinner party. I had served cheese casually but wanted to learn more. I read enough from books to write a pitch letter, then skimmed six books. By the time I started writing, I knew what I was talking about. I felt comfortable with this technique because the article was short. I made my major points, filled them in, and I was done.

You might structure a story by playing the neophyte and taking the reader on a journey as you become more knowledgeable. Jeffrey Steingarten favors this technique in his *Vogue* essays. It soon becomes clear, however, that he has researched the subject thoroughly and cleverly leads you down a path.

Professional: Beginning writers are sometimes perceived as lazy, or as dabblers. People think there are special rules for food writing, that it's not as demanding as other kinds of writing, says Andrews. "Because food writing is kind of trivial or unimportant, they think they don't have to be as accurate, because they're not writing about the president, they're writing about Wolfgang Puck." I'm glad he's honest enough to say so. In my own experience, when I tell people outside the profession that I write and edit on the subject of food, I get a curious look, as in "Is that really a profession?" Some people also think food writing is a hobby and an excuse to eat and travel well. Close. It's actually a *profession* where you get to eat and travel well, if you're doing it right. The standards for being a professional food writer are not rocket science. Always:

1. Be polite in your transactions, particularly when asking for help, and thank people who have helped you.
2. Be thorough and accurate: particularly when spelling names and stating titles.
3. Make deadlines and provide exactly what you've said you were going to write, or what you've agreed to write; cooperate with your editor to the best of your ability.
4. Avoid hissy fits or prima donna behavior (if you want more assignments).

A good storyteller: "On a very basic level, you have to be capable of transporting your reader somewhere else, just for a minute, and do that by showing them where you're taking them," explains blogger and author Molly Wizenberg. "Evocative, vivid writing that plays on the senses is crucial." The best writers notice the nuances that are often very universal in our lives, she says, such as obsession, where something in us becomes obsessed too. The best writers can put us immediately in their shoes.

Not stuck in nostalgia: When I wrote my first food-themed essay, it was about my mother and her cooking. Eventually I learned I was not alone in writing about food and memory. It's common to want to write about your family, particularly the person who taught you how to cook. This desire parallels the way people start out in fiction writing, working from autobiographical information. It's what you know. The information is easily accessible because it's right there in your brain.

When I teach, students tell me of their desire to write nostalgic memories. I've heard it so often I've decided it's a normal part of the process. Sure, start with your recollections. Practice setting the scene, putting the story in context, and adding a few recipes. Starting is different from publishing. If publishing is your goal, you must say something new. I actually did get the essay about my mother published in an international magazine. It focused on her inability, as an immigrant, to master Western foods like sandwiches, spaghetti, and meat and potatoes. It was funny and bittersweet, but most important, it had an angle that made my story different from the same old thing editors see repeatedly: Most editors don't see a lot of memoir pieces about having a mother who was an Iraqi Jew from China who cooked funny Western foods.

Editors see lots of nostalgic writing that turns them off. Magazine editor Goldstein says she sees too many story pitches "for the good old days, the grandmother, the sentimentality for everything done by hand lovingly. We all had childhoods and we all look back lovingly, but I'm more interested in the edgy stuff, things that help us understand more about ourselves or who we are." Bill LeBlond, editorial director of Chronicle Books, once told a crowd at a cookbook proposals seminar that if he had to read one more book proposal from people who learned about cooking at their grandmothers' knee, he would throw up.

I'm not trying to dissuade you from writing about your family. If you know how to shape your writing, it's certainly possible to write a cookbook, memoir, or essay focusing on a family theme. Take, for example, *In Nonna's Kitchen: Recipes and Traditions from Italy's Grandmothers* by Carol Field, which succeeds for a couple of reasons. It's about Italian food, and Americans are obsessed with Italian cooking. Field is an accomplished cookbook writer, and it was not her first book. And it's about several grandmothers who have spent their lives guarding their culinary heritage, not just about one grandmother who cooked for Field. *Monsoon Diary: A Memoir with Recipes,* by Shoba Narayan, chronicles family rituals and love of food, but also discusses her trouble adjusting to an arranged marriage and shatters stereotypes of immigrant life. Her funny, sparkling narrative doesn't hurt either. It might have something to do with her Masters in journalism from Columbia, where she was awarded a Pulitzer fellowship.

I'm not trying to depress you either, but I'm not the cheerleader type who says anyone can do it. These two writers paid their dues to get to where they are today. They work very hard on their writing, and so must you.

Ethical: Along the lines of persistent visits to restaurants (à la Mimi Sheraton) is the issue of ethics. Food writers must have a strong sense of who they are and whom they represent. They get offered many free things, particularly food and travel. The best writers pay their own way or, if they're lucky, a publication pays their way. Otherwise, a writer might feel indebted to a restaurant or tourist association, and be less likely to write that the fish was overcooked or that a food festival was boring. Inevitably, food writers get to know other people in the business, such as chefs and public relations people, and sticky situations can result.

A food writer's job is to be honest. Reviewer Richman explains that good food writing is "not press trips to Tuscany, not free meals at restaurants, and not the adoration of famous chefs where you sit around saying 'yum yum' to everything put in front of you."

Careful with language: When I asked experienced food writers what they dislike most about other food writing, the number one complaint was the use of too many adjectives, clichés, and flowery metaphors, where, instead of crafting beautiful sentences, writers rely too much on strings of adverbs and adjectives to move the story along. That means avoiding writing sentences like "The huge artichoke on the garnet dinner plate was a sage-colored flower waiting to be devoured, its leaves pointing skyward, concealing the hidden treasure within." Metaphors compare by saying a thing is something else, such as "the artichoke was a sage-colored flower." I'm not telling the reader anything new. "Hidden treasure within" is a cliché because it's not original. And while I'm critiquing, "was" doesn't carry the sentence forward with strength or interest.

Veteran writer O'Neill keeps rampant and vague adjectives at bay by evolving her taste vocabulary, even after decades as a food writer. Her main tool is a taste diary she kept for ten years. One of her mentors suggested using such a diary so that later, if she was writing about a raspberry, she could go back and consult her earlier impressions. Generic descriptions are just as bad as overwrought ones. Here's an example I found just now when I picked up a national food magazine and turned to a recipe:

"These beans are fantastic served with grilled chicken and rice. And if you have some nice chicken stock on hand, you can use it instead of water to cook the beans." Why are the beans fantastic? Do they complement the chicken and rice a certain way, and if so, how? Texture? Flavor? What is "nice" chicken stock? There's no way to know. While vague language won't ruin the recipe, a more specific introduction helps the reader imagine making the dish and serving it. Suppose the beans, with their dark red color, provided colorful contrast to the white rice, or the stock was deeply flavored. Specific writing is always preferable. Allegra suggests you learn to use a tool like Rodale's *Synonym Finder* to find the right words, because "you can only say 'delicious' so many times." To help you along, I've listed useful adjectives on page 161.

Writing about food isn't just about describing flavor and smell, anyway. Food may be the subject of a story, but the point of the story can reside in recounting, reporting, and finding the right details, as well as in the history, associations, implications, and of course, the context of the story itself.

According to O'Neill, another way writers can go wrong is when they write advertisements for themselves rather than guide the reader on a journey. Further, some writers get confused between knowledge for the sake of empowerment and knowledge for the sake of showing off. I've read lots of showy writing. It's the self-satisfied I'm-sitting-here-eating-truffles-on-the-balcony-of-a-terribly-expensive-hotel-in-Piedmont-and-you're-not approach. This type of writing implies the writer thinks he's excruciatingly important, which in turn implies his readers are not. Insulting your readers does not endear you to them.

All the writers interviewed here write in the first person, but they pull it off because of their experience, writing style, solid reporting, and research. They separate the narrator from themselves—the writer—so they are not building a story based on confession. They don't say "I" in every sentence. Even though the writing involves them, it's not about them. It's about engaging readers in a great story. Steingarten always writes in the first person as a "naïve narrator" who knows less than the author. But he doesn't believe he has to be consistent. He tries different styles in the same piece, such as using a conversational tone and then a businesslike tone, and has tried switching from first person to second person (speaking to the reader as "you," as in "you walk into a bar . . .").

Related to this focus is too much navel-gazing. When I was a magazine editor I found many of my writers' first drafts filled with minutiae, particularly in the beginning of the article. I call this the "deep dive," where writers move quickly into the small details. They get so involved in the story they lose perspective. "You need a sense of levity and relief," advises O'Neill. "If you just go around being what you think, you become a caricature of yourself. A writer is a prophet, standing on the mountain screaming. Once you're no longer a siren, you are no longer really a writer."

Writing Exercises

1. Write a paragraph about your passion for a certain food. Use show, not tell; show your passion instead of telling readers ways that you are passionate. Show would be, "I meant to stop myself after the first five handfuls, but before I knew it, I looked down and saw an empty, grease-stained cardboard bowl, with a few shiny kernels sticking to the bottom." Tell would be, "I really love popcorn."

2. Write two paragraphs about your favorite dish, using no adjectives. This is not just a description, but details about different ways you've made the dish, where you've eaten it, or who joined you at the table. At first the writing will look stark and spare. Now go back and add specific adjectives to make the story sparkle. Limit yourself to three.

3. Go back over your paragraphs from exercise 2 and change any generic nouns to specific ones. For example, change "room" to "kitchen" or "meat" to "duck breast." How do you like the result?

3

Getting Started

I f you've always wanted to write about food as a career, how do you get started? What kind of work do you want, and what kind of qualifications do you need? How do people move up the food chain to become food writers?

Fortunately, lots of answers exist. Above all, you must enjoy learning. That's what keeps the best food writers growing and moving forward. They're interested in many subjects, not just their area of expertise. You probably have the same kind of enthusiasm about food, so the next step is to back it up with knowledge. If you're feeling intimidated about your qualifications, this chapter will show you how to pump up your background and skills before you ever write a word. Credibility is an important part of getting a writing job and being taken seriously. The more you have to offer in terms of knowledge and experience, the more likely you are to succeed.

Part of learning about food writing is finding out what jobs exist, what kinds of qualifications you need, how to get started, and how others began their careers. One day you'll have a story about how you got started. Learning how to do it will make you more confident. All you need is a plan.

What Types of Jobs
Can a Food Writer Have?

Food writers write all kinds of things: cookbooks, blogs, newsletters, news, restaurant reviews, feature articles, travel guides, recipes, product labels and more. When I tell people I'm a food writer, their mouths water as they imagine my glorious life of eating. They imagine I hold court in expensive restaurants every night, get baskets of fine wines and pâtés delivered to my office, have chefs fawning over me, hold elaborate dinner parties, jet to Italy on assignment to do a story on pasta . . . Well, no. That's not my life. It could be someone else's in the food-writing world, though, if it was ratcheted down a notch— perhaps that of a top author or food personality who writes for the biggest, glossiest magazines with big budgets and expense accounts.

No two food writers do exactly the same job. We are a tough bunch to categorize. Many people do a little of everything, as you'll see in the "Week/Day in the Life" stories in this chapter. And what they do changes over time. Most recently I've become a blogger, have ghost-written a chapter of a cookbook for a well-known author, and collaborated on a cookbook.

Here's a breakdown of the most common categories of food writing, so you can see what kind of work writers do and how much the jobs overlap:

Food blogger: Most food bloggers don't blog full-time. For some, it's the first time they've ever written about food, and it's a fun hobby. Blogging provides an easy way to try out food writing, particularly recipe development. Some people fall in love with food blogging and find that, as they build readership, they want a professional blog. Others have been writing in other mediums and turn to it as another way to express themselves and promote their work. It takes just a few minutes to set up a blog. What takes longer is keeping up the pace of posting regularly, learning photography, and dealing with comments. To learn more, read chapter 4 on becoming a blogger.

A DAY IN THE LIFE OF A FOOD BLOGGER AND WRITER

Tara Weaver writes Tea & Cookies (www.teaandcookies.blogspot .com) from Seattle, "a collection of essays, photos, recipes, and other adventures written by Tea, a writer, home cook, and avid traveler." Her first book, called *The Butcher and the Vegetarian: One Woman's Romp through the World of Men, Meat, and Moral Crisis*, evolved from her blog. Here's Tara on blogging:

The best thing about being a writer and blogger is that every day is different. I start my mornings answering email and blog comments and questions. I'm grateful I don't have a baking-focused blog, which is more technical. My friends who do get questions like "Why didn't my macaroons turn out right?" There are so many variables; it's impossible to give an answer.

Questions tend to be about ingredient availability, restaurant suggestions, or how to become a writer. It takes time to answer, and it's rare to receive a thank you. This is definitely part of being a blogger; manners often disappear on the Internet. I've been lucky so far, but friends struggle with mean or attacking comments and how to respond (ignore, delete, or engage?). As my site grows in traffic, I suspect I will get more of these.

By midday, I'm off email, I hope. Here's where the day can get interesting. I might be writing or cooking, or off on some adventure, like visiting a spice store, an organic farm, or checking out a new farmers' market. Because I have wide parameters for what I cover, almost anything I do might end up being a blog post. There is possibility in everything I experience, taste, learn. Yesterday I spent the day wild mushroom foraging in the Washington woods. That's definitely going to end up on the site.

Because of this, I am always taking pictures. There is nothing worse than wanting to write and not having the photos to go along. I also try to improve my photography. The web is such a visual medium; I don't think you could have a successful food blog without them. I use photos both to illustrate my writing and to punctuate it, to make the reader slow down and take a breath.

Photography is only one of the technical aspects of blogging. I'm also continually trying to educate myself on the issues involved in running a Web site. It's easy to start a blog, but if you want to grow one you either need to learn web development or hire someone to do it for you. I have moments where I seriously consider getting an office job just to have in-house tech support.

I also write for print outlets and I've written my first book, though blogging definitely put my writing career on the fast track. The idea for the book came out of a blog post, and the book sold in part because I had developed a platform and readership. Sometimes it's hard to juggle blogging and writing for print (I must remind myself that I cannot hyperlink on a book page). Print publication takes a long time, and when I was on my book deadline it was hard to muster energy for the blog. It's a balancing act I don't always do gracefully.

I'm choosing more to write about things on my site, rather than pitching them to a magazine editor. I worked as a freelance writer and editor before I started my site. Luckily, I'm able to catch most—though not all—of my own typos.

At the end of the day, I do a little of everything, and we won't even talk about self-employment taxes and record keeping. The variety struck me recently when I saw food blogger Jaden Hair's cookbook, *Steamy Kitchen*. The book is full of innovative recipes and photos she took herself. I realized she'd done the work of four people: recipe developer, writer, stylist, and photographer. That's what you're juggling as a food blogger. It can be hectic, but it can also be a lot of fun.

Freelance writer: Many food writers are freelancers, writing for magazines and newspapers. The advantage of working for yourself is working when you want, as much as you want, from your own home and kitchen. Here's the hard part about it: Most write as a sideline to something else because it's hard to make a decent living as a food writer. So in addition to writing, freelance food writers might also cater, work in restaurants, become private chefs, attend cooking school, develop and test recipes for companies, take people on food tours abroad, or teach cooking classes. Writing for corporations pays better—writing press releases, Web site copy, developing recipes and curricula for chefs—but those jobs usually go to experienced cookbook authors who have paid their dues.

Some freelancers work full-time, but most do not. Full-time staff jobs are even more rare. When you see stories in newspapers and magazines, the full-time employees—editors, senior editors, assistant editors—have written some of them in addition to doing their regular jobs.

Syndicated writer: Usually a self-employed freelance writer, this person writes a regular column that a syndication service sends to many newspapers around the country. Most freelancers, however, write a story that is published in one place.

A WEEK IN THE LIFE OF A FREELANCE WRITER

Laura Taxel is a full-time freelance food writer and restaurant reviewer in Cleveland, Ohio, and the author of *Cleveland Ethnic Eats: The Guide to Authentic Ethnic Eats in Northeastern Ohio*. To give you an idea of what the life of a food writer entails, I asked her to write to me, diary style, about what she accomplishes in a busy week. Here is her report:

Monday: Wrote my weekly blog covering the local food scene for *Cleveland* magazine, then tried to finish a feature for a national trade publication about chefs who are preserving local, seasonal fruits and vegetables by doing their own pickling. Before I was quite done, it was time to get out of sweats—how I love having a home office—shower, and head out to lunch with a radio reporter who's interviewing me for a series on how the restaurant business impacts the local economy. Made a quick stop on the way home at the grocery store so Barney [Taxel's husband] would have something for dinner, as I would be out for the monthly gathering of our Cleveland chapter of Les Dames d'Escoffier International (LDEI).

Tuesday: Started the day at the dermatologist. I wanted to talk rash but he was determined to get personalized dining-out recommendations first. As guest speaker at a luncheon, I told stories about northeast Ohio restaurants, the people who run them, and the extraordinary food they serve. Then I sold and signed copies of my book. Dinner was at an Indian restaurant that a reader had recommended. If I think it has something to offer, I'll include it in the next edition, which I update every two years. In the meantime, I'll post my impressions on my Cleveland Ethnic Eats blog (www.clevelandethniceats.wordpress.com). When I returned home, stuffed with rice and lentil patties called idli, fried lentil doughnuts; and dosai, crispy, paper-thin, rice-flour crepes, I had to put in a couple of hours at the computer, checking social media pages, sorting through the daily flood of emails—reading and answering to the most important ones, and responding to comments on the blogs.

Wednesday: A research morning. Did some background reading for a story about traditional winter holiday foods and the meanings they hold for people. Then had two phone interviews, one with a food historian and the other a local woman who's made wassail and plum pudding for thirty years. Invested two frustrating hours struggling to find a way to organize all the material I've gathered for this piece into a coherent story. After numerous false starts and nothing to show for my efforts, I switched gears and spent the rest of the day tracking down sources for an article about the country's first Wine MBA program.

I'd been invited to a VIP reception for the opening of a new restaurant. I go to at least a couple of events like this every month, but decided I needed a quiet night at home. Because my husband was at a function of his own, it would be a good opportunity to focus on my new book, a cultural history of Cleveland's 100-year-old public market. The manuscript, co-authored with a friend and fellow food writer, isn't actually due for a year, but I know from experience how fast those twelve months can go by. Nonetheless, I talked myself out of it. Made an omelet with eggs and feta from the farmers' market, threw together a salad with greens from the garden—simple and scrumptious—read, and went to bed early.

Thursday: Spent most of the day at my desk. Completed an article for an airline magazine and emailed it off, then caught up with invoicing and filing. Ate lunch, threw in a load of laundry, then worked on an assignment for the city magazine about dim sum and where to find the best selections in town. Always looking ahead, I also crafted a couple of story pitches. One was about the growing popularity of food trucks for an industry publication, the other, for a regional travel magazine, proposed a short guide to a food lover's weekend in Pittsburgh. Had dinner at a restaurant I'll be reviewing. The kitchen deserves the hype it's been receiving. Everything I ate, from soft-shell crab in honey-mustard dressing to skewered scallops with chervil oil and celery root puree, and crispy duck breast, seared foie gras and grit cake, lived up to its promise.

Friday: Had to take my car in for repairs so I visited a Korean grocery store that was on the way. Chatted with the owner to the extent it's possible when neither speaks the other's language. We both did a great deal of friendly head nodding, smiling, pointing, and handshaking. I might include his store as a stop on the Elderhostel ethnic food tour I'll be leading next month. Late in the afternoon, I met with folks from the Cleveland International Film Festival to help plan a fund-raising event. My husband and I throw an annual party in his photography studio, where three or four great local chefs bring food, talk about themselves, and chat with guests.

This was a good week but too much running around. With deadlines looming, I know that I'll need to spend Saturday and Sunday writing. I don't mind because I genuinely love what I do and feel lucky, in this changing media landscape to still have opportunities to tell and sell stories.

Would you like to change places? Taxel has been a food writer for twenty-five years. When I told her that her job sounded like a dream, she answered, "My work isn't a fantasy, it's quite real: Lots of fun, simultaneously demanding and difficult, and poorly compensated. How's that for bringing it back to earth?"

Cookbook author: While these self-employed writers concentrate on writing cookbooks, most also write freelance articles and consult. They might develop recipes for industry as well, for food retailers, food manufacturers—any company that might take out an ad, produce a newsletter, magazine, or book, or put recipes on its Web site. Cookbook authors are paid an advance to work on their books, which might take anywhere from one to six years, depending on how many recipes they develop and where they travel to do their research. Those who are well known with a significant fan base and publishing history may command an advance large enough to put off other jobs while writing the book, but this is rare. Almost all will have to continue taking on other sorts of work, because the advance will not support them.

A DAY IN THE LIFE OF A COOKBOOK AUTHOR AND WRITER

Greg Patent, based in Missoula, Montana, is a cookbook author, freelance writer, and co-host of a weekly public radio program, *The Food Guys.* He has written for *Saveur, Fine Cooking, Food & Wine, Woman's Day, Family Circle, Gastronomica, Cooking Pleasures, Relish,* and *Bon Appétit,* and was a regular contributor to *Cooking Light* for 12 years. One of his cookbooks, *Baking in America: Contemporary and Traditional Favorites from the Past 200 Years,* won a James Beard Award. His most recent cookbook, *A Baker's Odyssey: Celebrating Time-Honored Recipes from America's Rich Immigrant Heritage,* was a finalist for a James Beard Award and won the Cordon d'Or Academy Award.

Here's an email he sent to catch me up on his career:

These days I'm writing two food columns a month for my local paper, the *Missoulian.* "Yes, You Can Cook!" is less than a year old, all about cooking empowerment, feeding yourself sustainably, and taking control of what you eats. An online video accompanies each column. My second food column focuses on cooking and eating with the seasons.

I'm a toddler when it comes to my online presence, and after less than two years, I'm revamping my web site (www .gregpatent.com) into a baking blog, the Montana Baker, and transforming my food blog (www.gregpatentgetsyoucooking .blogspot.com) into a kitchen diary with lots of instructive pictures and videos. Every time I cook or bake something I have to keep reminding myself to "take a bunch of pictures," just in case I decide to blog about it. I also have a You Tube video page, a Twitter account, and I foster friendships on Facebook. Life is moving so fast!

Last year I published two dessert stories in *Cooking Pleasures* and a piece on pound cake in *Gastronomica*. I'm at work on a proposal for another baking book, my ninth cookbook, and this winter I'm teaching a course at the University of Montana to students aged 50 and older, *Chemistry in the Kitchen*. As I write this, the *Relish* issue with my article on low-fat chicken recipes arrived in the mail.

I can hardly believe how my professional life has evolved over the past few years, but I'm riding the wave and enjoying every minute of it.

Greg's culinary career began back in 1982, when he became a full-time spokesperson for Cuisinart, Inc. I'm always impressed by his enthusiasm and drive to conquer new technology, start new projects and forge ahead with another book.

Menu consultant, recipe developer, and tester: Freelancers may also be recipe developers and testers, working for corporations who want recipes based on their product, or for companies such as grocery stores who want a recipe for an advertisement. Menu consultants work directly for restaurants and usually have a background in the restaurant industry. They might be wordsmiths who write or check menus. "Developer" and "tester" are often interchangeable terms.

Restaurant reviewer: Restaurant reviewers at daily papers can be full-time employees, but most papers rely on freelancers like Laura Taxel. Sometimes the editor of the section will be a restaurant reviewer as well, or the full-time writers will do all kinds of feature writing in addition to reviewing restaurants. (For more on restaurant reviewing, see chapter 6.)

Newspaper writer: When staff writers exist, often they have migrated from another section of the newspaper. Kim Severson, now an award-winning food reporter for the *New York Times,* moved into food from regular reporting. It's rare to have a top reporter and investigative writer devoted to food. Other reporters migrate from the sports or business departments, or become restaurant reviewers after writing movie or book reviews. *New York Times* restaurant critic Frank Bruni previously headed the *Times'* European bureau office. If you want to work on a newspaper as a full-time writer whose beat is food, you may have to become a journalist first.

~~~~~~

A DAY IN THE LIFE OF A NEWSPAPER REPORTER

How does a food reporter at a daily paper cover her beat? I called Kim Severson of the *New York Times* and asked about a typical day:

> I wake up at 6:30 A.M. and immediately hit the email to see what's come in overnight. I subscribe to several RSS feeds and listservs. The USDA might have a package of news releases, and there are emails from grocery manufacturers associations and restaurant associations. A host of food institutions might have a valuable story idea. I can see how something's trending, like the peanut recall, when the emails keep coming. They keep growing until I see enough to know I want to pursue it.
>
> I probably get 100 emails a day, most of which are people wanting a story or pitching a story, or press releases. A dozen

restaurant p.r. people might want me to go to an opening, look at new menu, or taste a new dish. A similar amount comes from food companies who have new products. There are people who are outraged about something and think I will want to write a story about it. I used to try to answer every email, but I can't anymore. It's too much.

I use Twitter a lot for reporting, tracking bloggers, hard-core food politics people, media reporters, and pop culture reporters. I'll glance through the last 100 tweets, and see, for example, what's going on with school food programs, or that someone in Omaha gets jailed for doing sous vide. There's a little boot camp of about 200 people who send info, who help me scan this wide world. Then I'll go check a round of websites, then read the newspapers. I make breakfast and coffee and sit down with my 2 year old.

I come into the office between 9 and 10 A.M., and if it's a reporting day, I get on the phone. I have lots of conversations about what I'm trying to find out. I might make a dozen calls, or 30 or five, if it's a short story. If someone tells me something newsworthy I have to find a verifier. The story may turn out to be ideas or trends for more stories. I write 50 to 60 stories per year.

All day long I've got my iPhone, and I'm checking email and getting texted while walking along. It's a bombardment. I've had to develop a skill set to triage info quickly and decide: Does this matter, is this something that could be part of a larger trend, does this really mean something in the long run? It's like a fire hose of constant info, and I dip in. People pay me to decide what's relevant and important. I'm not a daily news reporter. I can pull back and let things develop.

I also do blog posting for the online Diner's Journal. The *New York Times* has a high standard for a blog post, so I have to report out stories a little more. If I hear that a chef got arrested from two people at the restaurant, I have to find out if it's true, find out what happened, and get verification. Other bloggers might just print it, and then update it later. We don't do that.

I don't go to many press conferences. Usually I want to be in front of the story. The press conference is almost like a tip sheet, and it's too late by the time it happens. Because I mostly cover policy shifts, I have to get story out the day before.

When I go out, I'm doing interviews with people, trying to find people, trying to talk to anyone but a government official. I will spend the day with someone I'm profiling, like hanging out in a cafeteria if writing about school foods. Or I'll try to find activists in school food reform movement, school administrators, or suppliers. I think, "Who in the story would someone not be talking to, who are the non-obvious people?"

I'll spend a few days reporting hard, and then take a few days to write. There's a day's worth of editing with my editor looking at it and making suggestions. I also have to think about visuals.

Sometimes I will take a video camera out with me or work with a video crew. We'll do some stand-up stuff, where I say, "I went out to discover . . ." After that, I work with video person to produce a 3-minute video. Sometimes there's a slide show. The photo editor will assign a photographer, and I'll help the web producer write captions. I think about how I could tell the story differently, with cool graphics online and reader comments.

Most of the time, it's good old-fashioned reporting, finding the underlying cause of things, finding out the truth and presenting it to people. How we present it will change, but gathering and figuring out what matters and creative ways to present it is still important. People who are under 30 think in different ways than I do, but they're still interested in what their neighbors are doing.

Today reporters need to be more branded, have more personality. Before it was not about me, and I tried to stay out of the story. Now there's a hunger for people to know more about my opinion or me. I wasn't 100 percent comfortable with this change, but at this point, it's 'what the heck?' I've got a lot of editors looking over my shoulder who will keep me from crossing lines.

Severson worked as a reporter, restaurant reviewer, and assistant city editor at other daily newspapers. She crossed into the food beat at the

San Francisco Chronicle, winning national awards for news and feature writing. She joined the *Times* in 2004 to write about food and cultural trends.

~~~~~~

What You Need to Break In

How did food writers like Taxel, Patent, and Severson get where they are now? Did they work in restaurants, or get degrees from places like the Culinary Institute of America? No. Of the dozen or so top writers I interviewed for the earlier chapters, all said they didn't think a food background was essential, because the bottom line is whether you know how to write, interview, research, report, and develop stories. Only author Molly O'Neill said she "doesn't even look at those who don't have a food background" when she hires freelancers to do research or write for her. "I want somebody who has worked in restaurants, catered, traveled, or who went through a ten-year apprenticeship. That's what it takes to have taste." However, she allows there's always the exception to the rule. A. J. Liebling, the *New Yorker* writer and book author, had no background in food, but, according to O'Neill, had a "great capacity for joy and appreciation, and he learned."

Some in the food writing business even think too much of a food background is a liability. "It's important to be open, to research, to not accept the norm, to explore and discover new findings and research thoroughly," says Knopf cookbook editor Judith Jones. "Sometimes if you think you know too much, it's limiting." Others believe it helps to come into the field from an entirely different background. "Some of the best don't necessarily start with food, they end up with food," says *Gastronomica* editor Darra Goldstein. "Bringing a certain approach to life, or intellectual activity to food, can make for an interesting mix." Jeffrey Steingarten was an attorney before becoming a food writer for *Vogue*. But more importantly, he was a funny guy, having honed his humor writing at the *Harvard Lampoon*.

What are the best ways to break in? The easiest is if you are already a published writer and choose to change your focus. I started out as a general newspaper reporter and later edited magazines about restaurants, automobiles, computers, and city life. I knew how to write, research, interview, and get published. The hard part was gaining enough knowledge to write about food and earning credibility as a food writer.

The second easiest is if you break in from the food world as a knowledgeable cooking professional, food historian, culinary school graduate, food retailer, or food producer. Amanda Hesser wrote her first book, *The Cook and the Gardener: A Year of Recipes and Writings from the French Countryside,* after cooking in France in a chateau with a live-in gardener. That was before the *New York Times* hired her. Certainly, the book added to her desirability.

How to Get an Education

What if you're not already a writer or someone with a background in food? You can still succeed by getting an education. Even people with writing or food-industry credentials have to fill in the gaps. No suffering is required. Studying, when it comes to food writing, is a pleasurable act. You like to eat, don't you? And you like to read good food writing, right? All you need to know is what to study, how to find classes, and how to network. But let's start at the beginning. One of the first things you need to know is how to become discriminating about food.

Taste, taste, taste: When I embarked on a food-writing career I felt intimidated by writers who seemed to know everything about food, including how it should taste. I wondered how I would learn this skill. The answer, fortunately, was to do something I did already anyway. "Taste, taste, taste," says Goldstein. It's impossible to be discriminating if your palate isn't developed.

"Eating a lot is the first thing," agrees *Los Angeles Times* food section editor Russ Parsons. But eat with an open mind. "People try to fit food into categories—it is this, it isn't that," he warns. "They compare it to how it fits their preconceptions. The point of view of the novice can be overdone. You can only play the fool so often until people ask themselves why they are reading your work."

There's no such thing as being right or wrong about how food tastes, says *Saveur* magazine co-founder Colman Andrews. "You need to know something about your subject matter, but it's pretty much understood by the reader that if you're commenting on a dish, you're offering an opinion, not a cold hard fact. Some people have a more experienced or sophisticated palate. When you taste a $200 bottle of wine and you don't like it, I hope you have the courage to say that. When the chef's specialty is brought out like a religious relic and you don't like it, you're still the boss."

What if you don't like certain foods? Andrews says that's fine, because it's impossible to argue with the way people react to food and flavor. The issue is what you tell the reader. Let's say you hate caviar, he says. "That's fine as long as you're not saying no one should eat caviar because it's too salty and pops in your mouth."

In *The Man Who Ate Everything*, Jeffrey Steingarten decided the same day he was appointed food critic for *Vogue* that he should get rid of his food phobias—such as Korean food, anchovies, Indian desserts, and lard—by eating all the things he didn't like to see if his opinion might change. "Scientists tell us that aversions fade away when we eat moderate doses of the hated foods at moderate intervals, especially if the food is complex and new to us," he theorized at the beginning of his book. To his surprise, he liked almost everything except blue food. "In just six months," he writes, "I succeeded in purging myself of nearly all repulsions and preferences, in becoming a more perfect omnivore." He goes on to say that he eventually attained such a Zen-like state that all the food on the menu at a Parisian restaurant looked appetizing, making him unable to order dinner. You'll read more about developing the palate and how to approach individual tastes in chapter 5.

The companion to developing a discriminating palate is reading for knowledge, not just pleasure. This process takes time, kind of like studying Buddhism—you never stop learning and trying to improve. It's easy to overlook this commitment. Reading some articles, you may think that you could write something just as good right now. Depending on what you read, it's possible, but unlikely. I used to enjoy reading Caroline Bates' reviews in *Gourmet* magazine, and admit to fantasizing about what it would be like to have her job. When I read Jeremiah Tower's memoir I was startled to learn that in the 1970s, Bates reviewed Chez Panisse while Towers worked there as a chef. Bates had been a restaurant reviewer for more than three decades! Of course. Why would a national food magazine hire an amateur? She paid her dues, and so must you, depending on how far you want to go.

HOW SOME FOOD WRITERS GOT THEIR START

Colman Andrews, co-founder of *Saveur* magazine, used the pseudonym Persona to write restaurant reviews in Los Angeles for an underground newspaper called the *Staff,* and then moved on to the *Los Angeles Free Press.* "Persona was an imaginary person who wrote very flamboyantly, used food puns and had been everywhere and done everything," he recalls.

Author **Molly O'Neill** worked as a chef for ten years and studied cooking at La Varenne École de Cuisine in Paris. She co-founded a restaurant in Northampton, Massachusetts, then moved on to run restaurants in Provincetown and Boston. While a chef in Massachusetts, she got a call from an editor from the *Boston Globe* daily newspaper, asking if she would write a story. The editor of the city magazine there read the published story and called her.

"He told me that if I wanted to be a real writer, I'd come work for him," says O'Neill. "I was young and stupid, so I did. Fortunately, he was a brilliant editor and working for him was one of the luckiest things that ever happened to me. Writing about food was my reward for writing about business, cops and robbers, and news. He taught me how to be a reporter and how to write cleanly and on deadline. He was supportive and he was a merciless critic."

At some point O'Neill wrote a letter to M. F. K. Fisher and "asked her if she would help." Fisher said yes. "So I went to Sonoma and, for about ten years, I went back every year to visit and to work on my writing."

I found this so astonishing that I asked if she thought a beginner could write the same kind of letter today. "The fun part of food— the grassrootsness of it, the small townness of it, the discovery of it, the sense of Wild Westness of it—is over," she replied. "There's less tolerance for learning curves, less room for serendipity. Training figures larger than chance. Having said all that, if you are talented and willing to work like a galley slave, you can find out a lot about yourself and how the world works by making a living in food. And the walls around the highest echelons of the food world ain't all that high."

Russ Parsons had been a sports writer at a newspaper in Albuquerque for ten years and never thought about becoming a food writer, even though he loved to cook. Because the paper was small, he was able to branch out into general feature writing and music writing. One day he got an assignment to write about a woman who was named cooking teacher of the year by *Bon Appétit.* He took her class as part of his research for the story, and found he enjoyed it. He became an "obnoxious hardcore foodie, read voraciously, took more classes, and went to bed with a stack of cookbooks." Friends let him work in their restaurants.

Parsons grew dissatisfied with the way the paper covered food, where copy editors took the "rip and read" approach, ripping stories with no local angle off the wire and running them. He told the editor he wanted to write about food, and got a six-week tryout, editing and writing for the food section. He became the paper's restaurant critic after six months, and is in his second term as editor of the food section.

Cookbook author and freelancer **Greg Patent** won second prize in the junior division of the Pillsbury Bake-Off when he was a teenager. Instead of pursuing a career in food, he got a PhD in zoology and embarked on an academic path. He made the jump to food writing in 1982, after he became a television cooking teacher as a hobby. Once the daily newspaper in his town of Missoula, Montana, ran a story about Patent's standing as a finalist in a cooking contest, they let him write a local food column.

During her job as chef at the Swallow restaurant in Berkeley, former *Gourmet* editor **Ruth Reichl** became a restaurant reviewer for a San Francisco magazine, a gig she got from a customer who was an editor at the publication. She went on to freelance stories for *New York* magazine and eventually was appointed food critic of the magazine's sibling, *New West,* a California regional magazine.

Freelance writer **Alan Richman** started out as a newspaper news writer, sportswriter, feature writer, and columnist. Later he switched to magazines and got a staff job at *GQ* magazine, writing features, pro-files, and a wine column on the side. "The editor in chief asked if I wanted to make it a food-and-wine column instead. I jumped at the chance, since I'd rather eat than drink." Later he became a freelancer for *GQ*, *Conde Nast Traveler*, and *Bon Appétit* magazines. He never worked in restaurants nor graduated from a cooking school, yet has won several national awards for his writing.

Vogue Columnist **Jeffrey Steingarten**, a former attorney, wrote satire and parodies for the *Harvard Lampoon* while a Harvard law student, and tried out for a job at the *New Yorker* before his appointment as food critic for *Vogue*. He met Anna Wintour in 1979, years before she became editor in chief of *Vogue*, because he knew her husband a bit. Wintour became editor of *Home and Garden* magazine. She asked several writers, including Steingarten, to try out for a new, more serious column about food. The assignment was microwaved fish, 800 to 1,200 words.

"I said I didn't even know how to microwave," he recalls. "She said, 'We'll get you a microwave.' I said I can't have just one, as there are several manufacturers, and different features and power levels. She said, 'How many did you need?' I said twelve. She paused. She said, 'Well, okay, we'll get you twelve microwaves.' In the end I only got three because the fuses started going." Steingarten turned in 4,200 words. The magazine printed about 4,000. "The pattern was set," he says. "I turned the assignment into a first-person adventure, not perfectly well, but that's what I've been doing ever since, making some jokes along the way." Later Wintour went to *Vogue*, and Steingarten followed shortly thereafter.

Asked if there was a slight difference between an attorney's salary and a full-time columnist's, Steingarten admitted he should have saved more. When negotiating his salary, he asked if Wintour would pay him "as much as a New York plumber makes annually." He got it the next year.

Writer **Calvin Trillin** was a successful freelance writer, working for national magazines, before he began writing about food for *Life* magazine in the early 1970s. Later Trillin traveled around the country for fifteen years for a *New Yorker* series called U.S. Journal, writing a 3,000-word feature article every three weeks. When he got "worn down on reporting," he wrote lighter pieces for comic relief, covering topics such as Cincinnati people arguing about chili, or making the rounds at the Breaux Bridge Crawfish Festival.

"I had neither the credentials for nor any interest in inspecting, say, a serving of Veal Orloff for the purpose of announcing to the world how it measured up to what dog-show types call the standards of the breed," he writes in his foreword to *The Tummy Trilogy*. "I wrote about eating rather than food, and I wrote as a reporter who was enjoying his work rather than as an expert."

Laura Taxel was a general freelance writer when she sent a humorous essay about barbecuing to a local magazine. The editor said she could use a piece with lots of advice instead. Taxel gathered information from friends and the Kingsford Charcoal Company and turned in a rewritten article. "The editor liked the results so much I ended up with a monthly cooking column that lasted almost three years, and so began a career."

Inspired by M. F. K. Fisher, **Amanda Hesser,** co-founder of Food 52 (www.food52.com), decided to become a food writer and began by studying cooking in Europe. Later she worked for La Varenne École de Cuisine in France for two years, testing dozens of recipes for a book by Anne Willan. She met the school's gardener, who inspired her first book. In New York, she freelanced before being hired as an editor and writer for the *New York Times.*

As for **me**, after journalism school I became the editor of a fourteen-page women's section of a newspaper, filling it with recipes from the paper's wire service, plus wedding and feature articles. The publisher of a city restaurant magazine, who wanted a new editor, approached me for the job and I accepted. In this new job I visited restaurants and wrote features about chefs and restaurants. I went on to a career as a magazine editor, then became self-employed in my 40s and got back into food writing.

Even though it sounds daunting, if you can pay your dues by tasting, reading about, and cooking food, it doesn't get any better than that. Doing so just fuels your passion.

"You will embark upon an educated journey," explains David Leite of Leite's Culinaria (http//:leitesculinaria.com). "As you go along, there will come these 'aha' moments where you put together all these bits and you can talk intelligently about a rack of lamb or two types of apple. You realize you've moved to another level."

To increase your knowledge, read food writing, whether books of nonfiction or fiction, magazines, newspaper food sections—anything you can get your hands on that interests you. Here are my suggestions:

Read great books: Like tasting, reading is a pleasurable way to increase your knowledge. If you don't like to read, you will find it difficult to write. Below is a list of books compiled from recommendations from people I've interviewed for this book, plus my own suggestions. It reflects the work of authors who are primarily literary nonfiction food writers, not recipe writers (see more about great cookbook writers in chapter 7). I have not included books by anyone interviewed within these pages. Please assume that whatever they've written is magnificent or I wouldn't have bothered.

The list below is of classic narrative food writing, which I'm defining as an American love affair with French cooking, mostly. Some of these books are hard to find and some are out of print. You may have to special-order from bookstores, contact libraries, and peruse used book sites or used bookstores. But it will be worth your time. You can cook from these books but they offer so much more than just the subjects of food and cooking. You'll find beautifully drawn portraits of people's lives and times.

- James Beard, *Delights and Prejudices*, 1964. An erudite memoir with recipes from a great American gastronome.
- Jean-Anthelme Brillat-Savarin, *The Physiology of Taste: Or Meditations on Transcendental Gastronomy*, first published in France in 1825. Lively and amusing meditations, examinations, and discussions on food, cooking, and eating. Try to find the version translated by M. F. K. Fisher.

- Samuel Chamberlain, *Clementine in the Kitchen,* first published in 1943. A cook introduces Americans to the charms of French cooking.
- Laurie Colwin, *Home Cooking: A Writer in the Kitchen* and *More Home Cooking: A Writer Returns to the Kitchen.* Novelist Colwin, who died in 1992, wrote two memoirs that are a mix of warm conversations, practical advice, and recipes.
- Elizabeth David. Try *South Wind Through the Kitchen: The Best of Elizabeth David,* a collection of her best writing and recipes compiled from nine books written between 1955 and 1977. You'll find long sentences, and sensuous depth and detail about food and ingredients.
- Roy Andries De Groot, *Auberge of the Flowering Hearth,* a 1937 adventure about his visit to a mysterious French inn in a hidden valley. Also see *In Search of the Perfect Meal: A Collection of the Best Food Writing of Roy Andries de Groot,* a collection of essays by this gifted writer and gourmand.
- M. F. K. Fisher: She wrote narratives about food as a metaphor for life, with an exacting, sensuous vocabulary, and sharp wit. Her style was new in an America accustomed to recipes and instruction. *The Art of Eating* condenses her first five books from 1937–1949 into one volume. It includes *How to Cook a Wolf, Consider the Oyster,* and *The Gastronomical Me.*
- Edna Lewis, *The Taste of Country Cooking,* 1976. A joyful and evocative memoir of American country cooking from the granddaughter of a slave.
- A. J. Liebling, *Between Meals: An Appetite for Paris,* 1959. A *New Yorker* writer reports on eating in the now-vanished Paris of the 1930s.
- Harold McGee, *On Food and Cooking: The Science and Lore of the Kitchen.* So much more than a reference book, combining culinary lore with scientific explanations.
- Angelo Pellegrini, *The Unprejudiced Palate: Classic Thoughts on Food and the Good Life,* 1948. A charming look at the good life of food, wine, and cooking from a passionate Italian-American cook and gardener.

- Waverly Root: *Eating in America: A History*, 1994. With Richard de Rochemont, this former journalist chronicles an erudite and fresh history of American food and eating customs.
- Joseph Wechsberg, *Blue Trout and Black Truffles: The Peregrinations of an Epicure*, 1953, devoted to the eating-places and vineyards of France.

If you prefer to sample many authors and styles of food writing at once, here's a list of suggested compilations:

- *The Best Food Writing* anthologies, an annual collection featuring many of the writers interviewed for this book.
- *Through the Kitchen Window: Women Explore the Intimate Meanings of Food and Cooking*, 1997. It's out of print but still one of my favorites.
- *The Wilder Shores of Gastronomy: Twenty Years of the Best Food Writing*, 2002, from the journal *Petits Propos Culinaires*. A collection of essays that includes many written by writers in this chapter. The journal began in 1979 and has been out of print for many years.
- *The Penguin Book of Food and Drink*, 1998, celebrates a century of gastronomic writing, including humorist S. J. Perelman's "Farewell, My Lovely Appetizer." (Many food writers, including Jeffrey Steingarten and Alan Richman, revere Perelman's writing style, most of which is not directly about food writing.)
- *Endless Feasts: Sixty Years of Writing from Gourmet*, 2002. A banquet of food and travel writing, profiles and memories, with an introduction by Ruth Reichl.

Read great magazines and newspapers: Read the national food magazines, such as *Food & Wine, Cook's Illustrated, Fine Cooking, Cooking Light, Saveur,* and *Gastronomica* to keep up on trends and as a continuing form of education. Read newspaper food sections online, particularly those in the *New York Times, Washington Post, San Francisco Chronicle,* and *Chicago Tribune.* You might also like the Food News

Journal (www.foodnewsjournal.com), a daily list of the best food writing from newspapers.

Read food blogs: Subscribe to several so that they arrive in your email or on your browsers' home page by RSS feed. You'll want to devour blogs on the local scene, those who are well known and those who cover your favorite subject, whether it's baking, gluten-free cooking or pizzas. See chapter 4 on blogs to learn more.

Follow food writers on Facebook and Twitter: Most food writers have discovered social media by now, so it's an easy way keep up with them and possibly to develop relationships.

Study cooking: Take cooking lessons through adult education classes, a community college, retail stores, or privately. Many professional cooking schools hold weekend classes for the public. Cookbook writers sometimes hold private cooking classes in their homes.

Or work in a restaurant for a while. Russ Parsons, as a general newspaper reporter, wrote a story on a cooking teacher, and by taking her class realized he wanted to learn more. He took more classes, began assisting her, then friends let him work in their restaurants at no pay. "After I really immersed myself, I felt comfortable writing about food," he says. Working in restaurants isn't for everyone, but you'll get to see chefs in action, see how the back of the restaurant functions, and learn techniques and tricks cooks use to get dishes to the table on time. Perhaps a restaurant would let you watch, rather than cook.

You don't even have to leave the house to study cooking and food. You can learn a tremendous amount from television today. Watch cooking shows and shows about food. My favorites are the old-timers—Jacques Pépin, Julia Child, and Martin Yan.

Study food writing: Go to food-writing classes and conferences. The oldest is the annual Symposium for Professional Food Writers at the Greenbrier in West Virginia. If that's not possible, find food-writing classes in your city or online. Continuing-education classes sharpen your writing skills. Look for classes in your community on nonfiction writing, memoir, and personal essay. (See the Appendix for more suggestions.)

Get a degree in journalism or food studies: Get a degree in food studies from New York University, Boston University or the University of Adelaide in Australia. Most universities take a more interdisciplinary approach to food studies and offer classes through departments that include anthropology, psychology, and nutrition. Journalism programs are offered at universities around the country. The Master's Degree program at UC Berkeley offers the added attraction of Professor Michael Pollan.

Internships are one of the big benefits of studying at a college or university. During my studies as a journalism student I landed two internships: one at a city magazine, and another at a national magazine. The first internship resulted in a cover story (totally rewritten by the editor in chief, but hey, no one had to know). Freelancer Mary Margaret Pack worked as an intern at the *San Francisco Chronicle* while a student at the California Culinary Academy. By the time she graduated, she had a handful of feature stories to show as credentials for future freelancing queries. Both these internships came about because of arrangements the school made with publications.

During college studies in journalism, *The Cake Mix Doctor* author Anne Byrn interned at her hometown newspaper every summer and Christmas break, where she formed relationships with people in the food section. Her coup at the paper was scooping the story of Elvis's death. Living in the South, that was a big deal. She was a junior in college. "It was a Sunday night," she recalls. "That was my shift. There was no one else to write the story."

Travel: Experience firsthand how food is sold, how it tastes, and how people prepare food in their own countries. Watch food preparers in markets and on the street. If possible, meet home cooks and watch them in the kitchen. Visit the night markets of Asia and farmers' markets in Europe. Rent a place with a kitchen and try cooking something unfamiliar. Go to big and small restaurants to taste the local food. Take culinary vacations led by experienced cooks and chefs and get to know them. Buy cookbooks about the food of places you've visited.

Network: If you are a cooking teacher, entrepreneur, or other food professional, join the International Association of Culinary Professionals (www.iacp.com) so you can attend the annual conference and receive the directory of members. To meet other people interested in food, join the American Institute of Wine & Food (www.aiwf.org), or local groups where you can meet people with similar interests. Attend food-based events in your community. If you are a food blogger, join BlogHer (www.blogher.com) or Food Buzz (www.foodbuzz .com) to meet other bloggers in your community.

Byrn says she can't emphasize enough how networking has aided her career. While in college she majored in home economics in addition to journalism. When she graduated she heard about a job from a home economics networking group she had joined. Some of its members were food writers. The opening was for a food writer at the *Atlanta Journal.* She got the job in 1978 and worked there until 1993, at which point she became the section editor.

Believe you will move forward, and be patient: "Sometimes when you throw yourself into the moment you find out you are more learned than you think," says Leite. "Past experience can suddenly coalesce and you know more than you thought you did." On the other hand, it will take a long time because food writing is a skill that must be practiced repeatedly. You must spend an extraordinary amount of time learning about food and writing, says O'Neill, just as you would spend years learning how to play the piano well. But persevere and most likely it will pay off in the end.

Writing Exercises

1. Make a plan of five things you can do to move your knowledge base forward and get closer to writing about food. For example, buy a magazine subscription; take a cooking class; join a chat room. What are the things you need to do to succeed? Give yourself a deadline for accomplishing these five tasks.
2. Investigate two of your favorite food writers. Read as much as you can about them to discover how they started out. If they have written books, this information might be in a foreword or introduction. "Google" them to find interviews or profiles. Write a short report on how each of them got where they are today.

3. Read one of the books on the list on pages 52–54. Choose a style of book you might like to write. Write a 250-word book report on what you enjoyed about the book most. Evaluate the author's writing technique, subject matter, structure, and whether the book held your interest.

4

Get Published with a Food Blog

In the previous chapter, you learned about the path to print publication, where it can take months. In this chapter, you'll learn a simpler way to jump into food writing instantly: blogging.

Food blogs, if you're still not reading them (where have you been!), began as web journals and have evolved to be more like soapboxes. The best have a strong personal voice and message. Many include recipes and posts that are much shorter than feature articles in magazines and newspapers. They're meant to be spontaneous, based on news of the day or events in the blogger's life. The best blogs engage and develop a loyal community of readers.

Blogging is the most exciting area of food writing today. Food bloggers are pushing boundaries, writing about food in ways that print can't. There's immediacy to their writing, a kinship among fellow bloggers, and exhilaration in saying whatever they want, unfettered by editors.

After initially ignoring food blogs, some print publications have embraced them. *Gourmet* experimented with blogs before its demise, *Saveur*'s online site has a regular column dedicated to "sites we love," and Molly Wizenberg of Orangette (www.orangette.blogspot.com), has a regular column in *Bon Appétit*. Newspaper food writers, particularly reviewers, now blog and have large established communities of readers. Book editors and literary agents read blogs, always on the lookout for the next talented blogger worthy of a book contract.

In this newest chapter of *Will Write for Food*, you'll learn about why you should start a blog, how to begin, what to write about, how to develop your voice, how to post good photographs, get noticed, what's involved in turning a blog into a book, and whether you can make money. Along the way, I've interviewed and referenced the best and most exciting food bloggers, who will encourage and guide you.

If you're already blogging, you'll find lots to think about in terms of developing your voice, why certain bloggers succeed, taking your content and photography to the next level (particularly about how personal your posts should be), ethics, going from blog to book, putting ads on your site, and keeping up the energy to post. Get your pen out. You'll be generating new ideas for blog posts as you read.

Why Blog?

Quite simply, it's the easiest way to jump into being a food writer. Jump in and publish your first post within an hour. But more importantly, there are no gatekeepers. In the diminishing world of newspaper and magazine food writing, it's harder than ever to get your foot in the door, particularly for essay writing. Editors don't answer email queries for story ideas, budgets are small, space is tight, and competition is fierce. Even if you do succeed in print, your piece will be reviewed by an editor and may be edited or even rewritten. Having coached beginning writers who want to freelance, and seeing how hard it is, I now suggest they start a blog.

I started one myself, to see what it's all about, and as a way to continue the work of this book. If you haven't been there, see www.diannej.com/blog. It's been so much fun to write whatever I like, and satisfying to get a response. When I'm done, I press a button and there's my work, published on the web. I've been delighted and amazed by the response and my new community online.

Cookbook author, freelancer writer, and blogger Dorie Greenspan is just as enthusiastic. "When I started a blog, I wanted everyone to start a blog," she explains. "Now I feel like everybody has a blog. I would say start it because you have something you want to say, you have something to share, and because it would be fun." (Her blog is at www.doriegreenspan.com.)

"I respect connoisseurship and expertise. I love that there are experts in every field, and I love seeing their work. But I also think there's a place for people who are learning, for people who have something to say and want to share it, and every blog finds its own readership."

These are all great reasons to blog. Now, here are some others: First, blogging is all about you, and who wouldn't love that? It's a conversation with readers about events and ideas that interest you. It's all about what turns you on, what you cook, taste, discover, learn, and share. Writing about your own life is so much easier than writing about anything else, because you are the expert on your own experience.

Another reason to love blogging is that you'll write and publish immediately. There's no turnaround time. "I was in Paris and went to a new pastry shop, where the pastry chef was turning classics around and making them in new ways," continues Greenspan. "I'm no longer an active freelancer, but here I could write about it immediately. I took a few pictures and boom, there it is. It's so instant.

"Would that have made an interesting piece for a magazine? By the time it's published, it would be old news. It's fun to write at the moment you're interested."

That's the beauty of blogging. Not only can you publish immediately, but you can write about whatever you want. When Heidi Swanson started 101 Cookbooks (www.101cookbooks.com), she did so to cook from the cookbooks she had gathered and never used. Now she writes her own recipes and adds stories about travel. "My site is really simple," she told me. "It's my life where it intersects recipes. I can weave in travel, day-to-day tasks, whatever I like. I love to cook and always find something inspiring. I can't imagine not writing my blog."

Another more practical reason to start a blog is because it gives you a way to build a platform immediately as a writer. A platform is your visibility to readers, and it's important if you want to move forward in your career. It shows editors and agents that you have a following, and it creates a springboard to other opportunities. If you want to freelance, now you have writing samples to show. If you want to write a book, the content in your blog gives you a good starting point, and its readership shows that people are interested. Furthermore, you have to sit down and write, regularly, so you're already doing the job.

The readership is a further reason to start a blog. An unexpected joy I get from blogging is the community of writers and thinkers who read my posts and leave comments. I spend a lot of time alone at my desk, and the willingness of other bloggers to post their comments and insights gives me a thrill, a feeling that I'm part of something larger. I've become part of a community, a far-flung network of enthusiastic writers who contact each other for questions and support. The camaraderie among other bloggers is another terrific part of blogging. I've helped others and they've helped me, particularly with the technical issues.

Here's what a longtime food blogger, Adam Roberts of the Amateur Gourmet (www.amateurgourmet.com) says about the benefits of his blog. "Aside from the fact that lots of people will read what you write on a daily basis (which is always exciting), you get to act as your own editor, producer, director, publisher and secretary. You can make money from ads (though not enough to act as a super incentive). You can find a way to channel your creative energies (hence all my films and songs and EXTREMELY LONG posts like this one).

"And, best of all, you have a great reason to really explore the world of food: both in the kitchen and out in the world. If I didn't have a food blog, I doubt I'd cook all the stuff I cook or eat at as many places as I do. I do most of it so I can sit down later and process everything that I just experienced, for better or for worse. And over time you've created this gigantic record of your journey. If you click my archives and read the posts I posted my first couple of weeks as food blogger, I think you'll detect a marked difference in my competence level, my knowledge and my confidence both as a writer and as a chef. Food blogging pays off."

For some people, their blog is their life story. David Lebovitz (www.davidlebovitz.com), whose tagline is "Living the Sweet Life in Paris," says he doesn't think of himself as a food writer, but as someone writing about his life. "That's how you keep readers," he advises. "You never know what people are going to respond to. It's being personal, talking about something engaging, having a conversation."

Choosing a Software Service

Before you begin writing, you need to know some technical basics of getting your blog started. You'll have to decide which blogging software service to use and on whose server. Each service has different templates to fill in, customizable by you. Here are some of the most popular choices:

- Blogger, owned by Google, at www.blogger.com. A free service, Blogger is easy to use. Your blog will be hosted on Blogger's own server, which means the address will end with blogspot.com.
- Moveabletype, at www.moveabletype.com. It's a free service for personal use, but if you plan to have ads or sell books, you have to pay. Some big bloggers including Lebovitz and Elise Bauer of Simply Recipes use this software, customized by a designer.
- Typepad, at www.typepad.com. While Typepad will host your blog, it is not free because the target customer are businesses, not individuals. The cost is anywhere from $8.95 to $89.95 per month, and typepad.com will appear in your address. Supposedly, customer support is better because you pay this monthly fee. Some say the interface is easier to use than Wordpress.
- Wordpress, at www.wordpress.com. Wordpress is easy to use, includes many design templates (sixty at last count, some customizable) and hosts your blog free of charge. You'll have an address that ends in wordpress.com.

As I mentioned, the downside of these blogging platforms is that their name (blogspot, typepad, wordpress, etc.) will appear as part of the address of your blog name, unless you pay to move the software to a host service company. Doing so means choosing your own domain name which does away with the name of the software host. Most bloggers recommend you get your own domain name immediately. It makes it easier for people to find you by just typing the name of your blog or your name into a search field, rather than having to know which blogging platform you use.

When I started my blog, for example, the address was www .diannejacob.wordpress.com. After a few months, I moved my blog to the company that hosts my Web site, and now the address is part of my blog, www.diannej.com/blog. Registering for a domain name is inexpensive, beginning at $10 per year to use the name you choose. Some companies offer free registration for the first year. Next, find a company to host your Web site. That costs anywhere from $25–$150 per year, depending on which service you choose.

To customize your blogging software further, hire a designer. Make sure the designer understands the blogging software you use, and be prepared to shell out anywhere from $500 to a few thousand dollars, depending on the scope of the project. Get recommendations from others, shop around, and obtain a few bids to compare prices. Check the fine print on blogs you like as sometimes the designer will be listed with a link.

No matter which service you use, most blog templates have standard design elements. A header appears on every page of your site and shows people the name of your blog, like a newspaper masthead. Customize yours with colors, fonts, illustrations, or photographs. Below it, each post begins with a headline. Under each post, readers are invited to comment. On the side, the widgets you install create items such as a list of your most popular posts or a list of links to favorite sites, called a blogroll. Most blogs include a bio section, often called the About page. We'll talk about that in a moment.

Come Up with a Title

Blog names are usually more personal than book titles and make a statement about the person or the spirit of the blog. Avoid inside jokes and titles only you can understand.

Some titles are evocative or literary, such as:

- Orangette
- Chocolate & Zucchini
- In Praise of Sardines

Many are autobiographical:

- The Amateur Gourmet
- Cooking With Amy
- Gluten-Free Girl
- Homesick Texan
- Hunter Angler Gardener Cook
- The Paupered Chef

And many are clever or funny:

- Accidental Hedonist
- Blog Appetit
- Cake Wrecks
- Smitten Kitchen

The best way to find out if your title ideas work is to try them out on friends. If you get a blank stare, keep going. Also avoid difficult words to spell. You don't want people to continually mis-type your blog's name into their web browsers.

Create an
About Page or Section

An About section or page explains why you started your blog and what you hope to achieve. If people like reading your blog, they'll go there to find out about you. Grab their attention by explaining your blog's philosophy in a sound-bite-sized sentence. At Smitten Kitchen (www.smittenkitchen.com), it's "Fearless Cooking from a tiny kitchen in New York City." At Steamy Kitchen (www.steamykitchen.com), it's "Fast, fresh and simple for tonight's supper."

Post enough content to let your readers get to know you. It will make them more likely to connect and comment. It's not meant to be your life story, however. A few paragraphs are sufficient. Stick to the subject of your blog. Self-deprecating humor, if you know how to do it, works well. Here are three examples of About pages, where the voice and personality of the bloggers come through clearly:

Deb Perelman of Smitten Kitchen, www.smittenkitchen.com: "Deb is the kind of person you might innocently ask what the difference is between summer and winter squash and she'll go on for about 20 minutes before coming up for air to a cleared room and you are soundly snoring. It's taken some time, but she's finally realized that there are people out there that might forgive her for such food, cooking and ingredient-obsessed blathering and possibly, even come back for more. When she's not prattling on about galley and grub, Deb is a freelance writer focusing on topics from technology to the daily grind, and a freelance photographer with a focus on travel and, of course, food."

Clotilde Dusoulier of Chocolate & Zucchini, http://chocolate andzucchini.com: "Chocolate & Zucchini is a blog written by Clotilde Dusoulier, a 24 25 26 27 28 29 30-year-old Parisian woman who lives in Montmartre and shares her passion for all things food-related—thoughts, recipes, musings, cookbook acquisitions, quirky ingredients, nifty tools, restaurant experiences, ideas, and inspirations. The blog was created in September of 2003 as an outlet for someone who feared her friends might tire of hearing about what she cooked/ate/baked/bought, though they didn't seem to have a problem with being fed dinner. One thing led to another, a bit of media attention was received, articles were submitted to and published by newspapers and magazines, a book deal was signed, a day job was quit, and a new life as a full-time food writer began."

Pim Techamuanvivit of Chez Pim, www.chezpim.com: "Pim grew up in Bangkok, was shipped off to study in other places, and somehow found herself living and loving it in the San Francisco Bay Area. She quit her Silicon Valley job in 2005 to pursue a career in food: the writing, reporting, and anything interesting thereof that comes her way. Her recipes, writings, and photographs have since appeared in the *New York Times*, *Food & Wine* magazine, and *Bon Appétit* magazine. She's also moonlighted as a judge on Iron Chef America. Chez Pim chronicles her globetrotting adventures—and misadventures—in the world of all things edible, from vibrant street-side fares in Asia to the refined world of Three Michelin Star restaurants in Europe. Pim also cooks a mean pot of curry."

The only thing I'd change about these About pages is that they're written in the third person. The rest of the blog is written in first person, so I see it as inconsistent. I understand why people do it. It feels uncomfortable to write what "I" did, kind of like bragging. "Pim cooks a mean pot of curry" sounds less egotistical than "I cook a mean pot of curry." But since you write your blog in the first person, try writing your About page in first person too.

When you're done with the text, add a good quality headshot. It doesn't have to be a professional photo, but you don't want a shot that's blurry, low resolution, shows extraneous details in the background, or has little contrast (more about photography later). Your photo is part of your online persona, so don't shy away from it. It helps people connect with you.

Other pages you might consider adding, once your blog gets going, are a policy page about accepting review items or products (more on that later), a list of contest rules if you plan to give away products, or a Frequently Asked Questions (FAQ) page if people keep contacting you about the same topics. Readers of Lebovitz's blog often want Paris restaurant recommendations and information about living in France, so his FAQ provides this information, saving him from answering the same questions individually in emails. At the bottom of your blog page, add information about copyright— that everything on the site belongs to the author, and any reprints are only by permission of the author.

What to Write About

One of the top reasons people start blogs is to write about their life and experiences. Food blogging can be just about that, because there's no end of topics based on your life, such as a kitchen tool you can't live without, a trip abroad, mastering a challenging recipe, ranting about a school lunch program, or reviewing a new cookbook.

When you begin a blog, you might not have much of a focus. I've seen many new blogs based on loving food, where people just want to express their knowledge, joy, and passion. For some, blogging is a way people discover what they're passionate about. Initially, though, a broad theme, such as "I love food," can feel overwhelming or vague. Try to distill your interests down to a theme or structure. Carve out your niche. Don't worry about a tight focus. Some blogs are based just on bacon or pizza (two popular topics with lots of material).

Dusoulier of Chocolate & Zucchini says she tries to write about "new things, things I've not written about before, or haven't cooked before, to keep myself and readers interested. I'm that way in general in life. I don't like to rehash things. I don't watch movies several times. I'm most excited about a recipe when I've recently overcome something, when I've tried something new and it turned out well. I want to share it."

Whatever you find yourself thinking and talking about most could be the focus of your blog. To figure it out, pay attention to which magazine articles catch your eye, which food shows you watch most, which books attract you, which cuisines you cook most, or what you're doing when you lose track of time.

In one of the early food blogs and easily the most famous, the Julie/Julia project, Julie Powell took on cooking her way through Julia Child's *Mastering the Art of French Cooking*, and posted about her trials with herself, husband, job, and blog readers. She gave herself a challenge, and you could do the same. Blog to explore and master a new subject, to cope with a crisis, or to reflect. But be careful. If you're too self-indulgent, readers will not respond. Strike a balance, inject humor, and look for ways to connect with your readers.

How to Make People Care

At this point you're probably thinking, "Why should anyone care about what I have to say?" Good question, and a valid one. If all you want to do is document what you ate, probably few people will. Your job is to make readers care. Food blogging is about more than your performance in the kitchen or a list of the dishes you ate at a restaurant.

Instead, develop your storytelling skills so readers keep coming back. Use humor, self-deprecation, confession, guilt, and suspense. It's about drawing readers in, and whether people can relate to your experience. It's about eliciting emotions and reminding readers of events in their own lives.

One way to write about food is to approach your material in a new way, says Lebovitz. "What do you say about vanilla ice cream that hasn't been said before?" he asks. Ask what's interesting about your subject or figure out a quirky approach.

Conflict always gets people going, if you can be entertaining at the same time. "People love when I'm butting up against the bureaucracy of France or a nasty salesperson, but nobody wants to read a six-page rant," says Lebovitz. Author and blogger Michael Ruhlman, at http:// blog.ruhlman.com, likes conflict as well. "My most successful posts tend to be rants where I fly off on something, and get hundreds of comments."

Even blogs comprised of recipe posts are not just about what someone made in the kitchen that day. Three of the biggest and most successful food bloggers, Elise Bauer of Simply Recipes (www.simply recipes.com), Ree Drummond of The Pioneer Woman Cooks (www .thepioneerwoman.com/cooking), and Heidi Swanson of 101 Cook-books, have built huge databases of recipes, and perhaps that's how new readers find them initially, when searching a recipe for a particular dish. But what makes readers stay or return?

Here's Drummond's recipe for acorn squash roasted with lots of brown sugar and butter: ". . . But the holidays are approaching. And the holidays are a time for celebration, not restraint. I wonder how many consecutive years I'll tell myself that before I can no longer fit through the door of my house? Oh well. I'll cross that bridge when I come to it." Now, haven't you been there many times, wondering how much weight you'll gain over the holidays, but wanting to make an indulgent dish anyway? Drummond reveals her vulnerabilities and writes as though she's talking to a sister or a best friend, even though you don't know her. She also tells you to go ahead and enjoy yourself, and who doesn't love that message?

Bauer is close to her parents and often writes about them in her recipe headnotes. Here's an example from the headnote of Spicy Veg-etarian Chili: "Those of you who have been reading Simply Recipes for a while probably sense (rightly) that my father is a committed carnivore. Thus you may appreciate that dad, spending an afternoon making this vegetarian chili with vegetables he bought at the farmers market that morning, would only put so much care into a meat-free chili, his din-ner, if that chili were darn good. . . . Of course my mother did have to convince dad that no, we didn't need steak in addition to the chili, (because) the beans were full of protein." Ostensibly, the piece is about chili, but it's really about her family members and their dynamics and her contentment with the arrangement.

For a post on pineapple rice, Swanson got eighty-three comments. Read her lead and see if you can figure out why: "I've been to Hawaii two times. Once when I was sixteen, and again when I was twenty. Once to Maui, once to Kona. I remember it being lush and vibrant, achingly beautiful. The more miles you put between yourself and the resort areas, the better it got. I think I'd like to go back at some point, so when I realized there was an Edible Hawaiian Islands publication I subscribed to it with the hope that I'd discover farms, producers, markets and restaurants to seek out when we finally get around to going. The latest issue arrived in the mail the other night, and while flipping through it, I came across a recipe for a pineapple rice salad. I rarely cook with Hawaiian flavor profiles, but this looked too good to pass up. . . ."

Suddenly it's not about the rice. It's about being young again, traveling to exotic places, remembering the beauty and lushness of a tropical place, and subscribing to a magazine to be reminded. We've all been there. These universal themes are what draw us in.

In each case, these bloggers write about their own lives. They are experts at engaging your emotions and making you react. They present ideal scenarios, such as deserving a rich holiday dish, or living happily with parents, or memories of a trip to an exotic place.

The best bloggers know how to make you identify with them. "My hook, as you all know, is that I'm an incompetent louse who really wants to learn about food," jokes Roberts on the Amateur Gourmet. "Hence my blog details my adventures making mistakes and learning the ropes."

If you can be as funny as Roberts, you'll win readers easily. Here's an exercise: Try writing as if to a witty friend, where you feel compelled to be witty too. Imagine her across the table as you tell the story. Leave in the uncomfortable or messy parts. Try to make her laugh until she snorts and doubles over. Then write the same way you would talk, and don't take yourself too seriously.

Jaden Hair attributes some of her chatty style on Steamy Kitchen to dictation software with a headset. Once Stephanie Stiavetti of

Wasabimon (www.wasabimon.com) tried it, she said the software changed the way she wrote, because it made her language so much more conversational.

While yes, blogging is all about you, it's different from writing in a journal, which no one sees. You have readers. At first they might be your family and circle of friends, but eventually, strangers will come to your site. Look at who they are, why they care about your posts, and what makes them comment. Blogging is about reaching out, not just documenting your life. Connect with them further.

One way to do so is to use universal themes, the kind of subjects everyone understands: love, failure, curiosity, and loss, for example. No doubt your readers have also made a dish that went horribly wrong, or tried a new ingredient and learned from it, or fretted about growing older. And that means deciding about how personal to get, a subject of some anxiety among bloggers.

How Personal Should You Be?

Up to now I've been practical about how to write your post. I've talked about why to blog, how to come up with good content, and structure it for optimum impact. But that's not all there is to writing for a blog. What all good blogging has in common is the ability to evoke emotion from the reader. To do that, you have to get personal.

As in the samples of recipe headnotes I mentioned earlier, evoking emotion means getting in touch with your vulnerability and letting readers identify with your situation. That requires honesty and, to some extent, courage. "Believe it or not, people want to know things about you," explains Roberts on The Amateur Gourmet. "People want you to air your dirty laundry. People want to know if you're happily married, if you like your job. People want to know if you're dyslexic, if you used to be bulimic, if you're a recovering Republican. People really want to know if you're gay (believe me). Tell us who you're dating, tell us who broke your heart, but do it in the context of food. Remember this is a food blog, not a confessional."

You may not be comfortable with divulging this level of information, but if you are, pouring your heart out can make a difference to your readers. Consider what Charity Lynne Burggraaf, a food photographer, says in an interview on Wasabimon: "What I have found to be the most important thing to put into a blog is your heart. Which was something I tried to separate from my writing for a long time on my blog (might sound strange, but I didn't want to get too emotional—as it is my work). But I was amazed at the amount of support I got when I decided to open myself up a bit and talk about my mom and her battle with breast cancer this past year. Come to find out that my most popular posts often don't have to do with food at all!

"I've found that people are interested in my life, and not just my work. Heck, if they wanted to see my work they could visit my Web site! I'm learning that by opening myself up, it in turn creates a sense of community and a great support system of foodies and photographers— something I've often heard about and been a part of on the outside—but I'm still in awe of it happening on my own little blog. And I'm grateful for it."

Michael Ruhlman believes the personal part adds value, and he's not paranoid about it. "I'm not concerned that someone's going to kidnap my kid because they're reading my blog. If that was going to happen it's not because I'm writing about it. This is all so new, but if you don't feel comfortable, don't write about it," he advises. Criticizing people is off limits, he has learned. "You risk alienating people when you don't have to. Why alienate readers when you can bring them in? I can't afford to lose a single reader."

Clotilde Dusoulier, on the other hand, doesn't feel comfortable with private matters. "I see some bloggers who talk about their relationship to their mother, or a marital situation or break up, or a struggle on an emotional level. I don't do that on my blog.

"It's not that I think it's wrong. I'm in a very happy place, so there's not a lot of turmoil to discuss. If it doesn't have anything to do with food it doesn't come up. I'm very careful about my friends and family member's privacy as well. I don't reveal things about them they wouldn't like to read about online, and I'm vague about who I'm with. I don't reveal about people anything they haven't expressly told me it's okay to share."

Instead, says Dusoulier, she gets personal in tone. "It's chatty enough. I try to draw people in as if they were guests at my table. If I met them in person I would probably be the same way as I write."

Another person who's known for getting personal is David Lebovitz. "I have broader boundaries than most people," he admits. I asked him whether any of his posts might have been too personal. He pointed me to one with photos of a huge meringue he tried to flush down his toilet. Three days later, he wrote a second post, accompanied by a photo, because the meringue was still there. It was hilarious, and that's one of the best parts about David's posts. He's willing to not take himself too seriously.

"If done right, blogging is fun," says Drummond in a guest editorial on www.wepc.com. "Make it fun for you and for your readers. You don't have to be a cut-up or a comedian. But in this day and age, when everything around us is so weighed down and heavy, don't be afraid to take a picture of your toenails, draw a parallel between your chipped polish and world peace, and call it a day."

Regardless of how much you share with readers, a big part of writing is trusting yourself, believing what you write is worthwhile and valuable. Particularly if you're going to be vulnerable, you can't move forward if a negative voice in your head pops up. This voice makes unhelpful pronouncements, such as "You're no good at this," or "Why would anyone want to read this junk?" I call it the Internal Editor.

Everyone has one. You wouldn't believe how many top bloggers I interviewed who told me they are not very good writers. But they don't let that voice stop them, and neither should you. Nor can you get rid of it. It's a part of you. I've dealt with this voice since I began writing professionally in 1975.

"It's the editor voice that stops you from writing," confirms Shauna Ahern of Gluten-Free Girl and the Chef (www.glutenfreegirl.blogspot.com). "I think of a cramped librarian with a bun, yelling at me for putting my feet up on the desk. The more you can gently tell the editor to go get a cup of coffee and come back, the more you can trust your instincts. You want to be wild and funny and vulnerable and very much yourself. Then she can come back later and make it into a better piece of writing."

That's when the internal editor has value. Invite her back to help you edit. Personify the voice and tell her, when she arrives, that there's a purpose to her comments and you value them, but to please help only when you need it.

Develop Your Voice

Related to the topics of evoking emotion and not taking yourself too seriously is your voice. While I've discussed voice in another part of this book (see pages 13–18), nowhere is it more important than in a blog. "Blogs are dependent on the voice, they live or die based on it," says Ruhlman. It's because people go there to read about you: what you think, how your day went. You need a conversational voice, less formal than a book, and more personal than a magazine or newspaper article. The key is to make it memorable and uniquely yours, so people could know it's you just by reading a few sentences.

"More important than a concept, more important than anything, really, is that quality that makes all great writing worth reading and that's your voice," advises Roberts of Amateur Gourmet on his Web site. "Bring yourself into your food blogging and everything else will follow. When I first started, I wrote a ridiculous food song every Thursday night and sang it for no good reason. You can still hear them on the lower left hand of the site. Why are those there? Do they really have anything to do with food? Of course not. But they give you a sense of what I'm about."

In one of my first blog posts, I looked at what makes a great food blog. The number one characteristic was a strong personality. The bloggers you read are fun, intelligent, opinionated, and creative. They make you think, and make you learn. No matter what they're writing about, you want them to be passionate and well informed.

The actual subject matters less if you're a strong writer with strong opinions. "When I started my blog, I wrote about anything I felt like writing about, and I still more or less do, and that's what makes my voice unique," says Ruhlman.

But writing with a strong voice does not happen right away. "It takes a while to find your voice, to have an aura, sense of who you are," says Dusoulier. "Keep at it, and don't expect much initially. Try to craft it." In other words, you can't be Michael Ruhlman right away. He was already a successful author before beginning his blog. Dusoulier, on the other hand, was unknown and got there through sheer perseverance and enthusiasm.

FIFTEEN WAYS TO WRITE YOUR LIFE THROUGH FOOD

Shauna James Ahern, a former high school English teacher, writes in a strong, happy, and irrepressible voice on Gluten-Free Girl and the Chef. You don't need food allergies to read about life with her chef husband and her passion for cooking. Here's Ahern's suggestion list of how to write about life and food, culled from a Leite's Culinaria class she gave about voice:

- Read avidly, at least 10 blogs, and more than one magazine. Be voracious. Gobble up the information.
- Eat well. You probably eat better now than before you started reading about food writing anyway.
- Pay attention to everything. We rush through our days and we miss most everything. Take notes. Ask yourself what food reminds you of. It's amazing how much we filter out.
- Write. A lot. Write every day.
- Allow yourself to write lousy first drafts. We have so much anxiety about writing, so many bad teachers who taught us writing was about spelling and grammar. (But remember, first drafts don't get published, even on a blog.)
- Write to connect, not to impress. It kills good writing to think it has to be amazing every time. You don't think that when cooking.
- Play.
- Figure out what fascinates you about food.
- Use strong verbs, rather than was, have, going, being. Make your writing vivid.
- Avoid adjectives, if possible. Focus on dynamic verbs instead to make your subject sing.
- Think film. Show people your world and how you see it. Think like a camera, pulling back, getting the close-ups, and doing flashbacks like you see in films.
- Forget taste. Listen instead, and describe the sounds.
- Point sideways. Allow yourself to go down trails and expand on what you find, and then see where you end up.
- Think about how you construct sentences.

- Remember to give yourself in every word. Choose each word consciously, to create sentences that are your own. No one else could write the sentences I write because no one else is in my head, with my experiences and memories and expectations. The more we reveal ourselves, the more other people will connect.

Writing Your Post

Now that you've learned the basics of starting a blog and contemplated what to say and how to say it, it's time to write a post. Your biggest challenge might not be what you think: Writing a blog is a commitment. To be successful, post at least twice a week. It keeps you engaged and keeps you connected to your readership. Some people post more often than that. Dusoulier says she posted twice a day for a year when she started Chocolate & Zucchini, on top of a full-time job.

Set up a schedule of which days of the week to post, or start a few drafts for those days when your brain turns to mush. While David Lebovitz says he has no schedule, and posts whenever he likes, he also confessed at a conference that he might have as many as forty drafts going at one time, some that will never be published.

It might help to make a list of ten potential ideas, even if they're just a sentence long. That way you'll frame the subject of your blog and keep on topic. If you're really organized, write extra posts on timeless subjects, and save them in drafts.

It's one thing to think up subjects for your blog, but another to figure out how to frame or develop them. Here are a few suggestions:

Start a conversation. Bring up a topic, tell a story about it, and ask what others think.

Hook onto the news of the day. Have an opinion about the latest survey on junk food, or on a winning chef contestant on television, or discuss a newspaper story with your own spin. Get your post up quickly so people can find it when they search on the news event.

Make an argument. You believe donuts are unfairly maligned or coriander is the world's most versatile spice. Speak your passion and voice an opinion. It's also effective to be a contrarian sometimes when everyone else is busy agreeing.

Tell a story. Did you talk with a memorable character at the farmer's market? Did a pie become a colossal flop? Look for moments like these to make a larger point about your life, moments everyone can relate to where they think, "That's what I would do," or "I've been there," or even "I would never do that."

Talk about a book, movie, or product. They don't even have to be new. Perhaps you looked through your cookbook collection and became inspired to try a recipe, or you thought about a treasured utensil you can't live without.

Give away a product. Givaways are a terrific way to boost visibility of your blog. Most bloggers just announce a giveaway, with no strings attached, then pick a commenter at random and mail off the item. If it's a product given to you for free, and you promote it, however, different rules apply. More on that later.

Hook on to an upcoming event. Add a twist to stand out, such as "Ten Vegan No-Fail Dishes for Thanksgiving."

Surprise your readers. Write something unexpected, or spin a well-worn story and give it an unusual twist.

Regarding how long a post to write, the idea is to keep it short. When I first started researching blog writing online, I read on several sites that the maximum word count for a post is 250 words. You won't always be able to keep to that, but it's a good rule of thumb. You want to be mercifully brief. Make your point and get out. Blog readers only expect to spend a minute or two on your site.

Lebovitz points out that, more than other types of writing, blog posts that go on too long can be boring and cause readers to click away. "Most people are reading on small screens and have their hands on the mouse," he points out. "I suggest people go back and tighten up the post, removing anything that isn't helpful, compelling, or vital. It's likely readers won't miss those things either, and that will give them a chance to concentrate on what is important and interesting."

Once you've determined your content, learn how to structure a blog post. There's a system writers, particularly journalists, use to keep people reading. It's because readers decide at every step of the way whether to keep going. Like you, they're busy and want to know if the investment of time is worth it. Here are ways to keep them on the page:

Start with a good title or headline. This is your first point of entry for readers, so work hard on a good one. Keep it short. Study headlines in aggregate food news sites such as the Food News Journal (www.foodnewsjournal.com) to see what works. When brainstorming title ideas, try one based on these ideas. The headlines are real:

- Ask a provocative question, such as: "Is Your Credit Card Bill Making You Fat?"
- Be intriguing: "Why I Would Spend $200 on Dinner."
- Make people curious: "Ten Dishes You Must Make this Fall."
- Provide expert guidance: "The CoffeeMeister Talks Coffee Filters."
- Make a list: "Four Chocolate Questions Answered."
- Reassure readers, as in: "Freezer Jam: A Baby Step to Canning."
- Take a stand: "In Defense of Michael Pollan and a Civil Food Debate."
- Go for humor, especially with a potentially dull subject: "Dude Food."
- Make the description irresistible: "Baked, Buttered Corn."
- Be a little outrageous: "Blowtorch Prime Rib."

Follow with a lead paragraph. A compelling introduction reels people in with just enough detail to keep them interested and willing to continue. Tell a story, recite an intriguing statistic, or use the same techniques outlined for writing a headline. A good lead restates and expands upon the headline.

Set up your story. Learn to repeat. Tell people what you're going to tell them (headline and lead), then tell them (body). Later, you'll tell them what you just told them (conclusion). It makes readers feel comfortable about continuing.

Make one key point per blog post. Use the body of the post to expand upon your title and lead. Engage readers' emotions and connect with them.

Know your audience. It's easier to engage readers if you know who they are. Decide whom you're talking to and what they want to know, and then give it to them. What keeps them up at night? What makes them laugh? What are they obsessed about? What do they fear when cooking?

Also remember that readers only come for a few seconds. If they don't like what they see, they hit the back button. Adam Roberts of the Amateur Gourmet knows what people want to find on his site. "Spending time on a blog is like spending time with a person," he explains. "Imagine yourself at a party surrounded by people all of whom care about food. Would you rather talk to the sullen person with the digital camera who's standing near the cheese and crackers and mumbling about the levels of flavor in raw milk cheese? Or would you rather stand next to the high-spirited, highly animated talker who's telling a harrowing tale of a near-death experience with caramel? I know where I'd be."

On the other hand, don't pander to your readers and write just what you think people want to read. "There are things I could do to dial up my readership," admits David Lebovitz. "Everybody wants recipes. If I just did chocolate recipes three times a week, that would work." But he'd be bored out of his mind, and soon, writing his blog might stop being fun. Strive for a balance of what you enjoy and what readers want.

Own your topic. Write your own opinion, but offer value. Interview an expert for background, or read up about your subject. Offer fascinating facts based on food history or cooking technique, or contextual information about the place you visited. Flesh out your story to add telling details.

Try not to assume that everyone knows what you know, especially if you're a fanatic on French chocolate, or passionate about Peruvian food. Make sure you're talking to readers at the right level. Back up and explain. Hold their hands if you think they need it. Fill in details they might not know.

"Remember that your reader may never have made a scone before, or never deseeded a jalapeno, or doesn't know what a good cheddar is," says Ahern. "I want to encourage people to move into the kitchen, to invite them to the table."

Don't try to be the end authority on every topic, on the other hand. Says Ree Drummond of The Pioneer Woman Cooks on www.wepc .com: "Now, if you have a specialized blog about baking and you're a trained pastry chef, then go ahead! Be an expert! But if you're merely imparting what you believe and understand about parenting, politics, religion, or current events, just keep in mind that at least 50 percent of your readers will have a legitimate opinion that's often diametrically opposed to yours. And that doesn't make them necessarily wrong. Not that you have to compromise what you believe; but always consider that others won't agree with you, and leave a little wiggle room for healthy, intelligent discussion."

Add links. Connect to other blogs and websites to give your site more depth and richness, particularly if you're referring to information on another Web site. I love using links because they let me keep my posts shorter, but provide depth for those readers who want it. For a post that mentioned Nora Ephron, one of my favorite writers, I linked to a long and well-written Wikipedia entry about her books and screenplays, so readers could find out more.

Part of adding value is doing the research so your readers don't have to. It's a way to pack your post with more details without making it longer. Plus, the people you link to will find out and might link back to you, which increases your exposure.

You'll also want to link back to an earlier post, whenever possible, to keep readers on your site.

Lebovitz cautions linking to sites that aren't reputable or those that may disappear over time. A reader contacted him recently about a site he'd linked to, Filthy France, about dirty streets. It had become an explicit porn site and she was surprised to find it on his blog.

Write a close or conclusion. Tell them what you just told them, or circle back to the theme of the lead and restate it.

Review your text for density. Before you post, make sure you've created short sentences and short paragraphs. People are in a hurry. Break up your text with subheads and links, which appear in a different color. Use commas when necessary, but not every time, and often not before the word "and." You don't want to slow people down.

Review your text for errors. Before you click that "publish" button, check for typos, spelling mistakes, grammatical errors, and other faux pas that make your blog post look unprofessional. Unlike print, where your writing goes through a copy editor and possibly a proofreader, you're on your own here to catch all mistakes. Read over your text and headline several times, including in "preview" mode. If you can, let it rest for at least 24 hours. Poring over your post with fresh eyes is a great way to catch mistakes.

As Deb Perelman of Smitten Kitchen said on the Food Blog Alliance Web site, "When I see a site just swamped with errors and obvious spelling mistakes that could have been easily picked up by a spell-checker, I lose interest. If this person doesn't care enough about their readers to put their best site forward, why should I spend my time there? I like it when people seem like they really care about what they're doing."

Post often, at least twice a week. "I've got to do that or I'll lose people," says Ruhlman. "I don't write long posts because people don't have the time and don't finish and get bored. It's different from reading a *New Yorker* article, because it's less well written and I didn't take a long time to hone and condense. It's a more spontaneous act."

A Word About Recipes

It seems as though most food blogs are recipe blogs. If you're writing your own recipes, please read chapter 8 on the subject of developing, testing, and writing recipes. Otherwise, here are few issues to address about writing recipes online: using photos, adding links, and giving credit. I'll also address using recipes by others.

Because blogs are such a visual medium, it's helpful to show photos of more than just the finished dish. Some bloggers, like Ree Drummond, are all about the process, posting up to 50 photos for one recipe. You don't have to include that many, but it's useful to show your readers what a sauce looked like before and after you reduced it, or how finely you chopped the onions, or what a simmer looks like.

The key is to post photos that add value. A shot of you pouring olive oil into an empty saute pan doesn't tell the reader anything, nor does a photo of an orange on a countertop. A photo of mise en place (prepped ingredients ready for cooking), on the other hand, is popular and effective.

Build in links within your recipe whenever relevant, as another way of adding value. A recipe Dorie Greenspan posted required making caramel. "I was able to refer people to an incredible link on David Lebovitz's site about making perfect caramel," says Greenspan. "Before I would filter the info, and now I can send readers off, and it more than doubles the information."

When readers have questions about your method or ingredients, refine your recipe immediately. That's the beauty of writing online. In print, you'd have to wait for the next printing or edition.

If you're using other writers' recipes, it's essential that you give credit. Whatever you do, don't post a recipe exactly the way it appears and claim it as your own. If your Aunt Helen hand wrote a recipe for angel food cake on an index card and doesn't remember where she got it, do an online search to see if you can determine the original author. Aside from that, all you can do is tell people about Aunt Helen and her recipe, so no one thinks you've stolen it. Besides, now you've got a unique story to tell as a creative headnote.

If you're reviewing a cookbook or want to use a published recipe, you have two options. Either adapt the recipe and explain how you have changed it in the headnote, or ask the publisher for permission to print it exactly as it appears.

Write Book Reviews

If you're an avid reader, you might review cookbooks and other kinds of food books on your blog. Start with books from your library and eventually you could build enough credibility to get on publishers' lists of reviewers. If you make it, you will receive complimentary books with the expectation of a review, but it's not mandated.

Most food bloggers I know who do reviews have a policy: if they don't love the book, they don't review it. I'm not a fan of this kind of thinking, and I believe it leads to mediocre reviews that are always raves. The best reviews are balanced opinions. They are mostly good, but also point out weaknesses in structure, clarity, voice, accuracy, and other issues. On the other hand, there's not a lot of point to a purely negative review.

Strive for middle ground or higher, be polite but constructive, and if you didn't like the book, explain why. When you are done, imagine you are the author and read your review from his or her perspective. I bring this up because the Internet sometimes lacks civility, and negative reviews can affect the author's sales.

Here's an example of constructive criticism from Nora Ephron on the Food 52 Web site (www.food52.com): "There are a lot of tomato recipes in *Canal House Cooking*; after all, it's a summer cookbook. One is for a tomato sandwich. I love tomato sandwiches. I had one every day last summer until the tomato blight. There's nothing wrong with having a recipe for a tomato sandwich in a cookbook, but it's not singing to me because I already know the song. There's also a recipe for stuffed baked tomatoes served over pasta. This sounds good. But oddly enough, the recipe says that it takes ninety minutes to bake the tomatoes. I don't understand this. I've been baking stuffed tomatoes for years. Who needs ninety minutes to bake a tomato? (This reminds me, by the way, that one of the recipes in *Canal House Cooking* is for a pork loin cooked in milk. We all remember this recipe—we learned to make it when Marcella Hazan put it into her first cookbook. The recipe in the *Canal House* book is almost exactly the same as Marcella's, except for one thing: it takes 60–90 minutes longer, to reduce the milk. This seems weird.)"

To write a serious book review:

- Read the whole book, even if you skim parts of it.
- Look up the competition as a point of comparison.
- Read about the author and familiarize yourself with his or her previous work, so you will have a context in which to review.
- Consider the book's target reader. If it is not you, consider whether it's appropriate and useful for that reader.
- For cookbooks, make at least three of the recipes so you know whether they work. If you loved the book, now you can say why with authority. As explained above in the recipe section, if you want to include recipes from the book, you cannot type in published recipes without the publisher's permission, unless you adapt the recipe and explain how you did so in the headnote.
- If you loved the book, explain why with "show not tell." Show readers why with examples, rather than just writing, "I loved it."

Many book reviewers also do giveaways at the end of their review as a way to build blog traffic.

Good Photos are a Must

It sounds obvious, but good photos of food are critical on a food blog. "Unlike political or music blogs that focus on things that rarely have a visual component, food is something tangible, something you can hold, and something you want to see before you taste," says Adam Roberts on The Amateur Gourmet. "And the fact that you see food before you taste it—the fact that how the food looks often affects whether or not you want to taste it—makes photography an integral part of food blogging. Any food blogger can write on and on and on and on about a piece of pie or a fish eyeball they ate at El Bulli, but more than in any other form of blog (and maybe I'm overstating) when it comes to food blogging, a picture's worth 1,000 words."

Matt Armendariz of Matt Bites (www.mattbites.com) concurs. "A food shot is special when the photographer or stylist (or even blogger) has a real connection to the food," he says on www.digitalphoto graphyblogs.com. "This appreciation and love really shows in the final frame; you simply can't fake it. I've never met a successful food photographer that wasn't also a foodie. There's a reason for this.

"When buying photography or art directing a shoot I look for two factors: my emotional reaction and the technical factor. Does the food photo wow me? Do I want to reach in and take a bite? And is the photo high quality, unique, and technically well executed? I'm willing to forsake one side if the other side excels."

Now, you may have no idea how to get photos like that. You have a few choices. You can buy food-specific photos on stock photo sites helpful to bloggers, such as iStockphoto or Veer, which cost a few dollars per photo. They are sister sites of Getty Images and Corbis, both of which are aimed at corporate clients. But if your blog is based on cooking, you'll want photos of your own dishes and baked goods. Another option is to search for non-copyrighted images. It takes a lot of searching, however, to find good photos, particularly those large enough to feature.

Be careful. "Many bloggers and readers have a tenacious memory and will alert the original copyright holder about possible copyright infringement. So if you intend to use a photo, podcast, etc. from another blog, ask for permission, and host it on your own web space, giving proper credit with a link back to the original source," says Nicole Stich of Delicious Days (www.deliciousdays.com).

Your best choice, and the one that will serve your blog best, is to become an excellent photographer. You might resist this idea at first, because you see yourself as a writer. But part of being a blogger is taking charge of all the parts: you're the publisher, the writer, the photographer, the marketer, and the technical support person.

I've talked with great photographers and researched the websites of the best food photographers thoroughly to guide you as you develop your own style. Here are their tips:

Always carry a camera. You never know when you'll be inspired. It might be at a market, a restaurant, a grocery store, a farm, or just driving down the street, spying a neighborhood tree loaded with ripe persimmons.

Get a decent one. A small point-and-shoot camera is fine for when you're on the road, but if you can afford to, you may want to take the route of many serious food blog photographers. They use a digital single lens reflex (dSLR) in AV (aperture priority) or manual mode, so they can shoot in low light without a flash. Lebovitz said on the Food Blog Alliance that getting a digital SLR camera was "the single most important thing" he did to improve his blog, and that an SLR camera makes taking a great photo much easier.

Whichever camera you choose, get one with macro mode, so you can get in close, and one with high ISO spreads. The last one is important if you shoot indoors at night, advises Makikoh Ito on the Food Blog Alliance.

Take lots of photos. You don't want to take just a few, and then discover they're blurry or the contrast is too gray. David Lebovitz says he takes 25 to 50 photos for each published shot.

Lauren Ulm of Vegan Yum Yum (www.veganyumyum.com) says she averages around 100 photos per recipe, which she whittles down to a handful for each post. "Buy a large memory card for your camera to make sure you have enough space for all those photos," she advises on her Web site.

"I try overhead, straight on, close up, environment shots, and many different angles. My photographs start out boring and move towards interesting as I shoot. It's hard to explain how I plate or frame, but it involves a lot of photos and looking at each photo and saying, 'Hmm, the image looks too bare,' or 'I need to figure out how to emphasize this particular quality of the dish.' As I said before, the more photos you take, the better chance you have of getting that perfect shot."

Study your composition and props. Advises Deborah Perelman on Smitten Kitchen, "Try as best as you can to identify what you like about what is before you, and find ways to make that the very essence of the picture. That's why photography is an art and not a science—

you're letting your image tell a story about something. Look at the picture—is this what you wanted? How can you make the part that charmed you speak louder? Take it again. And again."

Look at food magazines and cookbooks to see how the food stylists do it. Clip photos that appeal to you and study them to figure out why. Most food is brown, so use a splash of color to make the shot more interesting, such as a garnish, a colored plate, or a pretty tablecloth under a white plate. Says Perelman, "A little food styling can go a long way. I'm not really into props or overly composed food. It's not a pinafore—its dinner. I think plate smears and lightly rusted spatulas are honest, and I find that warmly appealing, but much of this comes down to personal taste. That said, white plates (as opposed to our sage green ones that seemed such a good idea at the time) that are not too patterned and a little garnish or a fork propped just so can add a lot to a picture."

Lauren Ulm offers these tips on props: "White will always, always work. Square dishes always look classy. Smaller is better—small dishes are easier to fill up with food, which prevents your plate from looking bare."

Beware of busy backgrounds. Look for a solid color instead. Some food bloggers buy inexpensive foam-core boards and paint them different colors to use for solid color backgrounds. Bauer of Simply Recipes recommends using wooden cutting boards. "The wood is warm and works well to show off the food," she writes on her site.

"I believe background is just as important as the subject, and that's led to some interesting discoveries," says Matt Armendariz on DigitalPhotographyBlogs.com. "Because the background is usually thrown out of focus in food shots it's not so much what the actual surface is as the color of the surface. Plain corrugated cardboard becomes a beautiful tan color when blurred, cheap art paper is handy, napkins and fabrics do wonders, too. Just make sure your object is large enough. Other than that, use anything. You'll be surprised how pleasant every day items can be."

Work quickly. Food must look fresh. Salads wilt, sauces congeal, ice cream melts. Besides, if you're eating it for dinner, your family will be waiting to pounce on it.

Shoot in natural light. Shoot outdoors, if possible. Here's Lauren Ulm again: "When using natural lighting, don't place your food in a sunbeam. You want ambient, diffuse light. Things shot directly in the sun usually look too harsh, but again, it can sometimes work depending on the shot. The 'safest' set up is diffuse side-lighting coming from a nearby window." Buy vellum or tissue paper and tape it to your window to diffuse the light.

David Lebovitz takes most photos by the window with a tripod to keep the focus sharp. He also uses "a piece of Styrofoam propped up by a malted milk powder jar to fill in the dark areas." In warmer weather, he takes photos on his roof.

If you must use a flash because it's too dark, point the light straight up to get fill-in flash, rather than dead-on flash, which will cause too many shadows and bleach out your colors.

If you're cooking or baking, take photos during prep. "Don't get hung up on capturing the quintessential 'final shot,'" advised 101 Cookbooks blogger Heidi Swanson in *Food & Wine* magazine. "There are all sorts of great details that emerge throughout the cooking process."

Get in close. A macro lens or setting allows you to get as close as you want, to capture the drop of water on a freshly washed raspberry, or the crispy crust of a baked macaroni and cheese. You want your readers to feel as though they can taste the food through the photo.

Steady yourself. If you don't have a tripod, try blogger Josh Friedland of the Food Section's trick: He often uses the top of a water glass as a makeshift tripod. Lauren Ulm suggests a can of tomatoes or a pile of books for the same purpose. You'll want to use a tripod when doing macro photography particularly, advises Stiavetti, because the movement of your hands while you press the shutter button will cause blur.

Edit your photos. Adjust them by cropping, editing, and other techniques. Lebovitz downloads his shots into Apple's iPhoto and runs them through Photoshop. He posts them to his Flickr page first and then pastes them onto his site.

"Photoshop is a professional tool, with a steep learning curve," admits Bauer on Simply Recipes. "Years ago I subscribed to the tutorials at Lynda.com to learn this software. Lynda.com's tutorials are self-paced and very well done. For $25 per month you have access to a library of thousands of tutorial videos, and many are provided free, just so you can see how useful they really are. Lynda.com also has tutorials for Photoshop Elements, a more basic photo editing tool."

FOOD PHOTOGRAPHY REFERENCE
BOOKS, CLASSES, AND WEBSITES

Almost all the bloggers I interviewed in this section have comprehensive pages on their blogs about food photography. One of the best is Lauren Ulm's discussion at www.veganyumyum.com/2008/09/food-photography-for-bloggers. Also see White on Rice Couple photography tips at www.whiteonricecouple.com, and these books, workshops, and more websites on the craft.

Books
- *Digital Food Photography*, by Lou Manna. A basic guide on becoming a food photographer, including working with art directors and food stylists that also covers camera angles, lighting, and post-production.
- *Food Styling for Photographers: A Guide to Creating Your Own Appetizing Art*, by Linda Bellingham. This professional photographer has photographed for Baskin Robbins Ice Cream, Harry & David, and more. The book covers set-ups, lighting, and before, during, and final photos.

Workshops
- Culinary Entrepreneurship holds classes featuring instructors Matt Armendariz from Matt Bites, caterer Denise Vivaldo, and stylist Cindie Flannigan. Classes are based in California and include food styling and photography techniques for bloggers, plus food styling workshops and classes.
- Photo Styling Workshops has online classes on food styling techniques and prop styling. See the Web site www.photostylingworkshops.com for more details.

- Author Lou Manna lists food photography workshops on his Web site, www.loumanna.com.
- Boston University has hosted an International Conference on Food Styling and Photography every other year. See www.bu.edu/foodand wine.

Post-Production

Take classes at www.lynda.com to learn Photoshop and Photoshop Lightroom.

Websites

Many of the bloggers I've quoted in this section list advice on food photography on their blogs. For more, see:

- Still Life With . . . Little Nuggets from the Front Lines of Food Styling and Photography (http://stilllifewith.com). This blog is devoted to advice and observations on styling, shooting, props, and gear.
- Donna Ruhlman writes a blog on food photography through www .ruhlman.com. She also offers free medium resolution photos for food blogs. http://ruhlmanphotography.com/#/page/home.
- Nikas Culinaria Web site has a Food Photo 101 section. See http:// nikas-culinaria.com/food-photo-101.

Accepting and Reviewing Products

As you build readership on your blog, you're also building a target market for companies who want to get their cookbooks, kitchen equipment, and other goodies in front of your readers. Companies use blogs as an inexpensive way to get publicity, offering free products for both you and your readers in exchange for reviews or mentions in posts. And it's big business. Within a few months of creating my blog, I received a gift card, offers for giveaways, and a chance to win a free vacation if I created recipes about butter.

When I spoke privately with a blogger whose "star is still ascending," she said she gets so much free stuff that, were she to write about it all, she would never need any other content. And it's not just food. Companies have offered a free car for the weekend, plus free restaurant meals, free hotel stays, and hundreds of dollars worth of free food and kitchen equipment.

Some companies even pay bloggers fees to write about products in their own blogs, called sponsored blogging. If bloggers don't disclose that relationship to their readers, they will lose their readers' trust, something they've worked hard to build.

You will have to decide what you're comfortable accepting. Many bloggers have no problem taking free stuff. I've done it too, if it is of little value. Perhaps bloggers feel justified, since most don't make money from their blogs. At a BlogHer conference in 2009, Liberty Mutual surveyed 175 bloggers on responsible blogging and found 98 percent believed it is acceptable to receive a free product, and 87 percent believed it is fine to write company-sponsored posts. At least most mentioned transparency, disclosure, and honesty as key caveats to receiving free products and writing sponsored posts.

It's fine to plug products, books, restaurants, hotels, and trips, if within your blog's focus. The key is to always consider your readers first when writing an endorsement, not the company who gave you the freebie. I'm certainly not a fan of writing sponsored posts if you don't disclose you are paid (in some form, food or otherwise) to write them.

Mostly because of sponsored blogging, The Federal Trade Commission now requires American bloggers to disclose compensation when they endorse a product, place, or service, including free meals, hotel stays, and trips. The guidelines don't define payments exactly, but you'll be covered if you have a policy about how you handle free products and services from marketers. You have only your reputation, and having a policy makes you appear ethical and upstanding. Plus, if you keep your policy in a section on your blog, you won't have to disclose each time that you receive a free product.

Kath Eats of Real Food (www.katheats.com) has a "Bylaws" section laying out her philosophy on product reviews in a friendly, straightforward manner:

> As you guys know, product reviews and giveaways are a huge part of the food blog world. I feel that being able to sample products and give my opinion is a fun way to give you guys a personal account of what I

really like and what is just 'meh,' especially for new products or small companies that you might not otherwise know about.

Below is a disclaimer to let you know that I aim to keep my reviews as unbiased as possible. Here are the bylaws I follow:

- I try to review products that I feel fit within my 'eat real food' (or pretty darn close to it) theme.
- I always mention the first time that I try something that was given to me as a sample to review. I will always do this the first time you see me eat something, but I may not mention it the second, third, fourth, and hundredth time. I eat it to finish up the jar, box, or sample. I am assuming most of you are regular readers and will take note the first time.
- I absolutely would not write a good review about a product simply because it was free—my reviews are always my own opinions and you will find products scattered about that I have found sub-par. I let the companies who send the products know that my review will be my honest opinion.
- I do not accept payment to write good things about a product. If I like something, I really do like it. And I'm not afraid to say if I don't!
- I believe firmly in keeping the integrity of my blog and would never compromise my beliefs and standards for the sake of a payment.

Please note that any product you see on this blog may have been given to me as a free sample, so keep that in mind as you enjoy reading about my eats. And feel free to ask me about anything you see!

Some bloggers address public relations and marketing people directly. On David Lebovitz's FAQ, under "Sending Products & Reviews," he writes: "If you wish to send me a product, if I do accept it, I may or may not write about it on the site. I appreciate your understanding that this is my personal blog, I don't allow others to influence what gets published here. I don't accept products in exchange for a positive review or placement."

Here are seven recommendations on handling and endorsing freebies:

1. **Don't be greedy.** Take only what is relevant and appropriate for your blog. If you don't write about kitchen appliances, don't take them. Yes, some marketers are eternally hopeful and will keep sending products, but it seems greedy to keep accepting them. Also, it's a small community and people will gossip. Be careful about the value of a freebie. At some newspapers, reporters are not allowed to accept anything worth more than $25. Would you feel right about taking free coffee for a year? I wouldn't. What should the coffee company expect in return? You don't want to be beholden because of a costly gift.

    Do not take products to impress your friends, give as gifts, or sell. Return expensive products, unless the marketer says to keep them. With food blogging, it's easy to take things because you want to cook with them, eat them, or enjoy them as a consumer. Watch out for that impulse. It is different from taking them because you are a blogger. Be aware that the company is giving you this product because you are a blogger and they hope you will endorse or mention it.

2. **Don't promise endorsements of the product or experience.** Most marketers know not to demand a testimonial when they give you a product, but it won't stop others from trying. Don't agree to write about a product before using it, or at all. This also applies to giveaways. You don't have to endorse a product at length to give it away.

    Here's what a top blogger told me about guaranteeing coverage: "I always say that I will not guarantee that I will mention the product on my site and do also not want to be contacted afterwards if I will mention it on my site. In that respect, I only try to deal with companies that 'get it,' who don't have pr flaks who just want to hassle me endlessly. Most quality companies either have good pr teams or I deal with the owners themselves."

3. **Evaluate why to take a free trip.** Don't go if it is not relevant to your blog, but do go if it's something you want to learn more about. "I have accepted trips, but not to review a place, but for educational or social reasons," one mega blogger wrote me. "For example, Kingsford Charcoal sent me to Grilling University in

Arizona for a weekend. I didn't know how to grill, but wanted to learn. After I got back home I bought a gas grill, a kettle grill, and started grilling and experimenting. They also gave me a kettle grill (I asked for one), but that was three years ago. If this were today, I wouldn't have asked for the grill. I would still accept the trip if I thought I could learn."

4. **Don't always love everything.** Many bloggers feel they should only tell readers about the products and places they love. Life is short, and you only want to tell readers about the good stuff. If you must be relentlessly positive, strive for balance. List the pros and cons for more interesting reading and a more complex and balanced post. If you don't, after a while, readers won't need to read you to know what you thought. They will always find a rave review.

   Raving about products and places reads like promotional material. Instead, tell readers why they might be interested in that water purifier or manifesto on Korean cooking. Don't endorse a product or place specifically to satisfy a marketer. Let's say a big blogger mentions going to a restaurant. That's a coup. Who cares whether he loved it? It's all about the number of eyeballs who read about the place.

   If you're new to reviewing, read newspaper restaurant reviews as examples of the form of reviewing. Most of the time, reviews are positive, with a few cons. That's because a steady diet of negative reviews would be pointless, like telling readers every week where not to go. On rare occasions, reviewers slam a place. They won't slam a mom and pop shop, but if an expensive restaurant opens with tons of hype, reviewers will let them have it if the experience doesn't match up with the cost. For more on reviewing, see Chapter 6 on reviewing restaurants and page 83 for book reviews. Also see the Food Blog Code of Ethics, which tackles the ethics of restaurant reviews, at www.foodwolf.com.

5. **Be clear about product or shopping sections on your blog.** An Amazon store is self-explanatory, but other listings are coy. Whenever I see categories like "Shop" or "Recommends," I'm suspicious. I don't know if a company gave the blogger free product in exchange for a listing, or whether it's a product the blogger has discovered and wants to share.

6. **If a company pays you to write about their products, disclose it.** I don't like the idea, but at least it will be honest. I saw a post about a product and company where the blogger said they were a "client and sponsor." She gets my respect. Writers who endorse products represent their readers, not just themselves, and certainly not the companies they review. They are guides to tell readers whether it's worth their money and time. Protect your readers and respect them. Without them, no marketer would be interested in you.

7. **Put a permanent policy on your blog.** Tell readers whether you accept free products, how you go about your reviews, and other information that will make your blog credible.

How to Get Noticed

When you start a blog, you'll wonder who's reading it. The answer, initially, is no one, unless you tell people about it. So you start with a few friends, your mother, your co-workers, and maybe they tell others. Little by little, your readership grows.

But it won't grow that much. Your next step is to build your blog readership. Building readership creates community and buzz, both essential to a good blog. Here are twelve suggestions:

1. **If you have friends with food blogs, build a relationship by commenting on their blogs.** Drive traffic to your blog by commenting, but put some thought into it. Many bloggers say they can tell when people do it simply to draw attention. Try for a comment more thoughtful than "looks delicious!" By building a dialog with other bloggers, they'll want to read your blog because of the great content it offers. It's not considered good etiquette to ask for a link, so please don't ask for one. It's nicer to let it happen organically. Seek out other bloggers on Twitter and Facebook as well, and comment on what they're doing.

2. **Create communities to alert when you post.** You've got your Facebook following, your Twitter followers, and perhaps the folks who receive your monthly newsletter. Or create a custom

list of friends and colleagues to alert by email, and encourage them to share your posts with others. On social media, it's considered too promotional to only announce new posts, so make sure you do so between your regular comments.

3. **Offer subscriptions.** Make it easy for people to read every post. Install an RSS feed (Really Simple Syndication). When readers subscribe, your posts show up automatically as a link on their browser's home page. My favorite way to subscribe is through email. Google's Feedburner offers a free service that lets people sign up to receive your new posts in their email. Either way, people are more likely to read your posts when they're delivered, rather than remembering to visit your blog occasionally to catch up.

4. **Put the word out.** People like to know when others write about them. They might also want to link to your post, through their site or through social media. Also, if you think a particular blogger might enjoy your post, send an email with a link, explaining why they'd want to read it. They might even link to it, driving traffic to your site.

5. **Respond to comments.** When people take the time to type in their opinion or response, reply to their comment. At first I didn't do so, because I was concerned about artificially inflating the number of comments. Then I wrote a group comment, responding to two or three people at once. Now I enjoy writing back to people, letting them know I've read their comment and appreciate it. Don't just reply to reply, though. Be thoughtful.

6. **Comment on other blogs where the content is relevant to yours.** People who read your thoughts might click through to your blog. This will also help you get into the greater blogging community, a rich and rewarding aspect of food blogging.

7. **Join food blogging group events.** Go to a forum like Is My Blog Burning? or Stickydate, or a group like Tuesdays with Dorie, a blog where people bake from Greenspan's book. Once you get the hang of it, try hosting an event. It's a great way to get to know other bloggers who might link to you.

8. **Join a blogging marathon and write daily posts.** As Danielle Tsi of Bon Vivant (www.bonvivant.com) wrote on a Food Blog Alliance post, "This was a valuable exercise in grasping the nuts

and bolts of food blogging: taking a dish from concept to execution, styling and shooting it, writing and editing the post, publicizing the post and responding to comments and questions. It jumpstarted a blogging routine, grew Bon Vivant's readership and generated a host of new content to share on platforms like Foodbuzz, BlogHer and photography sites like Food Gawker and Tastespotting."

9. **Submit your photos to aggregate sites.** As Tsi mentioned, send your best photos to sites like Food Gawker and Tastespotting, as a way to generate interest in your site. Get to know what they like first, as they have specific aesthetic guidelines for submission. Be selective.

10. **Improve your photography.** Of course this isn't easy, but just having terrific photos can propel a food blog to stardom.

11. **Guest blog on other sites and use guests on yours.** It's a good way to exchange links, take a break, get someone else's perspective on your site, and perhaps reach a new or larger audience. Make sure the blogger's style and content, and size of post fits your blog. Show him or her your edits before posting. Explains Bauer of Simply Recipes, "Mostly I invite guest authors who I know personally, and know well, whom I trust, and whose voice on the site I think my readers would like. The one thing that is challenging is photos. Either the guest author has to include gorgeous photos or I have to photograph them myself. Two of my guest authors live close by, so it's easy for me to shoot the dishes they are doing."

12. **Hand out business cards with your blog name on it.** Go online to inexpensive vendors like Vistaprint and Modern Postcard and get colorful cards to hand out at events and conferences. Moo cards is another great one, where you can use your own Flickr images.

Increase Your Views

Many of the techniques listed above will affect how high your name, or your blog's name, comes up in a search engine like Google. They are called Search Engine Optimization (SEO) techniques, to help you place highly on search engine rankings. Readers will come to your blog from many sources. Some type your name in a search engine, so you don't want your blog name, or your name, to appear too far down on the list. Most will come to your site when they search for specific food or recipe keywords, such as "best mushroom pizza," and you want them to find your post on the subject.

Start using keywords in your title and text. Keywords are the terms people search on to find information. After you've written a post, use a free keyword tool, such as http://freekeywords.wordtracker.com, to determine which words people might use to find your post. Make sure the exact phrase appears in:

- the title
- the first sentence
- one main header within the post

If your keyword is two words or less, use it five to eight times in the post; if it's three words or more, do not use it more than a few times, or the search engine will see it as "keyword stuffing." Somehow, with all this strategy, you've got to make your writing appear natural. Crowding a post with keywords doesn't work, and may be detrimental to your search engine credibility.

Soon you'll want to see how many people come to your site, how many come back, where they come from, what they read, and how long they stay. Install software that gives you a report. One of the most popular is Google Analytics (www.google.com/analytics). It's free for the first five million page views, once you set up a Google account. One valuable part is the traffic section, which tells you where people came from to get to your blog. Here's where you find out what percentage of readers found you through a search engine or through links on other sites. It's fascinating to discover which sites drive the most traffic to you, and to discover new links you didn't know about.

Adam Roberts of Amateur Gourmet says it's the accumulation of content that matters. "The more you update, the more content you create; the more content you create, the more Googleable you become," he explains on his Web site.

"I've learned this watching my statistics: I get the large majority of my hits from Google searches for strange things that have nothing to do with food, only because there's some obscure word in the title. Clotilde (Dusoulier of Chocolate & Zucchini) explained to me once that Google has an algorithm that dictates how Googleable you are. It's based, I think, on how many people link to you and how often you update. So updating frequently has its rewards.

"But also, and more obviously, the more you update the more often people will check back to your site. The blogs I check most often are the ones I know will have new content every day. The more regular the new content, the more regular my visitation. I'm sure you can relate as a blog reader."

Try not to get too obsessed with the numbers. It doesn't do any good to check them every day. Over time, you'll get better at deciphering what they mean and whether to take action. Likewise, don't get obsessed with the number of comments. I admit I was a mess when my posts were met with silence, when I first started blogging. I begged friends to comment. Then, once people discovered it, I could relax.

If you find your site is lacking in comments, begin commenting on other food blogs that receive five comments or less per posts, suggests Sephanie Stiavetti. "Those blog authors will appreciate your comments and will likely come say hello themselves. This community building activity can help your blog develop a nice little following. Just make sure to keep it up."

While the advice I've given you here is practical and market-driven, there's also another part of blogging: The human side, where friendships and respect grow from being part of a community. Many famous early bloggers I've interviewed point to Elise Bauer of Simply Recipes as the one person who helped them understand their blogs and move forward. Later she launched the Food Blog Alliance as a way to spread the knowledge around to the thousands more who started food blogs. She sent me an email that sums up her graciousness:

"If there is one thing I would say to an aspiring food blogger, it would be to come at food blogging from a spirit of generosity. Be generous with acknowledgments, be generous with your expertise, and be generous with showering attention on and links to fellow food bloggers.

Pay attention to others and eventually some of them will pay attention back to you. This, I believe, is the super-secret-sauce to success."

Can You Make Any Money at This Thing?

Maybe you started your food blog for fun and don't plan to make money at it. As your readership rises, however, you might find you can put ads or sell products on your site and make a little income. The cream of the crop of food bloggers has managed to make blogging a full-time job, and yes, they make money. A few make six figures. But it's certainly no reason to start a blog, and for the great majority of food bloggers, there's no reason to quit your day job.

Money comes to food bloggers in several ways, including:

- a book deal that springs from the success of their blogs (more on that in a moment);
- writing blog posts elsewhere (anywhere from $5–$50 per post), such as on a city magazine's Web site; or writing an entire blog for a company;
- freelance food writing, consulting, and recipe development work based on the expertise they develop as food bloggers;
- pay for selling photographs suitable for framing; or merchandise such as aprons, note cards, and t-shirts with photos or logos from the blog;
- paid sponsorships if they use commercial products in photographs or recipes, as long as they disclose.

The most direct way to get income, however, is by putting ads on your site. You could start your own ad agency and sell ads one by one, but most people find that notion too time consuming. It's more realistic to go through channels designed for the web, such as Google AdSense, Amazon's Associate program, and ad networks.

Some bloggers set up a store, such as the ones offered by Amazon. Readers click through from their site to the products. If they buy, bloggers earn a commission. This is called an associate program.

Google AdSense, the clickable links that show up in blog sidebars, is free, and you don't need high traffic to get started. Bloggers choose a set of keywords relevant to their site, such as "low fat healthy." Google reads those words and puts up relevant ads. At first, you might make a few cents a day. Over time, as you build the content on your Web site and increase traffic, the amount can increase. Most publishers (the name Google uses) don't make much money from AdSense, however, unless they really work at it.

Bauer of Simply Recipes advises on the Food Blog Alliance that "decent traffic" to attract advertising is a minimum of 1,000 unique visitors per day. Even 500 readers per day might come to around $50 per month, enough to cover server bills and lunch. (Currently, she gets more than 100,000 hits per day, an unusual yet enviable position. Do the math and you'll see what I mean.)

If you have numbers as high as 1,000 unique visitors per day, join an ad network that solicits national companies to advertise. These companies include:

- BlogHer
- Federated Media
- Foodbuzz
- Glam Media
- Martha Stewart Circle
- PlateFull (General Mills)

Most of these ad networks work from a Cost Per Thousand (CPM), based on page views, and some are by invitation only. You could get paid $3 per thousand views, for example. With 1,000 visitors and a $3 CPM, you could make $3 per day, but 100 page views would come to only $9 per month, Bauer explains.

Once you look more closely at these networks, decide whether you like the advertisers and how they display products. Do you want ads for peanut butter, laundry detergent, or wrinkle creams? How about an animated dog running across your readers' screens? "So far, we've declined more than 50 percent of all incoming ad requests just because we didn't feel comfortable running them," said Stich of Delicious Days.

Choose an ad network that lets you customize which ads appear on your site, and reject ads you don't want. "Like it or not," says Bauer, "your readers will associate you with the ads on your site, especially the graphical (non-text) ads."

Ad companies have requirements about placement, such as "above the fold," a newspaper term that means the top half of the page. On a Web site, it's above the point where a reader would have to scroll. Some ask that you do not have any other ads on the page.

Some ad companies offer perks, such as links to your blog within their ads. At BlogHer, for example, a team of editors read the content every day and selects well-written individual posts, explains producer Jenifer Scharpen. "We aim to feature one blog per week on like-minded blogs. We also promote bloggers on BlogHer.com." Foodbuzz offers free dinners and community building events in many cities.

Some bloggers choose not to take ads, but I don't see anything wrong with it. For one thing, blogs are a lot of work, and I have nothing against getting compensation for all the hours bloggers put in. When I worked in magazines, I was the head of editorial, and several writers produced the content. On my blog, I am the publisher, the manager of tech support, the writer, the head of advertising (eventually), and the marketing department. I'm a one-man band. "We've got to wear more hats now, be versatile, be good businesspeople," says Michael Ruhlman.

I like what he wrote on his FAQ (Frequently Asked Questions) page: "I apologize for having to include advertising but blogging requires an increasing amount of time that I might otherwise use to make money for things like the monthly Visa bill, pork belly, and education. To justify the time I spend writing for the blog and responding to comments, I have to offset the costs with the small amount of revenue I get from advertising. It doesn't compensate me completely but, since I enjoy blogging, it sure does help."

Going from Blog to Book

Once you've been blogging for a while and have created a body of work, you might wonder whether the blog could be a springboard for a book. It's possible, but writing a book is not a cut-and-paste process repurposed from blogs. If that was true, readers would find little reason to cough up $30 for a print version when all the content still lives online.

Books launched from blogs have lives of their own, with new content. They must be thought of as their own product, separate from the blog. Plus, books are not usually made up of little bits. Readers want a narrative that hangs together, with a beginning, middle, and end, and that takes craft and time to produce.

Some publishing companies contact bloggers directly when they think a book would succeed. Jaden Hair was only six months into Steamy Kitchen when Tuttle Publishing contacted her with a cookbook proposition. That's unusual, however. Tuttle could see that she was an excellent promoter who knew how to engage with her readers. You'd have to have a measure of success first to attract a publisher. (To read more about developing a platform that would interest a publisher, see page 263.)

Typically books that spring from blogs fall into two categories: cookbooks and food memoir. Heidi Swanson of 101 Cookbooks has written two cookbooks since beginning her blog, and she's working on a third. Ten Speed Publisher Aaron Wehner says he met Swanson at an International Association of Culinary Professionals (IACP) annual conference in 2005. "We figured out we were neighbors, and we've become good friends. She's the gold standard of food bloggers, in terms of how well she's grown her site without changing the integrity of it."

Swanson points out that while a blog is ongoing, a book is a separate creative process with a beginning, middle, and end. Even her culinary point of view is different in her books. On her blog, she writes that an idea for a book can't be rushed: "Not long after submitting the manuscript for *Super Natural Cooking*, I started setting aside photos I loved, and continued to keep notebooks of my favorite recipes, ideas, and inspirations. I wasn't sure what I would do with them, or what would emerge over time, but I had a hunch something might. Or not. Either way, I don't like the idea of rushing these sorts of things. I've come to believe you can't really rush inspiration, it comes on its own schedule, emerging and intersecting my life when it sees fit. I just try to keep my eyes open."

The other category of book that evolves from a blog is memoir. (Read more about the form at the beginning of chapter 9.) While your blog may be about you and your experiences, they don't necessarily translate into a book. David Lebovitz says he only used two stories from his blog in *The Sweet Life in Paris* "because they fit and I liked them." The rest of the book, he said, was inspired by his move to Paris and the backstory readers asked about.

Besides, blog posts are short, and you can't just tack them together to make a book. "Even when a blog post is long, it's pretty short," says Molly Wizenberg of Orangette, author of *A Homemade Life*. "The book has a process of immersion, where I had to be comfortable with not always knowing where a story was going. I had to slow myself down. The biggest thing was finding a narrative arc. I didn't know how to write a continuous long narrative."

She began by making a list of all the recipes she wanted to include, then thought about the stories the recipes were attached to, and whether they had a place in the book. She wrote the stories out of order because it felt easiest, then tried to put the book in order and smooth out the gaps.

"I cut stories from the blog, pasted them into Word, then rewrote them," she explains. "Some parts are closely related to the blog, but in most cases I had to do a decent amount of rewriting or add details to make that story hang together with the rest of the book."

She compared a blog to a series of TV shows, and a memoir to a movie. "A series of cooking shows does not make a movie, just as blog posts don't make a book," says Wizenberg. "A movie has a plot, gets us invested in a character and a story line, and transports us somewhere else.

"The book was a place to write about things that felt too big for the blog. For example, I wrote about my dad twice in five and a half years. There wasn't space to tell the story comfortably. Sitting down to write a book makes a commitment longer than writing a blog post, and it gave me space to expand upon things I'd written, in service to a longer story I was trying to tell."

When it comes to photos, if your book will have them, you'll have to be a professional quality photographer to get a publisher to want to use your photos. Heidi Swanson feels strongly about using her photos in her books. "I'm not sure I would work on a book if I couldn't do both the photography and the writing," she admits. She says she loved the creative and collaborative process of working with a designer and giving feedback, but found all the decisions involved in writing a cookbook challenging.

It's an accomplishment, as a food blogger, to have a publisher accept your photos. Usually cookbook publishers use a professional photographer and stylist. As Jaden Hair explains on the Global Chefs Web site, "They rejected the idea to begin with, so for six months I practiced and practiced. I would send them pictures, they would print, review, and critique. They were very supportive of the idea and then finally I got to the point where they felt my photography was good enough to publish."

Both Wizenberg and Lebovitz wrote memoirs, where photos are not as essential as they are in cookbooks. Lebovitz's included some of his own black and white photos.

Keep Posting

Whether you're hoping for a book deal or satisfied with writing the short form, the secret to blogging is that you have to keep going, week after week, month after month, regardless of the response. If you have the stamina, perseverance, and the capacity for entertainment and information delivery, you are likely to succeed. Lebovitz, who adores blogging, admits he has dozens of posts in draft form, waiting for revision.

I wish I was that organized. Some days I have no ideas for my next post, and other days writing seems so easy I have no idea why I was concerned. Some days my posts land with a thud, other days the comments fly in.

"Do not expect an easy ride when you blog," confirms Sudeep DeSousa on Problogger. "You can put in a lot of hard work and then realize that nobody is commenting on your post and on the other hand you will write a one-liner and you will have the whole world talking about it. You will have days when you will be banging your head against the wall wondering what to post about and then there will be days you have so many ideas in your head that you don't know where to start. So be ready to enjoy the ride.

"Since all this hard work is going to use up your time," he continues, "You have to be prepared to give up something. For those that have a full time job—your personal life or work life is going to take a hit. Maybe some of your other hobbies or interests will get affected. So you need to decide carefully on the things in life that you are ready to forego in order to become successful as a blogger."

The best bloggers have a positive attitude about making their blogs part of their lives. When I interviewed Heidi Swanson of 101 Cookbooks, I asked her if she thought she would be blogging 10 years from now. "I hope so," she said with sincerity. She was smiling.

Another super-successful blogger concurs. "The blog is a part of who I am. It's become like a limb. I have to feed it all the time. I think of it as an engine that propelled me forward," says Dusoulier of Chocolate & Zucchini. "I look at the world through my blogger struggles. When I go anywhere I wonder if it's blogger material. I experience things more intensely because I'm asking myself more questions, not just living in the moment, so that I can talk to my readers afterwards.

"When I've found my groove and I'm not hung up on traffic and number of comments and whether I'm going to quit, it's so gratifying. It brings me so much in terms of interaction and feedback and ideas and inspiration. It's really worth every ounce of energy I pour into it. It has grown with me. It's really the key to everything else that I do."

On the other hand, Dusoulier sees the value of taking time off to rest and refresh, which means "not spending weekends working on it, not devoting all my free time to it, going to a restaurant and not taking pictures or notes. Unplugging. Taking a vacation where I don't blog or check comments and emails for a week."

The bottom line is that blogging can be hard work and time consuming, but it's got to be fun and worth it, however you define that, most of the time. Don't take it too seriously, and don't compare yourself to the food bloggers who have been doing it for years. Sit back, have a good time, and see what develops from your efforts.

GENERAL RESOURCES ON BLOGGING

While this chapter focuses on food writing, many sources show you how to be a better blogger, covering dozens of topics in approachable language. Here are some of the most trusted sources:

- Problogger, www.problogger.net. Dedicated to helping other bloggers learn the skills of blogging, share their own experiences and promote the blogging medium.
- Copyblogger, www.copyblogger.com. A free Web site to help you improve your online writing.
- BlogHer, www.blogher.com, a community for women who blog, includes an ad network and annual conferences on business and food.

Writing Exercises

1. Maybe you didn't flush meringue down the toilet, but surely you have stories about food that readers would enjoy. I just thought of the time my sister put whiskey and blue food coloring into her cake icing during a high school party at our house. None of her underage friends would touch the cake, even though imbibing alcohol was a priority.
2. Write a short story about a dish you hated when you were a kid, and how you've come to love it today. Provide the recipe, if appropriate.
3. Write about the cookbook you used most when you first discovered cooking. Find links to information about the cookbook or author and include them.

5

Becoming a Successful Freelance Writer

Writing for newspapers, magazines, websites, and clients satisfies many desires. It's a way to entertain and inform while unleashing your creativity and passion onto the page. It's such a thrill to see your own work in print. I'm still not tired of it, even though it's been over thirty years since my first piece ran in a daily newspaper.

Writing articles can be a long and frustrating process if you don't know how to get to a published story—and even if you do. Months can pass—even a year sometimes—before a story you've pitched to an editor appears. Editors are busier than ever, sorting through hundreds of story idea queries per month. Your job, on the other hand, is to come up with a story idea an editor can't resist, get the go ahead, write the story, get paid, and then do it all over again. I'm going to tell you how. As a former newspaper and magazine editor, I've evaluated and accepted work from writers for most of my career. Since 1996, I've been on the other side as a freelance writer as well.

In this chapter I'll give you insider information on different kinds of freelancing: mostly for publications, but also for corporate clients. You'll learn how editors assess a story. Editors and award-winning food writers offer advice on how to come up with, shape, position, pitch, pursue, and write your story idea, no matter what kind of publication or Web site you target or what type of writing you prefer. You'll learn about corporate writing, and about pay and even some strategies for how to increase it—no small task when it comes to food writing. And you'll get a short primer on tax deductions, so start saving your receipts now.

While this chapter does not cover restaurant reviewing specifically (discussed in chapter 6), it will provide valuable information on how to target and pitch a publication.

How to Come Up with Story Ideas

Let's start with freelance writing for publications. What should you write about? Your brain should be constantly generating ideas based on what's going on in your life and what you read. "You've got to be like a lint brush," says writer Barry Estabrook, a former contributing editor for *Gourmet* and founding editor of *Eating Well* magazine. "Ideas are cheap. Execution is harder. People tend to get too attached to a single idea. Come up with so many that you don't get obsessed with any one."

Notice he didn't say to write one story and then find a home for it. Many beginning writers take this path and don't succeed. The problem is that every publication wants a story written just for them. Since yours was written for you, you'll have to convince an editor that it's right for the publication's specific style, voice, and readers. That's why editors reject almost 95 percent of ideas and stories.

So back up and give your brain fodder for ideas. Here's how:

- Read food sections of newspapers. Keep a pen and paper handy and write down any ideas that come into your head. Tear out articles typical of those you'd like to write, either in subject or format.
- Do the same with food magazines, general magazines, and trade publications. This time, check writers' bylines against the mastheads of magazines to see what kind of stories freelancers write for each publication (See Appendix for a list).
- Find websites that take freelance work. Often the websites of publications are easier to get into than the print versions (See Appendix for a list).
- Visit bookstores to see what's new in the cookbook section.
- Notice trends in restaurants and food shops.

- Watch food shows on television.
- Visit farmers' markets and specialty food markets and producers.
- Spend an hour with your cookbooks, looking for subjects that inspire you.
- Look at your own life for ideas. If you just went through a kitchen remodeling, or you're planning a trip to a cooking school in Morocco, you might have a story.
- Figure out what kind of stories you're best at writing, based on your personality. For example, I'm a practical person who loves to explain how something works, or to help people get better at a task, so I'm attracted to service or how-to stories.

The act of wondering led me to write many articles that were published in an international magazine aimed at supermarket shoppers, published by Sunset Custom Publishing. I put myself in the shoes of readers, both in the market and at home. *What can you make with those yellow premade logs of polenta in the supermarket, and are they actually edible?* I wondered. That led to a story and recipes for a Busy Cook column, followed by wondering what to do with a can of tuna besides make a sandwich, and what to do with a box of frozen spinach. Next came how-to stories based on other questions I had, like secrets of a great buffet, how to order wine at a restaurant, and how to plan a cheese course for a dinner party.

Freelance writing tends to fall into two categories: general writing and specialized writing. General writing covers all aspects of food. If you find everything about food exciting, from cooking to farming to travel to history, you're probably a generalist. Specialists, on the other hand, write mostly about one subject in many incarnations.

Writing as a specialist can be a strategic way to build your business. Years ago, Estabrook established his expertise as a writer on seafood when he became a freelance writer. Previously, he had worked as a commercial fisherman, was familiar with the seafood business, and developed a keen interest in the controversy between fishing and conservation. After reading about an escape of farmed salmon in Maine waters, he wrote an article on farmed salmon for *Gourmet*. The editor of an environmental magazine saw the piece and assigned him a story on overfished sea bass. Another editor at the environmental magazine asked him to review a book about wild salmon depletion. A fisherman saw Estabrook's salmon article and invited him to spend a few days aboard a commercial fishing vessel.

That adventure turned into an article he pitched and sold to *Gourmet*. The fishermen on the boat told him about scallop divers they knew in Maine. He sold the story idea about scallop divers to *Gourmet*. See how naturally Estabrook continued his freelance career? Granted, he is a veteran of the food-writing community, but the story still makes a point: as his stories built on each other, they further established his credibility.

What Kind of Story Should You Write?

Coming up with story ideas is the first step. Shaping them into certain article conventions is the second. Here are some of the most popular for freelance writing:

Recipes: For many publications, recipe-based stories are a huge focus. *Cooking Light*, for example, prints around eighty recipes per issue, with almost all contributed by freelancers. Most of these stories comprise a short introduction followed by three to five recipes. The feature article might include small bits of side information on technique, a guide to choosing an unfamiliar ingredient, and information about its history, where to buy it, or how to serve it.

Think of a theme that helps readers plan, such as low-effort or low-fat dinners; or one that inspires them, such as Greek food for a party or slow-roasted stews for winter nights.

In the case of *Cooking Light*, you would want to avoid esoteric ingredients and keep the method straightforward. Before you submit a piece that includes recipes, familiarize yourself with the publication's editorial style. Don't call for asafetida, for example, if you don't see esoteric ingredients in any recipes.

For national food magazines, recipes need personality and confidence to appeal to an editor, something different from what readers can find free online. And the bigger magazines will test your recipes in a test kitchen, and may ask you to make changes if they don't like the result.

To write about seasonal cooking, keep in mind that national magazines have long lead times. *Cooking Pleasures* has a one-year lead time, and editors already form many story ideas during monthly meetings. For most national magazines, you might have to pitch a story more than six months in advance, so a story on indoor grilling during winter would be pitched in late summer. Newspapers, on the other hand, think a few weeks ahead, unless it's a major holiday like Thanksgiving. In that case, even seven weeks ahead is probably not too early.

Most food publications have test kitchens where people will make your recipes to ensure that they work. Often editors can judge recipes just from looking at your story idea. If you've read chapter 8 on recipe writing, you'll be in good shape.

Trend: Usually articles on trends are reported, meaning you interview and quote experts and sources, and come to conclusions based on their expertise. Some include statistics. Trends from other print sources sometimes lead to great queries for food-based publications. If you subscribe to nutrition and health newsletters, for example, you might reshape the trend stories and pitch them to food publications with a health focus. If you see positive research on elderberry's power as a defense against colds and flu, for example, dream up recipes for how to use the extract and syrup and send a query to a health-oriented publication such as *Delicious Living* or *Health* magazine.

Guide: Here you'll educate readers on how to make choices about a particular subject, such as how to buy organic, select winter greens, or brew exotic teas. Travel guides help readers find restaurants and specialty foods in a region.

News: In news reporting, you would interview several people and piece together their comments for an article on a breaking development. Most news reporting appears in newspapers rather than magazines, because it is a specialized skill requiring journalism. Examples would be breaking stories about mercury levels in fish or California's new rule banning foie gras.

Personality profile: Based on an interview with one person, such as a chef, restaurateur, food producer, retailer, or food personality, the focus is on an interviewee who has achieved recognition, made a significant contribution, or performs unusual work. You may need to include their recipes, tested by you.

Interview: Similar to a personality profile, interviews take the form of questions and answers that follow an introduction and brief biography of the interviewee.

Roundup: Usually a comparison or list, roundups help readers choose from a group, such as five kinds of Indian spices, or ten great Italian restaurants. If you're attracted to the idea of a roundup, find a publication with "Ten Best" kinds of titles.

How-to: Teach readers how to solve a problem or do something better. These articles can be technique based, such as how to make great mashed potatoes, how to find vegan restaurants in New York, or how to choose the right kitchen equipment. How-to or service stories are organized in a logical, instructional order, anticipating how readers think about a given task and the questions they might ask while thinking about it.

Human interest: These are stories about warmhearted people who do good deeds, such as soup kitchen cooks who feed 350 homeless people every day, or a group that sells baked goods for a cause.

Historical background: Pique an editor's interest by combining history with other forms listed here, such as destination or service writing.

Cookbook review: If your target publication or Web site include reviews, find out how they assign them. A magazine might get dozens of books every month from publishers, choose which ones to review, and hand them out to reviewers. If you find a small publication that publishes reviews, you could try writing one based on a cookbook you've purchased, and submit it. Use previously published reviews as models for how to shape your story. Be careful how you criticize—very few cookbooks are all good or all bad, and publishers are more likely to publish positive reviews than negative ones. For more on book reviews, see page 83.

Destination and travel: Food-based travel pieces might take you to a food festival, a region known for artisan foods, or a city famous for its restaurants. You don't even have to go anywhere, says *Los Angeles Times* Food Section Editor Russ Parsons. "Write about what's going on in your backyard. Don't be embarrassed by your limitations." He quotes a songwriter friend who wrote, "Some people can go around the world and not see anything, other people can go around the block and see the whole world."

For newspapers, try the travel section instead of the food section. I've found it easier to be published there.

First-person essay: Personal stories are the top choice of many writers but not the priority of most publications and websites. Editors are flooded with personal experience articles. Usually they don't publish more than one article per issue, if they publish any at all.

That doesn't mean it's impossible to get published, just that you have lots of competitors. Increase your chance of success by writing about an experience that relates to readers and their lives. What universal theme resonates for them? If it's just about what happened to you, then the response from editors can be "So what?"

When it comes to subject matter, you have lots of choices. Perhaps you:

- achieved a goal, such as graduating from cooking school or cooking a special feast;
- just returned from a fabulous food-based vacation (in a sidebar, give readers ideas on how to duplicate it);
- have a funny cooking, eating, or traveling experience, or one that should be avoided;
- had a life-changing or inspirational experience that will help readers cope with a challenge in their lives;
- did something for the first time, such as served as an apprentice in a restaurant;

- went to an event, such as a wine auction or family reunion with amazing food, or a food festival;
- are obsessed with a favorite food, or have a favorite story about food;
- cook unusual holiday dishes;
- volunteer in the food world;
- like to garden, hunt, or camp, or have some other hobby that could involve food.

A few places that take first-person essays are *Newsweek*'s "My Turn" column, the *New York Times Sunday Magazine,* and *Woman's Day, Family Circle,* and *Slow* magazines. *Saveur* magazine sometimes publishes a "Memories" column. In addition, magazines particular to some subjects, such as camping or gardening, are good prospects.

Regardless of the style or topic of your story, you must have a clear and imaginative focus, a fresh angle, and a slant appropriate to the publication. News and trends are always good. "You can't just repeat what other people have written," says *Gastronomica* editor Darra Goldstein. "Try and find your own new angle to it, your own discovery, instead of the same thing recycled many times." Sometimes it's enough to put a fresh take on a non-original idea. Said Jeanne McManus, former food editor of the *Washington Post,* in an interview, "I like pieces that broaden the discussion about food, that surprise you in that they take something—an ingredient, a technique—something that we think we all know about and slightly change forever the way I, the reader, think about it."

Magazines also change the editorial mix when a new editor comes on board, so check current issues. "Our newish editor loves a meaty feature, so we're including more profiles, reportage, even contrary-verging-on-controversial essays," confirms Ann Taylor Pittman, senior food editor at *Cooking Light.*

How to Target and Position Your Story

Your next step is critical, and one that many freelance writers fail to do: zoom in on a publication or Web site that's most likely to publish your story. Targeting means systematically finding the most realistic and appropriate place. Let's say I'd like to write a local story about the growing Vietnamese food scene in my town. Notice that my story idea is not a topic, but a trend. "Magazines are really of the moment, not a compendium or a definitive thing like a book or encyclopedia," said Martha Holmberg, former editor in chief and publisher of *Fine Cooking,* during an International Association of Culinary Professionals (IACP) annual conference. "We don't want the whole thing, we want a slice. Not the topic. It's what you do with that topic."

The topic of the story would be "Vietnamese food." If that's as far as I got, an editor would be likely to say, "So what?" A subject is not specific or intrinsically interesting by itself. If I change it to say that many markets and restaurants have opened in a particular neighborhood, however, now I have a trend story, one with news value that could be published.

The next question I'd ask myself is, "Who cares about this story?" The newspaper for that neighborhood might care, as might an alternative weekly and the daily newspaper. All are local, a key point. A national magazine may not want the story, because it focuses on a small region, unless it's targeted as a cool new neighborhood for foodies to explore.

The other part of targeting involves identifying an audience. This sounds obvious but I can't tell you how many story ideas I rejected when I was an editor because the writers didn't understand the magazine's reader base. If you want to write about food for children, target magazines aimed at parents. If you like exotic, expensive vacations, focus on magazines and websites with upper-income, traveling readers. It's not hard to figure out who reads the magazine if you review the content in a few issues, including the ads. Sometimes a magazine's Web site will list reader demographics under advertising information. Which publications interest you and share your values? In many cases you are the target audience and would therefore be good at coming up with appropriate story ideas.

Once you identify a possible place for your story, find up to a year's worth of issues and search for stories similar to your idea. This is harder than it seems, as some publications are not available in libraries and don't put their content online. Also, many industry magazines are free to qualified subscribers, which might not be you. Canvass friends and others who might keep the publications you need to review. Visit big newsstands. Respond to free offers for sample issues. For websites, read all prior stories in that category.

In the case of the Vietnamese food story, you'd look through the neighborhood newspaper to see whether it has published stories on food-based businesses, and if so, what kind. If you find none, you'd move to the weekly and focus on restaurants because the readership is more likely to eat out than cook. For a daily, again, review past issues to see how they cover local food trends, and reshape your story as necessary. Perhaps there's a first-person essay on searching for the best takeout roast chicken. If so, a story about the best takeout Vietnamese might be too obscure. Follow this same reasoning with any other publication you'd like to pitch.

You're probably wondering whether to pitch one publication at a time, or whether to send the same query to several at once. Speaking as an editor, I can't advise you to send custom pitches on the same subject to various publications simultaneously, unless they have wildly different readers. An airline magazine and a food magazine are not different enough for me. I wouldn't want readers to say, "You know, I think I just saw a similar story in a different magazine, written by the same person." This strategy will not win you any points with editors either.

Be realistic about which publication you target. If you've never been published, don't bother starting with *Bon Appétit* or the *Washington Post*. Find the smallest publications in your area, or a new Web site or small newsletter. They may not pay or may pay next to nothing. At this point, you shouldn't care too much, because you need clips to establish your credibility to a bigger publication.

Review food magazines for clues about what they want. Check the front part of the book for freelanced material. Figure out which pieces are freelanced by comparing the names to the staff names on the masthead. Estimate the length of features. Examine which stories are text driven versus recipe driven. Examine the structure of stories, such as how many sidebars and boxes they use.

Once you feel confident your story would fit the publication, list the most important points and subpoints to prepare for your query letter. Put the points in logical order, based on questions readers would ask.

Review the sample stories you selected for similarity. Notice the style and voice. Is the writer part of the story or invisible? Does the magazine hold the reader's hand in the instruction, or assume a certain level of expertise? Does the writer sound breezy or authoritative? If it's a trend story, find a statistic to make the trend credible. Do a word count of an example story and plan how many points you can cover in the same amount of space. If your story raises questions, do enough research to answer them. Notice whether the similar story includes sidebars—boxed smaller stories or lists. If so, come up with a few sidebar ideas.

Don't write the story yet. First take a look at what kind of publication is likely to publish it. Then write the pitch.

~~~~~~

HOW TO BOIL WATER: A LESSON IN POSITIONING

Martha Holmberg, former publisher of *Fine Cooking,* shows how food magazines have their own style, voice, and vision. Here's her take on how each pitch letter would slant a story on how to boil water:

Fine Cooking: I've boiled water for years, and I've developed my own method that's fast and produces an even boil. I'll include information on pot selection, the best source of heat, the benefit of using a lid, some do-ahead tips, and I'll give recipes for salted water, acidulated water, and water infused with a bouquet garni. I could do a sidebar on making a bouquet garni.

Cook's Illustrated: Good boiled water is crucial to good cooking, so we decided to experiment to find the best way to boil. I tried aluminum versus stainless, 8-quart versus 12-quart, with a lid, without a lid, gas versus electric, starting with hot versus starting with cold, and our results will surprise you: Cold water and no lid worked best.

Saveur: My Italian grandmother used to boil water for her pasta using the clippings from my grandfather's vineyard as fuel. Her agnolotti was soulful and satisfying, and I'd swear it was the fruity scent of that smoke that made the difference.

Bon Appétit: Boiling water is the focal point of an evening spent with good friends and good food. Charleston couple Bunny and Chad built their Craftsman-style bungalow kitchen with a special boiling bar so friends could gather and sip wine while the water does its magic.

Food and Wine: Enter the world of Trey, chef-owner of the white-hot restaurant of the moment. In his off hours, he craves nothing more than to hang with his friends at the renovated leather factory he shares with his designer girlfriend Giselle. Their casual evenings kick off with green tea martinis made from boiled Icelandic water and served in stemware designed by Giselle.

She's exaggerating to make her point, of course, that editors at each of these magazines have a firm idea of how their magazine differs. One of the main reasons they reject queries is because writers don't create enough of a slant to make the story appropriate. Another is because writers pitch a subject—boiling water—rather than a slant on boiling water. With Holmberg's clever examples, it's easy to see the difference.

Finding the Right Markets

Another way to decide who wants your story is to understand which kind of publication to target, what's realistic, and how to approach them.

National food magazines: Everyone wants to be published in one of the big food magazines. It's difficult to get a feature article accepted, though, unless you have written a cookbook, own a popular restaurant, have your own television show, are a well-known cooking-school teacher, have written for big magazines or newspapers, or apprenticed under a celebrity chef. Some magazines, such as *Cook's Illustrated* and *Taste of Home*, take no freelance articles at all.

That's fine. You can be realistic. Let editors get to know and trust you by writing short pieces. Look at departments in the front of food magazines and come up with an idea for a 250- to 500-word short, newsy piece. Saveur Fare in *Saveur* might profile a producer, a food festival, and a bakery. *Bon Appétit*'s Starters department has short creative pieces as well. Be innovative, inventive, and fresh, says Tina Ujlaki, executive food editor of *Food & Wine*.

While departments are usually collections of short work by different writers, columns are usually written by one person and provide clues on subjects the editors think are important enough to appear regularly. *Food & Wine* always has travel, restaurants, wine, and entertaining columns. *Bon Appétit* has regular writing on technique, healthy cooking, and restaurant recipes. *Eating Well*'s departments include two on nutrition.

Gastronomica, a quarterly magazine published by University of California Press, breaks away from the pack. It takes no advertising and includes none of the usual food photography. Editor Darra Goldstein says she welcomes articles from any field touching on the history, production, uses, and depictions of food. It's certainly easier to crack than the big glossy food magazines, unless you're only interested in recipe-based stories.

Regional magazines: The biggest cover several states, such as *Southern Living* and *Sunset,* two magazines owned by Time-Life. Both *Southern Living* and *Sunset* take freelanced food and travel pieces and recipe-based articles. State magazines don't necessarily do much food writing at all. *Texas Monthly* is an exception.

Trade publications in the food and beverage industry: *Restaurant and Institutions, Food Arts*, and *Natural Foods Merchandiser* are a few of the food-industry trade magazines that cater to specific audiences such as food service operations, restaurant management, and retailers and wholesalers. Many well-established freelancers work for these publications because they pay better than those oriented to consumers. If you are a chef, a caterer, or have worked in food service or production, industry publications could be an ideal outlet for you, as story ideas will come easily.

To learn more, try to qualify for a free one-year subscription to some food and beverage publications and study them for opportunities. There's even a thorough book on the subject: *Writing for Trade Magazines: How to Boost Your Income by $200 to $500 per Week,* by Kendall Hanson, although it came out in 1999.

National travel magazines: Many travel features in these magazines include information about restaurants and dining as part of a destination. For example, *National Geographic Traveler* publishes articles such as "Confessions of a Cheese Smuggler." In a department in *Islands* magazine, you might see a piece on "Anguilla, a wine and food lovers' getaway."

Women's magazines: Check the women's magazines for those with recipe sections, such as *Martha Stewart Living, Oprah, Family Circle, Yoga Journal, Health,* and *Woman's Day.* Some carry nutrition and diet-based advice articles as well. Chances are good that you need to be a published writer to get a pitch accepted at these national magazines. Competition will be fierce.

Food sections of daily papers: I'd like to be optimistic, but I'm not. Newspapers take less and less freelance work. Most dailies are part of big chains like Knight Ridder or Cox News Service. The chains swap employee stories between newspapers, so food section editors have lots of stories from which to choose.

The food section has a tight budget anyway, with most of it designated for buying food, maintaining the test kitchen, recipe testing, food styling for in-house photography, culinary demonstrations, and professional development for staff members, says Heather McPherson, food editor of the *Orlando Sentinel.* She fills a four-page section each week by writing her own stories and subscribing to syndicates for other content. "We take very little freelance because budgets in newspapers across the country are shrinking," says McPherson. "You make the most with what money you have. I won't pay someone to do something I can do."

Aim for a local angle for newspapers. Here's a tip from *Washington Post* former food editor Jeanne McManus: "I like pieces that show the pulse of the city in which we publish the food section, pieces about people doing real things in the world of food."

Weekly papers: Usually these are alternative papers written with attitude for people in their twenties and thirties who go to clubs and restaurants. You'll always find restaurant reviews, but the question is whether there's a budget to do other food writing. Weeklies usually work a few days to one week ahead.

Virginia Wood is food editor of the *Austin Chronicle*. She says she fills two and a half pages per week with restaurant reviews, profiles, company stories, and cookbook reviews. Her assignments go to seven regular freelancers. Wood said two of these freelancers were working chefs she'd known around Austin who changed careers and were interested in food writing. Two writers who were also trained chefs approached her with good ideas or impressive clips. A restaurateur suggested a mutual friend as the wine writer. The final writer is the spouse of one of her *Chronicle* colleagues. "I didn't go looking for people with food service backgrounds, but five out of seven of us have spent years in the kitchen, which I think informs our writing in important ways," she concludes.

Other weekly papers are community based and might be good prospects for first-time writers. Freelancer and cookbook author Peggy Knickerbocker started out at San Francisco's *Nob Hill Gazette*—"some silly thing about Thanksgiving," she recalls—and *North Beach Now*, with a story on the oldest cappuccino machine in the Italian neighborhood. From there she used her clips to approach the *San Francisco Examiner*, where she wrote a piece on cooking for people with AIDS.

City magazines: These tend to focus on restaurant reviews and capsule reviews to please their advertisers. Occasionally they profile specialty-food producers, such as an old-time candy bar manufacturer, or a piece on organic farms open to the public. They might have stories profiling local food people, or roundup pieces on where to get the best sandwich or coffee. Most produce an annual "Best Restaurants" cover story. The most sophisticated and most often copied city magazine is *New York*.

General and association magazines and newsletters: National magazines such as those of insurance companies, the American Automobile Association, and the American Association of Retired People are hard to crack, as are airline magazines. But all take food stories. Newsletters are a good option if you're starting out.

The Web: Your best bet is the web versions of companies and print publications, such as *Sunset* and *Fine Cooking*. Also see a list of sites that pay for freelance work in the Appendix.

What are the differences between writing for the web and writing for print? Freelancer Cheryl Sternman Rule says that web writing tends to be more personal and less fact based. It also pays dramatically less.

"Because websites aren't constricted by ad-driven pages the way magazines are, editors are often more flexible about word count, subject matter, and even deadlines," explains Rule. "The turnaround time, from submission to seeing your piece online, becomes a matter of days or even hours, rather than the six-month lead time common in magazines."

To her delight, Rule has found editors have encouraged her to express her voice. "Magazines and newspapers enforce a uniform style, so quirkiness isn't always valued. As a magazine writer, part of my job is to represent the magazine, not myself. I've found almost the opposite to be true online.

"Of course, there's a flip side to all this creativity: Pay is substantially, shockingly less. Web site editors are more likely to ask for supplemental material, such as photos and recipes, and they don't necessarily offer more money. And with competition especially fierce, writers have much less leverage to negotiate fees and rates online than they do in print."

Other freelancing opportunities: Contribute to anthologies, guidebooks, and reference guides. Look for opportunities in newsletters and on websites, based on what you know. When she was starting out, cooking school teacher and writer Thy Tran wrote the cooking chapter in *How to Fix (Just About) Everything*. For the book *Asia in the San Francisco Bay Area: A Cultural Travel Guide*, she wrote a chapter on the San Jose Vietnamese Community.

Write Your Query Letter

Now that you have chosen your target market and publication, and refined your story idea, your job is to spin the subject to fit the publication or Web site. Write a short query letter explaining your idea and why you are the best person to write the story.

Target the editor who receives query letters. If the publication does not list a food editor on its masthead or on its Web site, call the editorial department. Whoever answers the phone can help you. Usually it's an editorial assistant or associate editor, and part of their job is to field questions from writers. Don't be shy. You want to know a couple of things: to whom should you pitch your story, and the editor's email address. Get the correct spelling of the editor's name and be formal in your email. Say "Dear Ms. Ujlaki," not "Dear Tina," if you've never met her.

You might also find editors on social media, such as Linked In, Twitter, and Facebook, and at conferences such as those put on by IACP and the Symposium for Professional Food Writers at the Greenbrier.

Editors are flooded with query letters and reject almost all of them. When I was an editor my rejection rate was around 95 percent. Here's why queries fail:

- generic story idea, not targeted to the publication;
- too long;
- unfocused story idea;
- badly written, with a boring lead;
- just an introduction, no story idea. "If someone says 'I'd like to work for you, contact me if you're interested,' I'll never contact them," said Holmberg. Like most editors, she doesn't have time. She might put your letter and writing samples into a file, and mean to get back to them, but she probably won't.

Ideally, query letters are three paragraphs long. Here are the elements:

The hook: Grab the editor's attention with the same kind of lead paragraph you'd write for the story. Your first few sentences must demonstrate that you can write and that you understand the audience's mission and readers. Here's one from freelancer Janet Fletcher: "Everybody knows that broccoli is a great cancer fighter. But too many people overlook its cousins . . . that have comparable health benefits and underutilized potential in the kitchen. Kale of many kinds, kohlrabi, broccoli romanesco, and broccoli rabe are among (those) that deserve a wider audience."

If you reference a story or department, it shows you read the magazine and have thought about a story that is right for them. Editors will pay attention.

The pitch: Explain your story idea in specifics, in just a few sentences. If you can't, it's a sign you haven't thought it through closely enough. For a story with recipes, list the titles or make suggestions. State the length, whether it will fit in a particular section, and give a working title and a summary. If you have thought of other elements such as sidebars and tip boxes, mention them. Editors are thinking little pieces these days, so your ability to cut the story up into boxes will help you. Longer narratives are out, unless you're writing for the *New Yorker.*

Your credentials: State why you are qualified to write the story. The best reason would be that you have written stories like this before. If you have been published on an entirely different subject in an unrelated field, don't mention it, as editors will not see it as relevant. If you've never been published, bring up relevant work experience or personal experience or your blog. If you've already done some interviews or research, or have been granted access to a prestigious profile subject, these facts might compensate for lack of writing experience.

The close: Thank the editor and say you will follow up in a few weeks. If you have a deadline, such as you're leaving the country within a month, say so.

Multiple story queries might increase your chance of getting published if you pitch two or three ideas of one paragraph each. For one national magazine, I pitched three stories. They had just accepted one idea from another writer, didn't like the second, but wanted the third. For another magazine, I pitched two articles and the editor wanted both. The challenge is to be concise.

These days, almost every editor takes email queries. Put a few key words in the subject line with the word "Query" preceding them. Don't send clips as attachments. Editors have grown tired of big files that download slowly or arrive in formats they can't open. If your bylined pieces are online—even on your own Web site—put links in the body of the email and make the editor's life easier.

Check the email several times for typos, spelling errors, etc. Print it out and proofread it. If you send a badly written query with typos, or you have spelled the editor's name wrong, you'll turn the editor off and reduce your chance of being taken seriously.

SAMPLE QUERY

Here's a letter freelance writer Tracy Cuervels O'Grady wrote to *Relish*, a national magazine that appears in weekend editions of newspapers. She researched back issues and saw a freelanced story about using different types of cheese to make French, English, and Italian lasagnas. So she figured the editor would like the different renditions of pot roast. Tracey looked up one of the magazine's pot roast recipes and emulated the format.

Dear Jill Melton:

In the annals of New England culinary history, pot roast was known as a frugal dinner, since it calls for inexpensive cuts of meat like chuck, flank and bottom round cooked slowly in a covered pot. Perhaps for its practicality, it's also been a favorite pub offering. But now this old-fashioned Yankee dish is more appealing updated and infused with Asian, Indian, Italian and Mediterranean flavors.

While it's always been a standby at cantankerous Durgin Park in Boston's Faneuil Hall, where tourists enjoy eating up nostalgia, pot roast fell out of favor, replaced by more sophisticated meat dishes. Fortunately, at rustic Dalya's Restaurant in Bedford, Massachusetts the practical dish has an elegant incarnation, thanks to chef Udiel Restrepo. His Mediterranean version of this poor man's roast beef is more tasteful than its historic twin with dribbles of heady, fragrant truffle oil and garlic mashed potatoes.

In this article of about 600 words, titled, "Not Your Grandmother's Pot Roast," I will include recipes for Mediterranean pot roast as well as an Asian version (Chinese 5-spice), Indian (with aromatic flavors such as cardamom and cumin), and Italian (parsley, sage and red wine) version.

My articles have appeared in the *Boston Globe*, the *New York Times*, the *New York Daily News*, *Hallmark*, *Conde Nast Traveler*, and *Chocolatier*, among other publications. (She also included links.)

I would love to write for *Relish* so I hope you will consider my idea.

Regards,

Tracey Cuervels

The editor accepted the story, requesting Asian, Italian and Mediterranean versions, but not the Indian version Tracey pitched originally.

~~~~~~

Get a Response

You sent off the query. Now you wait. Typical responses range from two to eight weeks. Really. And often, you may get no response at all.

When you've waited an appropriate amount of time, send a follow-up one-sentence email by forwarding the original query. Be polite and professional. Ask if the editor has received the query and had a chance to read it.

Sometimes editors respond with some version of "I need more time." If I don't hear back, I email again, with a shorter note. "Be persistent," said Tina Ujlaki, executive food editor of *Food & Wine*, at an IACP session. "It takes a lot to get through, and it might mean we just haven't got around to it."

If you still don't hear back, don't phone. Even if you get editors on the phone, they will not know who you are, won't know where they put the query, probably won't have time to look for it, and will have to get back to you.

Waiting for a response can get frustrating. I've waited as long as a year. "After spending about three weeks sending queries and clips with no success, I'd get so depressed I took naps on the floor because if I slept in bed that meant I was really depressed," says freelancer Linda Furiya. But she persisted, and eventually an airline magazine hired her to do a roving feature on city dining. That article led to more assignments.

Some editors are so swamped that they don't bother sending any response at all. Be prepared for that outcome. Even established freelance writers complain that they get no response sometimes, so don't get too discouraged if it happens to you. The secret is to send out a few query ideas instead of one, so you're not so attached to the outcome. If you hear nothing, pitch a new story, or move on to a new publication. Don't give up. Refocus.

What if an editor wants your story? She or he will discuss length and deadline, and offer a fee. If you want the job and you're not experienced, take it and don't haggle over the money. It's considered impolite to do so before you have proven yourself. I've heard more established freelancers suggest you pause and say, "It sounds a little low," to see if the editor will offer more.

Sometimes, an editor might like your writing but doesn't want the particular story you've pitched. She might ask if you'd be interested in another story, perhaps one based on an idea she already generated.

Up until now, I've assumed you don't know the editor you're pitching. But there's another way to do it: network. If you meet editors at writer's conferences, industry events, through social media such as Linked In, or even by chance, your job is to be memorable enough that editors remember you when you send in a story idea. If you meet them in person, get their business cards so you can follow up on email. To increase the odds, query them the next day on a subject you brought up. Don't wait for six months, trying to get up the nerve. Get it over with. Six months from now, you might as well be a stranger.

If the publication or Web site published your work, it's your job to try to establish a relationship with your editor. The more comfortable an editor feels with you, and the more you deliver professional stories on deadline, the more assignments you will receive. If editors like one story, they might like more, so keep pitching ideas.

What About Pay?

It sounds silly to start this paragraph with a question like this, but in food writing, it's legitimate: you might have to write for free when you're starting out. Because competition is so intense, and because many publications and websites have a small budget, you might be asked to do so. On the plus side, your story will be published and you'll have a clip. You'll get the experience of working with an editor and working on a story. If you do a good job, you might get an assignment for pay. On the other hand, you won't get paid this time around. If in your gut you feel the editor is taking advantage of you or not taking you seriously, don't sign up for the job.

People contact me all the time to tell me they were asked to write for free. One of the most popular posts on my blog, Will Write for Food, is about a woman who started a blog and then pitched recipe-based stories to two regional newspapers, only to have both tell her they would not pay her for her work. I asked the community what they would have done. The consensus was that because she was just starting out, it was acceptable if the writer needed the clip to move forward with her career.

But she should stop working for nothing as soon as she has a few clips. Or barter: One quarterly magazine gave me a free subscription in exchange for two articles a year. That's better than nothing, and gave me a few tax write-offs.

I've since learned I can work almost for free by being paid close to nothing. I've received $25 for cookbook reviews, $30 for restaurant reviews in a guidebook, and $150 for a 3,000-word story. My experience is hardly unique, even for the big names. "I always dabbled in food writing as an aside but never planned to become a food writer. I never thought I could make a living as one, as the $50 and $75 I got for most of the food pieces I wrote proved," says *GQ* contributor Alan Richman of his early days in the business.

Why is food writing such a badly paid profession? A full-time free-lancer put it this way: She asked if, when I was a magazine editor in other fields, I had 100 people standing behind me willing to do my job for nothing. I said no. That's her situation, she explained. If she asks for more money, someone else will step in to fill her place for less, or nothing. Another freelancer wrote this when I told her about my book: "I'd better hurry and get my career more established, because I'm sure that once all those would-be's read your book and follow your advice, the competition will be stiffer than ever."

Even freelance writers at the top of their game don't feel well compensated. When asked about the hardest part of freelancing, Estabrook said, "Money. Even when you're making top rates at magazines and doing books, it's a financial grind. Competition is such that publications aren't really forced to pay more than they do for articles." He added that even if he wrote an article every month when he was a regular contributor for *Gourmet*, he would make $50,000–$60,000 per year, with no medical care. "That's a grueling pace you probably couldn't keep up."

Most food writers don't write full-time. They can't afford it. Says Wood of her regular writers at the *Chronicle*, "None makes their living as a freelancer, because it's almost impossible to do so." Again, keep your day job or work part time at other jobs unless your spouse or partner can support you, you have a generous trust fund, or you can arrange to win the lottery.

Write Your Story

During a break in a writing class I taught, a student approached me and said she was a terrible writer. I asked her how many drafts she wrote. "One," she answered. Whenever I tell that story to fellow writers, they laugh. Your first draft isn't *supposed* to be good. Anne Lamott calls it a "shitty first draft" in her excellent book on writing, *Bird by Bird: Some Instructions on Writing and Life*.

The first draft is whatever you write to get started, after you have done your research and completed your interviews. Make it awful, incomplete, and out of order—whatever you want. Then go back over it several times, filling in pieces, shaping and polishing your work. Good writing doesn't flow out in a single piece, fully formed. It needs revision.

Start with a compelling lead paragraph, called a lead: Draw in readers by piquing their interest. Spend a long time getting it right. The best way to do so is to review the leads of previously published pieces in the publication or Web site. Obviously those leads worked for the editor, so try to copy them. Here are a few more strategies:

- Base it on common experiences everyone understands. Here's a lead from an article in *Bon Appétit:* "As desperately as I wanted to overhaul my seventies nightmare kitchen—it was ugly and claustrophobic, and the oven was held together with grease—I was scared. Was there a way to do the job without losing my money, my mind, and my marriage? Here's what I found out."

- Put readers in the center of the story immediately, a particularly good technique for travel stories. Here's the first sentence of a story on Bangkok in *Bon Appétit*: "It's hard to miss the distinctive flavors of Thailand in bustling Bangkok, whether you're slurping noodles at an outdoor market or quaffing cocktails in a skyscraper bar."

- Give a telling anecdote about one person to illustrate the point of your story. An *Eating Well* story on sugar addiction begins: "Long ago, Peg Duvall fell into a trap. As a teenager in the 1950s, Duvall studied diligently and led a life surrounded by high school friends. But she had a hard time relaxing at night."

- For a how-to piece, hook readers by reassuring them it's going to be worth it. Here's a lead in *Fine Cooking:* "Learning to love beets isn't nearly as hard as you might imagine, because a roasted beet isn't so much a beet as it is a sweet and tender roasted vegetable."

Says freelancer Peggy Knickerbocker. "Capture your audience with something visual. I position the reader in the moment where I was captivated, and then go back and write the story. I have learned to write about something vivid, like kneading the dough, with little clouds rising into the air. *Saveur* taught me that."

Follow with a nut graph: Once you've drawn the reader in, explain what you're going to tell them. A nut graph bridges the lead and the rest of the story. It explains the point and tells readers what they will learn. Sometimes leads are so condensed that the nut graph is a sentence ending the first paragraph, as in the kitchen renovation story in the first example.

Near the top, tell readers why they should care, what's in it for them: Readers are busy. This is particularly true in newspapers, where you have to get to the point quickly. Readers want to know if this article will be worth their time. *Fine Cooking* accomplishes this in the first sentence of the beet story.

Hold readers' hands: You know where the story's going, but your readers don't. Drop a trail of bread crumbs all the way through. Reassure readers you're telling them what you said you would, and foreshadow what will come next. Readers don't like to be surprised. Prepare them for a story that takes a turn or covers several points.

If you're writing a recipe-based story, chances are good that you'll write a lead and nut graph, then go right into the recipes. In this example from *Cook's Illustrated*, a nut graph frames the story: "Years ago, in the kitchen of a university apartment, my Taiwanese roommate taught me to create a simple noodle dish that involved no more than boiling the noodles. It was a cheap, quick, meatless meal on which a student tired of Salisbury steak could subsist. Could I create something that recalled that satisfying dish, yet was a bit more substantial— more suited to a weeknight dinner?"

Make sure the body of the story follows a logical path: All stories have a beginning, middle, and end. Before tackling the middle, draft an organizational plan of points you wish to make. Each paragraph's first sentence makes the decision for the rest of the piece. Thoughts should flow in logical order from one topic to the next. Once you have a structure, if you feel more comfortable starting in the middle, go for it.

Strong close: Does your story have one, or does it trail off? In the conclusion, tell readers what you've already told them. If you've relayed an anecdote or created a theme in your lead, circle around to it again in the conclusion.

HOW TO INTERVIEW

- When you first contact your interviewee, politely explain the point of your story. Say where it will be published. If you haven't pitched the story yet, say you're calling to get permission to interview the person for a story. Once you have an interviewee's consent, your query letter has more teeth. Request a convenient time to come by or telephone. Say how much time you'll need.

- Try not to do the interview by email. Because people are busy they will answer with the smallest effort possible and then you're done. There's also no room for the best part, when the two of you spontaneously travel down a new path to new material. I do interviews by phone, on a headset, and type my notes. Some people tape interviews and then transcribe the notes.

- Create a list of questions by doing research and eliminating those that will annoy your subject, such as "What's the name of your award-winning cheese again?" Find out all you can by using a Web site search, or talking to people who know the person.

- Annoying questions are different from dumb questions. If your subject uses a word you don't understand, ask what it means. Feel free to ask "How do you know that?" or "How did it work?" when appropriate. Ask "Can you give me an example?" when something sounds theoretical. You're not the expert; you're the information gatherer, and you have to make sure you understand well enough to write about it later.

- Ask open-ended questions. Yes or no answers don't tell readers anything. Your interview will be over before you know it and you'll have no story. Ask questions such as "What led you to decide to? . . ." and "How do you feel about? . . ."

- Ask a surprise question. Sometimes even a silly question leads to an excellent quote.

- Focus. If you're interviewing Thomas Keller because a restaurant magazine wants to know how he runs several establishments at once, don't ask about his technique for making gnocchi.

- Remember that the interview is not about you. It is not a conversation, but you can sound conversational. Express interest, even skepticism. Do not state your opinions, sympathize, or add meaning to questions. Don't tell stories about the time something similar happened to you. You're not there to entertain or make friends with your subject.

- End when you said you would, and thank the interviewee for making time to talk with you. If you need more time, make another appointment. Send a thank-you note when you're done.

Edit Your Own Work

When you think you've drafted the story you want, your next step is to strengthen and shape it. Be ruthless. You might end up deleting half of it, moving paragraphs around, and rewriting the other half. None of this means you can't write. On the contrary, it means you are doing the work of real writers: revising. Here's how:

- Eliminate any throat clearing, where you have to warm up to get to the story. See if the lead starts a few paragraphs from the top.
- Eliminate repetition by saying what you mean clearly. Don't keep writing the same idea in slightly different ways.
- Write in active versus passive voice. Active voice means someone takes action: "John cut the crusty bread." Passive voice means the action is more removed: "The crusty bread was cut by John." Passive voice flattens your writing.
- Create action by packing your story with verbs. Powerful verbs make your writing more vigorous, and help readers move through the story.
- Adjectives are the curse of food writers. Find one specific word and cut the rest.
- Tighten every sentence, eliminating all other unnecessary words, particularly adverbs such as "very" and "really."
- Cut out tangents or put them in sidebars.
- Use "show, not tell." Don't tell readers you didn't like sitting at the dinner table with your dad. Show them what it was like. Put them there at the table with you.
- Revise by ear. Read your work out loud to feel its rhythm and flow. It sounds silly but it's an invaluable way to eliminate clunky sentences and find parts that need clarification. When you hesitate over a sentence's construction, examine how to revise it to read more clearly.
- If you have time, put your story away for a few days. When you come back to it you'll be more objective about what to fix and the fixes will be clearer.
- Edit for grammar, punctuation, and spelling. Proofread for typos. I can't emphasize this enough. There's nothing more

irritating to editors than a careless mistake. It makes editors worry that you're not as accomplished as you seem. Have someone else read your work to look for errors.

"My process involves a lot of thinking before, during, and after," says freelancer Alan Richman. "It's not about polishing words but polishing the thinking, making things more focused."

What are the hardest things about writing articles? To quote Knickerbocker, "To be a good journalist, take the profession seriously, get the facts right, and present something new and fresh. Combine accuracy with creativity and passion."

BOOKS TO HELP YOU BECOME A BETTER WRITER:

- *On Writing Well: The Classic Guide to Writing Nonfiction*, by William Zinsser
- *Elements of Style*, by William Strunk Jr. and E. B. White
- *Writing Down the Bones: Freeing the Writer Within*, by Natalie Goldberg
- *Bird by Bird: Some Instructions on Writing and Life*, by Anne Lamott
- *The Resource Guide for Food Writers*, by Gary Allen (useful info on style, grace, and writing aids)

Working with Your Editor

Once you submit your story to the editor, you may not hear back right away. Don't panic. Eventually your editor will read it and contact you about changes. Most stories need tweaking. Perhaps you left out critical details, or your lead is buried, or you need more information in certain areas, or the tone is wrong. Being edited is part of the process. Be polite and accept the requests.

If you are having control issues about someone changing your work, get over it. It will happen forever, no matter how long you've been writing. Yes, an editor can make changes you don't like. If you must object, pick your battle and make a reasoned argument, politely. Most editors, particularly on newspapers, don't even show you what they've done to your story before it is published. After a newspaper printed one of my restaurant reviews, I discovered that an editor interjected her own opinion, one contrary to my own. I called her and explained, politely, that my opinion was mine alone. She didn't do that again.

As a Freelancer, What Can You Write Off Your Taxes?

If you become a food writer, can you now write off all meals, research, and travel? Probably not, unless you can meet certain criteria.

The first test is how much time you spend on food writing. According to the Internal Revenue Service (IRS), if you put in at least 500 hours per year, you have a business. If it's less than that, you have a hobby.

The IRS allows no deductions for hobbies unless your hobby makes a profit. In that case, you can deduct expenses up to the same amount as your hobby's expenses. If you took a loss, where food writing earned you $2,750 but you spent $3,500 on food, travel, classes, and office expenses, you could deduct only $750 of the expenses. These expenses constitute a miscellaneous deduction and may be subject to further restrictions.

If you have a food writing business that takes up more than 500 hours per year, you may qualify for some tax deductions. Here are test questions the IRS might ask to determine whether your business qualifies:

1. **Do you keep records documenting your writing and research?** Doing so would indicate you have a serious business. Let's say you wrote a restaurant review. You need more than the credit card receipt to show as evidence. Keep notes on the meal, a sample menu, a map, a parking receipt, and a sample draft. For recipe development, keep versions of each recipe, with notes on how you worked.

2. **Do you have the expertise to run a profitable business, and have you hired experts or taken classes to help you in areas where you are not an expert?** If so, you may write off whatever expenses are ordinary and necessary for performance of your business. Let's say you

took a weeklong cooking class in Venice. You received a syllabus, kept notes, took photographs and researched restaurants, markets, and food purveyors, thus establishing a true business purpose for your trip: your desire to increase your knowledge and expertise of Italian food, thereby improving your marketability.

3. **Is it reasonable to expect a profit?** The more you can show you are in business to make a profit, the more legitimate your write-offs become. Here are a few examples:

- You want to travel to Turkey and write articles about your food explorations there. Querying editors before you leave indicates you are looking for profit-generating opportunities. Querying editors afterward might indicate you are looking for ways to write off your vacation. It doesn't matter if the editors reject the articles. What matters is your intent and record-keeping prowess.
- Let's say a newspaper paid you $75 for three recipes. The cost of groceries came to $100. While you didn't make a profit, expenses might be deductible if you argue that you are paying your dues, gradually increasing your exposure and experience to increase your marketability.
- You want to write a cookbook based on using kitchen appliances like rice cookers and food processors. Your purchase of kitchen equipment might be deductible if you can show that you also bought similar books for research purposes, wrote a book proposal, interviewed kitchen-shop retailers, and looked for an agent. Even so, since they are capital expenses, the deduction might occur over the life of the equipment as opposed to a full deduction on the year of the purchase.

Once you meet the above criteria for a business, you qualify for the right to deduct ordinary and necessary expenses for a self-employed business person, such as telephone bills, office supplies, and membership fees. Keep detailed files of your work-related papers, including copies of your notes, plus all bills and receipts.

Many food writers also cater, develop recipes, do food styling for photographs, act as spokespeople for brands, consult to industry, and teach cooking classes. The good news is these pursuits are interrelated and can be considered one business. Therefore the Venice cooking class may make you a better caterer and recipe developer, in addition to increasing your knowledge as a food writer.

This is a cursory discussion only. For more details, consult a professional tax preparer.

Three Ways to Make Decent Money

As I've said before, food writing doesn't pay. But there are ways to make more money if you're willing to recycle your work and change your notions about what to write about. Here are three suggestions:

1. **Recycle.** Freelance work can pay a little more if you recycle the same article to other publications. Most publications buy first North American serial rights, where the publisher has the right to publish your work first. It does not authorize their right to publish your work elsewhere, such as in another publication or on a Web site. After that you're free to sell it again, preferably to non-competing markets both here and abroad. For example, a piece you wrote on spa cuisine in Mexico might fit a travel magazine whose focus is more on travel and less on food. A piece on coriander might first appear in a magazine focusing on herbs, and then in a more general publication.

   By adding and subtracting according to the needs of other publications and websites, you can publish a similar story many times—and get paid each time. Just apply what you learned earlier about targeting and positioning. Do not disclose that the article was previously published. Magazines don't care unless you're going to make it a problem for them when they see your article in a competitor's publication just as their publication goes to press.

2. **Write for trade publications.** These publications, such as *Restaurants & Institutions* and *Food Arts,* have a narrow focus, though, and you must know enough about the industry and

have enough contacts to generate the right story ideas. If so, there are publications about manufacturing and retailing of groceries, beverages, produce, farming, and many others.

3. **Take corporate writing jobs.** The second kind of freelancing that pays is commercial writing, or writing for companies rather than publications. Cookbook author Janet Fletcher got into commercial writing serendipitously. She was pitching companies to become commercial sponsors for her new newsletter when one company offered her regular work. Her newsletter turned into a mini-magazine for a supermarket chain with seasonal stories, recipes, and product information. That job continued for about three years. Fletcher went on to write advertorials and special advertising sections that appeared in food magazines, and for ten years, wrote the newsletter of the American Institute for Wine and Food.

Now, after almost thirty years of food writing, a significant share of Fletcher's income comes from commercial work. She writes Web site copy and develops recipes for corporations and commodity boards. The nonprofit boards, such as the Almond Board and the Beef Council, hire her to write text aimed at professional chefs. For the Culinary Institute of America, she writes material for conferences.

In this kind of writing, you're usually "pitching a product or a place or a service," says Fletcher, "but it's a soft sell with an editorial feel to it." Commercial writing has its downside. Most of your work doesn't appear with your byline, so it's harder to build your portfolio. But if you're a reliable writer with good ideas who knows how to keep clients, you can succeed. "Find a need and fill it," Fletcher advises. "Look for companies whose Web sites are not very good, or who don't have marketing materials and need them. Approach independent public relations firms."

Public relations firms, marketing agencies, ad agencies, manufacturers, retailers, and non-profit boards and councils hire freelance writers for all kinds of commercial writing: press releases, brochures, Web site content, ghost-written first person pieces, press-kit materials, label information, scripts for videos, pitch letters, research papers, and speeches. They might also give you work developing and testing recipes. If you're just getting started in this area, you may be willing to take less to get a portfolio of work and establish credibility.

The bigger question is how to find work like this. Blogger Amy Sherman of Cooking with Amy (www.cookingwithamy .com) accepts most invitations to events, because she never knows whom she'll meet. At one meeting promoting travel in Alberta, Canada, she met a managing editor of a publishing house, who offered her a bimonthly column on a Web site. After joining the San Francisco Professional Food Society, she met a marketing professional who hired her to fix chef recipes and help her client attract bloggers to promote products, and another for whom she wrote a client's monthly newsletter.

"When you're self-employed, you're a small business person, and you have to know how to market yourself," she advises. "Most people have to do marketing. The sooner you get used to it and get good at it, the sooner you'll be successful." She considers her blog as a place to highlight her writing skills and expertise, providing a showcase for corporate clients.

IS SYNDICATION WORTHWHILE?

Some say syndication is a great way to make money. If you are an established writer, you can query a syndication service about submitting articles for distribution to major daily newspapers, community weeklies, newsletters, and Web sites across the United States and around the world. If the service accepts you, it takes 40 to 50 percent of sales. Sales are based on how many newspapers purchase your story or column and how much they pay.

These days, with reduced budgets and access to lots of free or inexpensive copy, newspapers are no longer a great market for syndication. In fact, one cookbook author told me he was only able to sell his column to one newspaper, which then demanded he also sell them all rights to print it. The syndicate will send payment if and when publications pick up your article or column. It takes a lot of publications to pick up your column to have it add up.

If you have a blog, you might find websites that aggregate blogs. Typically, however, they do not pay, promising you "exposure," in exchange for putting your copy on their Web site.

Syndication sites:
- List of syndicates, www.dmoz.org/News/Media/Services/Syndicates
- Creators.com, www.creators.com
- King Features, www.kingfeatures.com
- United Features, www.unitedfeatures.com

In conclusion, writing for pay is a competitive arena that requires good skills and creativity. Editors and clients like writers they trust who pitch well-defined ideas, understand what they want, turn in good work on time, and form a good relationship. If you can follow these rules and have a thick skin about rejection, you'll always be published. And despite recent hand wringing about the paucity of freelance work, dozens of magazines and websites still pay for good stories. I've assembled an impressive list in the Appendix.

Then there's the role of passion, my theme from earlier chapters. Says Knickerbocker, "I don't think I've ever written something that has been an assignment that didn't come from me. [Otherwise] I haven't been able to write well about it. It's always something that has moved me very deeply, where I just have to get something off my chest and have to write the story. Someone's going to buy it. They're going to feel the vibrancy and the clarity.

"I kind of can't believe my life worked out the way it has," she says, "that I get to write and be paid for it."

FOR MORE INFORMATION ON FREELANCING

Books:
- *Starting Your Career as a Freelance Writer,* by Moira Anderson Allen.
- *This Business of Writing,* by Gregg Levoy.
- *Writer's Market,* a directory published annually by Robert Lee Brewer.

Web sites:

- Association of Food Journalists, www.afjonline.com. Membership limited to writers and editors who spend at least 50 percent of their time on food news and are not paid by food producers, processors, or merchandisers.
- The International Food, Wine, and Travel Writers Association, www.ifwtwa.org. Open to food and wine writers, photographers who write, and established online journalists.
- Magazine news and database, www.woodenhorsepub.com.
- Mediabistro, a membership Web site, lists extensive tips for how to approach dozens of food magazines. See www.mediabistro.com.
- *Writer's Digest*, www.writersdigest.com.
- *Writer's Market* online, www.writersmarket.com.
- For information about grants and contests, see www.fundsforwriters.com.

Writing Exercises

1. I find how-to stories the easiest to write, maybe because I like to help people. Now you try it. Make a list of ten how-to headlines of stories you can write with your eyes closed. Perhaps you're an expert on piecrusts and your article would be about technique. Your headline will not be "All About Piecrusts." Instead, it will focus on how you are an expert giving out advice. "How to Make a Winning Piecrust Every Time" is a more specific, and more exciting, alternative. After you've written your list of ten headlines, pick one and make a list of the steps involved. Now you have the middle of a story. Once you write the beginning and the end, the first draft will be complete.

2. Recycling stories based on the same subject and research is a terrific use of your time and a way to generate better income. Think up three stories based on one subject written for a general consumer publication, then adapt them for an industry newsletter and a magazine aimed at mothers. Write a lead for each kind of story based on what the readership wants to know. I'll give you some

examples. A lead for a food safety story for a general consumer publication targets readers who prepare food without thinking too much about bacteria, and has a general lead about keeping the kitchen sanitary when cooking. A lead for a story for an industry publication quotes a government official discussing new labeling guidelines for meat. A lead for a publication aimed at mothers begins with the story of a child eating leftovers that have gone bad, and then discusses ways a mother might protect her family from ingesting the wrong foods. For each lead idea, I visualized the target audience and slanted the subject directly to them, addressing what might concern or interest them.

3. If you have not been published, come up with a story idea based on your own personal experience, and craft a query letter. A well-crafted query letter might be enough to sway an editor. Here's a sample story idea: "Since I returned to work after having a baby, I've had to plan ahead and buy cupboards full of canned and packaged food for my baby. My article will draw upon my experiences of sampling prepared baby food such as crackers and cereal. It will recommend the top five products for busy mothers, based on taste, ingredients, and value."

6

Secrets
of Restaurant
Reviewing

What could be better than going from restaurant to restaurant, eating exquisite food with friends, and then writing about it? Being a restaurant reviewer has to be one of the most glamorous jobs in the world. You dine for free at the best places in town, and restaurateurs and chefs fawn over you. Right?

Yes and no. You may often eat excellent, cutting-edge, and exotic food that would have strained your pocketbook in the past. But you'll also eat lots of mediocre and bad food, sample foods you might not like, go out more than you want, and work harder than you imagine. Additionally, chefs should not know you, if you're a credible reviewer. And you might find it hard to keep your weight down. As one reviewer told me, "Clothes always come in larger sizes."

The first secret you'll discover is that reviewing involves mediocre food as well as the good stuff. "No one sees you eating bad sushi sixty miles away from home on a Saturday night," admits Tom Sietsema, restaurant critic for the *Washington Post*. The Phantom Gourmet (www.phantomgourmet.com), a New England TV personality and critic, concurs. "For all the dinners that begin with ephemeral tastes of contemporary manna and end with culinary orgasms, there are three mediocre and at least one really bad meal," he complains. Some reviewers I interviewed told me about just plain bad food, and even rotten food that gives them food poisoning. But who feels sorry for them?

You might notice that not much is published about mediocre and bad food. Most publications and websites keep negative reviews to a minimum, unless the place is famous, expensive, or new and opened to great fanfare. Most editors and writers believe it's best to tell readers about places that excite them and give them a reason to go out, rather than telling them where not to go.

The second secret is that reviewing is difficult and time-consuming, even if all you do is write reviews. As a print reviewer, you may go out several evenings in a week. I went out three to four nights per week to write one review per week for *San Francisco Weekly*. Michael Bauer, executive food and wine editor and restaurant critic for the *San Francisco Chronicle*, who writes two reviews per week, goes out almost every night. Sietsema, reviewer for the *Washington Post*, heads out every day for lunch, sometimes breakfast, and sometimes two dinners if he's on deadline. He keeps detailed calendars because he makes upward of sixty reservations per month. *L.A. Weekly*'s Jonathan Gold, the first reviewer to ever win the Pulitzer Prize for restaurant reviewing, eats at 300 to 500 restaurants per year, and drives 20,000 miles per year in search of food.

The main reason for multiple trips is to go back to see if your experience was consistent, and to sample more food. One review may require two or three visits per week. On top of that, you have to keep from being recognized (more on this on page 166). You can make it easier on yourself if you plan and space out restaurant visits. Some critics plan up to three months ahead and might visit one restaurant twice over several weeks.

The third secret is that if an editor gives you an assignment, you're on your own. There's little chance of on-the-job training. If you're like other novices, you'll surely have a lot of questions, and that's where this chapter comes in. Even if you've already begun reviewing, you'll learn something new.

This chapter shares questions that came up for me when I started reviewing, along with insights and tips from some of the best reviewers in the country. Many come from *New York Times* restaurant reviewers, who continue to dominate America in matters of opinion about food, chefs, and restaurants. You'll find more tips on the Web site of the Association of Food Journalists (AFJ), www.afjonline.com, which lists a code of ethics and critic's guidelines. The AFJ, by the way, gives annual awards to the best critics in the country. Sietsema and Bauer, both interviewed in this chapter, are multiple winners. Alan Richman, a contributing writer for *GQ* magazine, also interviewed, has won multiple awards as well, more than a dozen from the James Beard Foundation.

As you read, you'll learn about the complex issues behind reviewing, particularly ethics, that make this field endlessly fascinating. You'll discover practical ways to get your first assignment, and if you blog, how to analyze a restaurant. You'll also find inside information and candid stories about how reviewers began their careers.

While this chapter mentions writing citizen reviews for websites such as Chowhound, Yelp, Egullet, and Citysearch; or for publications such as Zagat, it is not the focus, as my goal is to get you paid for your work. However, the information provided here will certainly make you a better reviewer if you start out in those mediums, particularly if you only want to review as a hobby.

How Is It Done?

First, as a reviewer, you have to choose where to go. At daily papers, the old "newsworthy" standard applies, explains Russ Parsons, food editor of the *Los Angeles Times*. Questions he asks himself include: "Is there a reason people should know about this restaurant? Are people talking about it and want to know about it? Is it unknown and very good? Is it hyped and not so good? Does it in some way reflect something important about the community?"

If you're a freelancer or food blogger, you might select restaurants on your own. Says the Phantom Gourmet, "Every new restaurant likes to claim it's pushing the envelope, but part of my job is to know whether what they are doing is truly new or just a new veneer on something that was already passé ten years ago."

To decide on restaurants, you have to be out and on the lookout, scoping out your town for new places that add variety to your reviews by price, location, or cuisine. Or you may have heard that a restaurant has changed chefs or made a major menu revision. Friends and associates will send you tips. Perhaps you want to go to an established place the publication hasn't reviewed for a while. Sometimes the editor wants a particular restaurant reviewed, or the paper expanded into a new county and the editor wants coverage there. Or you might propose a roundup of a particular type of restaurant, such as those with good bars.

If you're starting out and you want to be published in print, you'll have to write on spec and then submit it. (That means editors are under no obligation to run the piece or pay you, if they don't like it.) Make sure you read your target publication thoroughly first, for several weeks. If there's only one review per week by one reviewer, they might not want another. Analyze what sorts of restaurants are critiqued. Don't pick a coffee shop frequented by seniors if the paper wants only hip, expensive places in certain parts of town. Don't write a 2,500-word review if reviews top out at 350 words. Your safest choice for a review will be a new restaurant. But don't sweat it too much—the point is to impress an editor, who might give you an assignment for a new article if he or she sees promise in your writing.

If you're going to a fancy place, find out about the restaurant and chef, perhaps where the chef worked in the past, and who designed the restaurant, if design is relevant. Sometimes you can find old reviews online that mention the chef. Search for background about the chef. Sometimes your publication will have received a press release from a restaurant's marketing department, but most of the time you have to figure it out yourself. Try to get a menu. Representing a potential customer, call to ask about the chef's specialties and most popular dishes. If it's pan-Asian cuisine, for example, and the specialty is grilled ahi steak with ponzu sauce, you now have the opportunity to research the cuisine and how the dish is made, and then you'll feel more confident about judging it. While you're on the phone, find out directions, hours, and how to dress, if it's upscale.

Not all reviews are of upscale eateries, even though they are the majority. Some reviewers stake out food from immigrant communities, including taco trucks and restaurants where the menu might not be in English. "I have my thing," *L.A. Weekly's* Jonathan Gold said in a profile in the *New Yorker*. "Traditional—I hate the word 'ethnic'—restaurants that serve some actual hunger people have, rather than something they tell themselves they must have." He describes it as the "triple carom": the "Cajun seafood restaurant that caters to Chinese customers and is run by Vietnamese from Texas."

Regardless of which eatery you choose, your next decision is when to go. Reviews of dinner are standard, unless the restaurant relies on its biggest crowd at lunch. Monday and Tuesday are the most frequent chef's nights off. Friday and Saturday nights put the most stress on the kitchen. (Consider these for your own research, but they're not things to tell readers.) Go for lunch and dinner, but not just for lunch.

As for how many people to take, there's no right answer. Reviewing can be distracting. It's hard to taste, observe, and simultaneously participate in the conversation around the table. When you go alone, it's easier to soak up atmosphere, experience, and energy level. On the other hand, you may hate dining alone, and the downside is that you can't sample very much food. You could try taking one person who understands that you're working. Old friends or colleagues may let you concentrate and feel comfortable about not talking when you need to think. Most important is to choose people who will eat anything, and who will not take offense at rabbit, offal, or sampling ducks' tongues during dim sum. Make sure they understand that you might ask them to order particular dishes, not necessarily the menu items they'd like most, so that you can sample a variety.

Frank Bruni from the *New York Times* was systematic. In his memoir, *Born Round*, he says he picked a weekly target for review, and reserved a table for four. "I needed three companions to order different dishes and help me cover as much of the restaurant's menu as possible," he writes. "If I was making my first visit, I usually laid down only one rule for my tablemates: no duplicate orders. . . . If I was making my second or third visit, I'd call out the dishes that had been previously tried and shouldn't be ordered this time around." He preferred rotating plates as opposed to passing food on bread plates.

The best reviewers visit each restaurant at least two times, often three. If you go just once, you won't know enough to make decisions. Service, food quality, and atmosphere vary. One night service might be exceptional, and another night your waiter may be off having a cigarette while you're waiting for the bill. Going multiple times helps you understand and more accurately gauge the spirit of the place. Another reason to go back is to taste more food. Sometimes you'll taste the risotto Milanese twice to see if it has improved or if it really is as spectacular as it was the first time. Or you decide you need more dishes to get a balance between grilled, baked, sautéed, and roasted dishes.

By now you're probably breaking out in a sweat, anticipating your next credit card statement. Cost can be a problem. Will you be reimbursed? The short answer is: it depends. If you send two unsolicited reviews to a newspaper, you foot the bill. If you've been given an assignment, you'll probably be paid something. Later in this chapter you'll read more specifics about finances and payment.

What if You're Writing a Blog or Have Your Own Site?

If you're not interested in print reviewing and have established a food blog or Web site, you probably don't have the bucks for three visits to a swanky restaurant. Realizing this, some new restaurants hold preview dinners, where media attendees don't pay. Otherwise, most bloggers only go once, which makes their reviews less credible in the eyes of traditional media. However, food blogs often scoop traditional media, which annoys the heck out of print reviewers. To keep up, most big dailies have started blogs with breaking restaurant news.

Some writers offer rationalization for being hosted for a meal. On the Web site Tablehopper (www.tablehopper.com) about San Francisco dining, Maria Gagliardi explains, ". . . unlike Ruth (Reichl) or other newspaper food critics, I just don't have their big budget to eat out 'undercover' at a place three times. Remember, I'm a self-employed writer.

"So, yes, when I am hosted for a meal, the odds are good that I'm going to get special treatment of some kind (lucky me), or at least will be experiencing the best that establishment has to offer. Which is exactly what I want to share on Tablehopper: what I think is the best an establishment has to offer. It's why I refer to myself as a food writer, and not a critic. Since I'm not dining anonymously, I take full advantage of the wonderful access I am granted by dining as myself. I get to ask questions, meet people, try special dishes. There is sometimes the added perk of meeting the chef or the owner, and so I get to ask things like where did they get the inspiration to make Fernet ice cream. Those are the stories I'm after and want to share, whether I'm paying for my meal, or not."

Since I come from the print world, I'm still trying to get my head around this kind of reviewing. The good news is: there's guidance. See The Food Blog Code of Ethics (http://foodethics.wordpress.com), written collaboratively by Brooke Burton and Leah Greenstein, both food writers and bloggers.

Restaurant Checklist

Whether you're writing a print or online review, you'll look at a review from many angles, when you get to the restaurant. Frank Bruni says in *Born Round* that when he spoke with his editors about taking the job, they discussed "the ways in which restaurants were about much more than food—they were theatres, social laboratories, microcosms of their neighborhoods and their moments—and the ways in which a broad spectrum of journalistic experiences might help a critic capture that."

Let's start with an extensive list of questions to ask yourself. I've compiled the list below based on my own experience, interviews with reviewers, and information from the Association of Food Journalists. All questions may not be relevant, and some are more important than others. Questions about food are always paramount.

At the beginning: How are you treated when you make a reservation over the phone and when you arrive at the door? Do you feel welcomed? Perhaps you can arrive a few minutes early and take in the scene. How full is the restaurant? Are diners enjoying themselves? Are diners getting similar-looking food and service at each table?

The service: A good staff elevates eating to dining. Your waiter should be knowledgeable about the food and willing to find answers to questions you have or solutions to problems. Is your waiter attentive, overly chatty, or someone with an attitude? Do servers wait until you're finished before removing your plate, or do they let plates gather on the table? Does the waiter check in a few times? Are you told if your food is delayed? While you can complain to see how the waiter responds, your main job is to keep a low profile and not attract attention to yourself. How is the service at other tables? Do they get their food before you do, if seated at the same time or later?

The menu: Use it to examine the philosophy of the chef and restaurant. It's a good way to understand chefs' intentions, how courses flow, which flavors are important, whether seasonality is an issue, and the way they put flavors and colors together. Notice how categories are balanced. Is the menu pretentious, with too many foreign words not explained? Are the prices reasonable, given the surroundings and service? If it's an upscale restaurant, it might present a new menu every day, so you might not want to focus exclusively on particular dishes because they might disappear. If it's a corner family place, the menu may not have changed for years.

Evaluate the wine list: Are the prices reasonable, compared to the price of the food and other wine lists? Does the selection and presentation enhance the theme of the restaurant? Does a waiter or sommelier help you select? Are they knowledgeable about the wines?

Ordering the food: Taste as much food as possible, particularly signature dishes. Often the menu will list which dishes are most popular, or the waiter will point them out if prompted. Bring guests and taste their food. Choose a variety of dishes and courses, based on cooking techniques, ingredients, and styles.

Tasting the food: What is your gut reaction? Are flavors balanced and integrated? Is the dish exciting, fresh or made with quality ingredients? Is it over-salted? Is there too much cream or vinegar, or too little spice? Is it the right temperature? Is the food visually appealing and properly cooked? Does typically unappetizing food look good here?

The ambiance: En route to the restroom, walk slowly and evaluate the view or the dining room. How does the setting and style compare to other restaurants of its kind? Are the tables large enough and not crammed together, and are the seats comfortable? Is it too noisy, or the music intrusive? What about the clientele? Does the restaurant appeal to a certain type, such as hipsters, couples, or business folks? Would you take friends or family there to celebrate a birthday?

When you leave: How hard is it to get the check, and does someone acknowledge you when you leave? When you're out the door, what is your overall impression? Ask yourself whether you look forward to going back, why or why not, and whether you found dishes you can't wait to try again. What were the strongest and weakest aspects of the evening?

You're probably wondering how to remember it all. You can't, at first. Even the best critics had trouble initially. Bauer says he had the overwhelming feeling that he had to know everything, get it all down, and know every ingredient in a dish and react. "The first two years I was a basket case," he admits. "I didn't take notes—I had to remember. Talk about not having fun. I practically had an ulcer." Fortunately, his anxiety didn't last. Now he can have a good time and recall what's most important. "You don't have to remember every nuance of every dish," he advises. "Learn what you need to know. Let the other stuff go."

It's a good idea to take notes, but not at the table, because you won't want the restaurant staff to discover you. A notebook small enough to fit in your purse or pocket is a great place to assemble your impressions, preferably in a restroom stall or outside, after your meal. Or record your thoughts in a tape recorder after leaving the restaurant, perhaps in your car. Bruni says he used his phone to send text messages to himself, or stepped into the bathroom to call himself and give dictation into his voice mailbox.

If the menu is a daily printout, don't feel too guilty about stealing it. Later it will come in handy when you can't remember the name or ingredients of a particular dish, or when you want to evaluate the types of food presented. If you don't have a menu, some restaurants list dishes on their Web sites. Or have a friend call to ask for a faxed menu, but don't count on it if the restaurant is busy or too small to have a fax machine.

The Goal of a Review

Your job is straightforward: Point people in the direction of high-quality, brightly flavored fresh food, and paint a vivid picture so they can decide whether to go. You help consumers make informed decisions about where to eat. As a result, you may encourage them to try something new, educate them about new foods or cooking techniques, or inspire them to visit a new neighborhood. Most readers, however, will read your review for entertainment or information value, and may never visit the restaurant. That's okay.

Your goal is not to suggest how the chef might improve the food, because diners, not chefs, are your readers. If you want to feel superior by bossing chefs around, you won't succeed. Even the most powerful reviewer in America in the 1960s didn't take himself too seriously. "It burdened my conscience to know that the existence or demise of an establishment might depend on the praise or damnation to be found in the [*New York*] *Times*," wrote Craig Claiborne in his memoir, *A Feast Made for Laughter*. "Although I reasoned, correctly, that the judgment of the food critic did not invariably determine whether a restaurant would prosper or suffer mortal decline."

Writing a Good Review

Good reviews are honest, fair, exercise good judgment, and are authoritative and accurate. Honesty is critical because it applies even if your friends love a place but you don't. If you're objective, you'll be less likely to get caught up in the romance, like claims that Fred's Breakfast Nook has been making the best pancakes for fifty years. Does the restaurant follow through on its promise? It's your job to find out.

Honesty applies to how well you know yourself. Says Bauer: "People go to restaurants when they're feeling good, having a celebration, or getting together with friends, but for you, it's your work. You have to divest yourself of negative feelings and go into neutral. You can't crave beef when it's your last visit and you have to order salmon."

You get to know your own prejudices and beliefs. Try to keep your "personal pollution" out of the decision, advises Dara Moskowitz. Bauer doesn't like sweet sauces, for example, and says so if he's reviewing that kind of dish. I hardly ever ate red meat, was sick of chicken, and looked forward to eating fish. But I couldn't say every week, "The fish was good." I ate lamb, rabbit, bacon, and steak—whatever was on the menu. Biases can't get in the way.

Personal beliefs can become a problem if, say, you conclude the food didn't justify the high prices at a steak house. Could it be because you think steak shouldn't cost more than twenty-five dollars? If so, reveal your prejudice in the name of fairness. Check yourself by asking why you loved a dish. Is it because you love moussaka, or is it the way the chef prepared it, by doing something special?

Mimi Sheraton, former *New York Times* reviewer, says there's no cuisine that she hates categorically, and no food that she dislikes except tripe. She might hate a dish's representation, but not the food itself. "I don't think you should have preconceptions or apply previous experiences," she says. You can factor them in afterward.

She's also not the kind of reviewer who cuts the chef a lot of slack. "I'm not so much for explaining the philosophical goals of the chef. I'm not interested in whether the chef will be good some day, and not willing to eat something terrible to finance a chef's development. If a chef wants to serve chocolate on cauliflower, he should make it for himself and taste it, and not serve it to the public to see what they feel about it. I don't like experiments." What you eat at that moment is what you judge.

What About Negative Reviews?

The bottom line is your loyalty is to the consumer, not the restaurant. Think about the people who save up for a meal out, says Sietsema, who can't test-drive a meal and are counting on you to tell them the truth. You have to be negative when you really believe that something was bad. You don't have to be cruel or take cheap shots, though.

There's an unwritten rule in reviewing: Critics are harder on expensive restaurants, because a costly place takes a bigger bite out of readers' wallets. High-profile restaurants can take the hit, compared to a small neighborhood place that will suffer. As *Gourmet* magazine editor Ruth Reichl once said, "When a restaurant charges twenty-five dollars for a bowl of turnip soup, pleasant is not enough."

There's no point trashing a small restaurant in a magazine like *Time Out* because the magazine lists capsule reviews, which are positive by default. Amanda Doyle, associate editor of *Where* magazine in St. Louis, says she tries to be subtle when writing about small restaurants. If she had a long wait, for example, she will write, "It's too bad they don't take reservations." Sheraton would never give a negative review to an obscure restaurant. "What's the point of saying don't go to this place that you've never heard of?" she asks. Instead she'd end up not writing the review.

At publications where restaurants are advertisers, you could be told by an editor to soften a negative review because of potential repercussions. Often the publication ends up running no review at all to avoid a situation where the restaurant might pull its ad. In *Where* listings, Doyle says advertisers' capsule reviews represent about a third of all reviews and have first priority. She chooses the remaining two-thirds. Overall, negative reviews have fewer political ramifications in the chat rooms of Web sites such as Egullet.com, because the sites are not dependent on advertising.

What do you do when the food is uneven? Bauer once dealt with this issue by writing that a restaurant made "two dishes well and the rest not so well." Readers told him they went anyway, ordered the items he liked, and left happy. The restaurant met their needs. Sometimes everyone else at the restaurant is enjoying the signature salad with blueberries and pine nuts, but you don't like it. In that case, you say just that and explain why.

I like reviewers who use humor to make a negative comment more entertaining. Alan Richman loves a line he once read in a review of a Chinese restaurant: "The hot and sour soup only had to be one or the other." Here's Gold, writing about skewered coins of bull penis with a wincing simile, "It doesn't taste like much, this bull penis, pretty much just cartilage and char, but the spectacle is as emasculating as a Jonas Brothers CD."

Negative reviews can have consequences. Years ago, a friend of Bauer's owned a lunch-only place in Dallas. Bauer thought it would be fine to be friends, because he wouldn't review that kind of restaurant. Then this friend opened a high-profile restaurant, and Bauer had to critique it. "It was a mixed review, not all negative," he recalls. "I felt horrible, even though I was much more careful with the review." His friend never spoke to him again. More recently, Bauer learned that on three occasions, angry restaurateurs hired private investigators to follow him and check into his background after he had given their restaurants less than favorable reviews.

In the end, restaurant reviewing is the most subjective form of criticism in the world today, asserts Richman. "There are no standards for how food tastes. Everything stems from the taste buds and taste memory of the reviewer." Most of the time, a restaurant is neither very good nor very bad. It is somewhere between the two, and your job is to see the shades of grey. Reviewers also wrestle with the issue of whether liking the food is the same as the food being good. It's your job to separate these two things and reconcile them, because you have to have an opinion. This becomes an issue when you get hate mail with readers questioning your analysis. All you can do is pay attention to what you're eating, as in the Buddhist philosophy of mindfulness.

What Makes a Great Reviewer?

Today, powerful reviewers at daily papers and big magazines feel under attack from websites and blogs, where anyone can chime in with an opinion. They lament the loss of carefully crafted and detailed reviews. Great reviewers, they believe, have passion, knowledge, authority, a great writing style, and stamina. They write intelligently, from a frame of reference established through years of loving food. They discern quality, ferret out pretentiousness, acknowledge flavors that don't go together, and can point to why a dish works. They give the reader a feel for the place, its rhythm, and overall vibe. And they keep up their energy level and enthusiasm.

Passion is paramount. In Gael Greene's memoir *Insatiable: Tales from a Life of Delicious Excess*, she writes at the end, "I fully expect to go on eating and critiquing forever and that on my deathbed my last words will echo those of Brillat-Savarin's sister, who cried, 'Bring on dessert. I'm about to die.'" Alan Richman, whom Salon.com's Frances Lam called "the most decorated food writer known to man," still has it after many years of reviewing. He says he can't wait to see what a restaurant has in store for him. "I get a hop in my step," he enthuses.

He's also incredibly knowledgeable. You need a deep understanding of your subject to succeed. You already have experience dining in restaurants, you know and love food, and you probably love cooking. From there, you could increase your skill level by taking cooking classes. To supplement my knowledge, I twice took an eleven-week class in French cooking basics, repeating the course to understand the underlying principles and techniques of formally trained chefs. Joan Zoloth, former reviewer for the *Oakland Tribune,* took cooking classes to understand how a dish was put together long before she became a reviewer. She was just passionate about food.

Ruth Reichl suggests you train yourself. "There's not a school to go to," she said in an interview. "Work in restaurants for a while. Get a lot of experience. As I write in the beginning of *Comfort Me with Apple*s, (A. J.) Liebling was oversimplifying when he said, 'The primary requisite for writing well about food is a good appetite.' That's not enough. You need to have a lot of experience. You need to bite off as much of the world as you can. Travel. It probably means not getting entangled with too many responsibilities."

Reviewers also thrive on research about food and trends. Do you devour cookbooks, food dictionaries, blogs, and specialty online sites? Do you know the food scene in your town? Do you love to find unfamiliar raw ingredients in specialty groceries? Do you enjoy tasting the food of other regions or countries when you travel? Do you consult authorities when you have a question about tofu skins or a particular braising technique?

Critics understand and appreciate other people's cultures, even if they aren't experts in the cuisine. Education and research are particularly important when reviewing ethnic restaurants, where you learn how to approach an unfamiliar cuisine and what to look for in its elements. Some reviewers take along natives or experts in ethnic cuisine, such as people who have cooked a particular food all their lives, or cookbook authors. I almost tripped up when I wrote my first review of a Cambodian restaurant. I ordered a fish dish that is supposed to be mushy. I thought it had the texture of cat food. Luckily, I didn't write that. Although my editors had requested edginess, I would have gone too far by stating that view, which would have appeared disrespectful and uninformed. Instead, I went to cookbooks and spoke with experts to become educated.

Cuisines of other countries are more accessible in the United States than ever before, and reviewers have to step up to the plate. Earlier on, someone like *New York Times* food editor Craig Claiborne, who reviewed restaurants in the 1960s, only had to know about French, American, Chinese, and Italian food.

Today that doesn't work. "If you're going to review Japanese, Peruvian, Indian, Malaysian restaurants, you really need to have been to those countries and to have seriously studied what their food is supposed to do," said Reichl in an interview. "It's not enough to do it from a Western orientation anymore. You're dealing with a very knowledgeable public, and you can't be in the situation where the people you're writing for know more about the food that you're writing about than you do." She has called a consulate or embassy to see if an employee can accompany her to a restaurant to explain the food. At one publication, the art director was Korean, and Reichl took her to restaurants so she could find out about the food from someone who grew up with it.

No matter what challenges critics face, the best ones are excellent writers and storytellers. They know how to show enthusiasm and opinion without resorting to exclamation marks. They keep readers interested and entertained from the first to the last sentence. A well-written review conveys the critic's "sense of adventure as an eater and sense of joy in the experience," says William Grimes, a former *New York Times* reviewer. He describes his style as knowledgeable, but written with wit and a light hand. "Reviews should be entertaining," he says. "You shouldn't weigh people down with info that becomes a burden for them. Deliver information and lift it with a sense of humor." Grimes isn't just talking the talk. In a review of an Italian restaurant, he writes: "The big-hearted entrees can bring down a weak-kneed diner at fifty yards."

Jonathan Gold is a master of evocative detail. In a massive restaurant roundup for *Travel & Leisure,* he writes of a Chicago steak house as "a battered old place under the El with blood-rare strip steaks the size of catcher's mitts, baked potatoes the size of footballs, and the best martinis in the world. Beefy, happy men tuck into huge platters of garbage salad—a time-honored Chicago thing not unlike a great antipasto run through a paper shredder—and croissant-size shrimp with cocktail sauce." Can't you just see it? He's given you evocative visual information on the place, the food, and the diners in two sentences.

Some critics find writing the review harder than going to the restaurant, including the Phantom Gourmet. "Strangely, though, it can also be the most rewarding part," he adds. "Finding just the right word, describing a dish or the atmosphere in just the right way as to convey exactly how something tasted can be frustrating, but when achieved, fulfilling. This process takes nearly as long as the dinner itself."

Most reviews follow a similar format, and when you have to write within this format all the time, it can be challenging: they describe the setting, what's on the menu, the prices, the service, and ambiance. Then they go into the appetizers, entrées, and dessert. The worst are the "bite-by-bite" reviews where people just go through the meal, describing everything they had, says Mary Margaret Pack, food writer and restaurant reviewer for the *Austin Chronicle*. For variety, the *Post*'s Sietsema employs action, such as what people at the next table are saying and whether they're enjoying their food. Critics at alternative newspapers have the most freedom to mix it up by adding personal details.

As you can see, voice is an important part of reviewing. While it's not something you can fake, it's helpful to define it so your reviews are consistent. When I started out, I read the reviews of writers I admired to let their styles sink in. I tore out pieces I loved, particularly those with beautiful or witty writing, and collected them in a file. Luckily, Gold collected his in a book called *Counter Intelligence: Where to Eat in the Real Los Angeles*. A former music writer for *Rolling Stone*, he wrote reviews of neighborhood places for *L.A. Weekly* in the 1980s that are funny, irreverent, passionate, insightful, knowledgeable, and filled with witty references. At one point he left Los Angeles for *Gourmet*, and his voice changed. It was no longer irreverent, but more formal, with a kind of hushed tone. Now he was reviewing fancy, expensive restaurants, writing about truffles and foie gras, and his voice had to be appropriate to the publication.

Sheraton says perhaps it's because she's bossy that her voice is authoritative as a result. Experienced reviewers feel comfortable expressing their own opinions. That means not writing what your friends thought of the food. I once wrote that my girlfriend thought her glass of white wine at a Greek restaurant "tasted like Aqua Velva." Yes, it was witty, but I couldn't have defended her judgment if confronted. I could only defend my own point of view.

Because she's famous, Sheraton is not asked to write in a voice that reflects the publication. Many freelancers make their living this way, however. Compare reviews in an alternative newspaper to those in a daily paper. Each publication has its own style and voice, and the writers conform to those parameters. Smaller, alternative papers sometimes take a sassy, edgy tone in reviews, and editors will send yours back if it's not written that way. Often the editor doesn't explain the publication's style at the time of assignment, so it's up to you to figure out what's appropriate. The only way you can do so is by reading the publication first, and then picking the most appropriate adjectives to describe the voice (see pages 13–18 for a list).

What about actually describing the food? The best reviewers use specific language. Three of the laziest adjectives I know are "nice," "wonderful," and "delicious." Most of us have resorted to them at times. They are so vague that readers don't know what you mean, other than something positive. It's harder to develop a taste lexicon, but a developed vocabulary is critical to being a successful food writer. "What surprised me the most is how hard it is," says Pack. "I read other reviews and see people struggling with the same kinds of things I do with the language." Which word makes her cringe most? "Unctuous."

HOW WELL CAN
YOU DESCRIBE FOOD?

This list certainly isn't exhaustive, but it gives an idea of specific language. If you want more, read reviews, circle the words you like, and compile your own list.

Taste and Smell:

Acrid	Cooling	Peppery
Bland	Fruity	Perfumed
Buttery	Herbal	Piquant
Bright	Mellow	Robust
Briny	Nutty	

Texture:

Brittle	Foamy	Slippery
Chewy	Gelatinous	Velvety
Crisp	Silky	

Appearance:

Blanketed	Melted	Sprinkled
Caramelized	Mottled	Stuffed
Crumbled	Murky	Syrupy
Crusty	Plump	Tired
Drowned	Sheared	Trembling
Lackluster	Shiny	Wet
Leafy	Smeared	Wimpy
Limp	Spice-dusted	

Sound:

Bubbling	Fizzy	Sizzling
Crackling	Popping	Sputtering

Others:

Alluring	Denuded	Impeccable
Comforting	Depth	Liberal
Complemented	Dispirited	Satisfying

Ruth Reichl, in an interview, reminds us that writing about food isn't just based on describing it. "One of the things I was lucky to learn early on is that you can't describe flavor, but you can put someone into a space where they can understand what you're talking about. If you really think hard and you try to imagine what the flavor is, if you hold it in your mouth and your mind for long enough, you can make other people experience that taste. You don't do it by saying, 'It's salty, it's sweet, it's citric.' You have to paint a picture."

Two loaded words I avoid using in restaurant reviews are "expensive" and "authentic." If a publication rates restaurants by price, such as inexpensive, moderate, and expensive, and gives a range in its rating system, then readers will know what "expensive" means. Otherwise it is undefined, leaving readers to wonder. Using the word "authentic" has pitfalls as well. My husband loves Pad Thai, and ordered it often when we traveled in Thailand. Each restaurant served the noodles differently, even inside a thin egg omelet once. Which is authentic? After all, the name means something like "fried Thai-style."

Once you've left the restaurant, if you didn't ask your waiter about certain dishes and you still have questions, it's acceptable to call the restaurant and identify yourself. If you're not sure about the hint of ginger in the tomato sauce, ask about the ingredients. Ask how the chef made the chicken with deep flavorings. He might tell you he brined the meat for two days. (Ruth Reichl wouldn't agree with my suggestion, however. She says the last thing you want is a restaurateur saying, "She didn't know what she was eating, she had to call!")

When you're done with your piece, double-check all dates, name spellings, the address, telephone number, and hours. It's not a pain. It's part of your job, and better than getting a call from an irritated editor who just found out from a reader that you spelled the restaurant owner's name wrong (this happened to me).

The last characteristic of a good reviewer is stamina, particularly if you have to eat at the same place a few times in one week, or make conversation. Grimes points out that reviewing with guests at the table is an extremely social activity that takes lots of energy. "You are the host," he says. "You can't sit there silently, chewing." Plus, you have to be resolved to sample the same dishes. "How many crème brûlées have I tasted in the last two years?" moans Moskowitz. "A thousand? But other people have only ordered them five times in their lives, and they're excited about them. What keeps me going is their right to have a good anniversary dinner."

And then, you have to watch your weight. Part of having stamina involves the will to just sample. To quote Jane Stern, who with her husband, Michael, co-authored *RoadFood: The Coast to Coast Guide to 700 of the Best Barbeque Joints, Lobster Shacks, Ice Cream Parlors, Highway Diners, and Much More,* "We take a bite and if it sucks, we don't wait around for it to get better." I taste everything, but don't try to eat it all. That's why God made doggie bags.

Michael Bauer says questions about how he maintains his weight and health is probably the most frequent question he's asked. He says he moderates his alcohol intake, tastes the bread and butter, and takes part of the protein for his dog. He also works out on a treadmill Monday through Friday.

How Do You Find That Great Undiscovered Restaurant?

In addition to the coup of being the first to review a new restaurant, good reviewers always look for the finds. "Finds are hard to come by," admits Sheraton. Sure, people tell you about a great new restaurant they found, but "nine times out of ten it's a terrible place." She asks cabdrivers and waitstaff where they eat. She also walks around town, sees an interesting menu in a window, and checks out the place.

"Once you're known, you'll get all kinds of recommendations," she says. "You don't have to look for people to tell you about restaurants. You have to shut them up."

What About Educating the Palate?

Some reviewers think the ability to taste is an innate skill: people are born loving food and having a strong interest in it. Others think taste comes from experience. "Taste is a matter of experience that varies widely with age, ethnic background, locale and era," says Sheraton. And some think it can be taught. A good palate may have physical aspects and a different arrangement of taste buds that affect the experience of flavors. Cilantro, for example, affects people differently: they either love it or hate it.

Some reviewers say you don't have to be an expert in a cuisine to understand how something should taste. If you like a sauce, have a sense of whether it's well made, or whether flavors are discordant or lack proportion.

Bauer took the rare step of formally training his palate early in his career. He met his mentor, cooking instructor and author Madeleine Kamman, while working for a Dallas newspaper. He went to her cooking schools in New Hampshire and France, and then traveled around France with her for three weeks. "She really taught me how to taste sauces," recalls Bauer. "She would say, 'Can't you taste the carrot in that sauce?' We'd break it down. I had some really intense dining experiences."

I took a two-part course at a cooking school on developing the palate, where instructors doled out substances in small cups and your job was to identify them by smell and taste. We also learned how subtle changes affect a dish. My biggest surprise was when we squirted lime over canned tuna. It was sublime. Then we repeated the experiment with lemon juice. It tasted awful, even though it's common to squeeze lemon over fish and add it to tuna salad. Try your own blind experiments with different sugars, butters, salts—the possibilities are endless. Don't just taste. Study them, touch, and smell them.

What if You Haven't Worked in a Restaurant or Been to Culinary School?

You may be temped to think you have to go to culinary school to understand the palate, but only a tiny percentage of food writers have experience in the profession. This fact bothers some chefs, who ask how reviewers are able to judge food and restaurants without having been a chef or waiter.

Sure, it would help. But it's not critical. A reviewer's job is to advocate for the consumer, to represent the person who's spending the money. Most diners have not been chefs or waiters. They just want to know if they'll have a good dining experience and how much it will cost.

Restaurant experience can have its downside. You can't feel sympathetic and take the restaurant's side when something goes wrong, and you might become obsessed with technique and focus too much on how the food should be made, rather than communicating your impressions of the final product and the restaurant.

"An eminent food journalist need be a master chef no more than a connoisseur of Bach need be expected to perform the composer's preludes and fugues with immaculate precision," states James Villas, former editor of *Town and Country*, in a *Gourmet* article about Craig Claiborne, who was known not to be a very accomplished cook.

It's not essential that you cook, either. "Although I do not believe that one has to know how to cook to be a reliable restaurant critic, the knowledge certainly helps a critic to describe food convincingly and explain where it fails or succeeds," writes Mimi Sheraton in her memoir, *Eating My Words: An Appetite for Life*. "It is, however, no more necessary to cook well than for a drama, dance, or art critic to perform or paint."

Must Reviewers be Anonymous to be Effective?

The most powerful reviewers will still say yes to this question, even though bloggers rarely bother. To truly represent readers, no one at the restaurant should know who you are. It's impossible to write an objective review if restaurants know you're coming or recognize you. They will not treat you the same way they treat other diners. You will get special attention, more food, and dishes that have been fussed over.

Some reviewers announce themselves so they can get the best table and service. Others might agree to come back for a free meal. Any of these behaviors signals you can be influenced or bought. Restaurateurs will conclude that because they gave you something, you owe them.

Some print reviewers, in addition to bloggers, don't agree. Jane and Michael Stern, who travel around the country reviewing roadside restaurants and diners, often identify themselves. They say that while New York reviewers can make or break a restaurant, at tiny out-of-the-way diners, owners don't care. Once they made an appointment to meet a restaurateur and were stood up. He was more excited about the opening day of hunting season. Their situation is atypical, though. Most of the time, you'll be reviewing restaurants in your town.

It's easy to be anonymous when you first start out. Your first year will be fine, because people don't know what you look like, and if you pay cash or use a credit card in someone else's name, you're safe. Eventually, however, if you persevere as a critic, you're likely to be recognized because waiters who spotted you once at one restaurant can change jobs and spot you at the new place. When this happens, you have to play it cool. Realistically, the restaurant can't do much except hover, send over too many waiters, or send over too much food.

Perhaps the most famous written account of being recognized appeared in Ruth Reichl's early critique of Le Cirque, a snobby New

York restaurant, in the *New York Times*. The first part described her shabby treatment as an unidentified diner, and the second detailed what happened when the owner identified her: "Over the course of five months I ate five meals at the restaurant; it was not until the fourth that the owner, Sirio Maccioni, figured out who I was. When I was discovered, the change was startling. Everything improved: the seating, the service, the size of the portions. We had already reached dessert, but our little plate of petit fours was whisked away to be replaced by a larger, more ostentatious one."

The *San Francisco Chronicle*'s Michael Bauer has been a critic for decades, and recognizes the dilemma. "Ninety percent of the time I know when I've been recognized," says Bauer. The evening is going well and then he senses a difference. The waitstaff becomes nervous. He asks a guest to "look at the kitchen and see whether there's a knot of people by the door. Often the service and experience are better before they know who you are. Then reviewing becomes a balancing act. If service is still bad, you realize there's no way they can pull it together."

Serious critics take steps to disguise themselves. They make reservations in another name, pay cash, or use credit cards with someone else's name. They call from outside the office because many restaurants now have caller ID. They wait until their guests sit down before arriving at the table, sometimes through a back door. They don't go to functions attended by restaurateurs and chefs, such as a restaurant grand opening, anniversary dinner, or wine tasting, where they could be recognized. Once you start reviewing, you will likely receive invitations to events like these. While they are tempting, decline them.

WEARING DISGUISES

Top reviewers go to great lengths to disguise or alter their looks. Here's how the pros do it:

Ruth Reichl, former restaurant reviewer for the *Los Angeles Times* and the *New York Times*, gets the award for queen of elaborate disguises. Her book on the subject, *Garlic and Sapphires: The Secret Life of a Critic in Disguise*, is being made into a movie. A theatrical coach helped her with her first disguise when she moved to New York. The woman told her, "You can't just put on a wig. You have to inhabit it," said Reichl in an interview. The woman had Reichl create a backstory for her disguise as a middle-aged Midwestern woman. Some of Reichl's other disguises were Aunt Betty, a nondescript older woman with lace-up oxfords who was not treated well at restaurants; and Brenda, a big boisterous redhead whom waiters loved and for whom they brought extra food.

Reichl became the people in her disguises. "I had voices for them," she admitted. The newspaper auctioned off the costumes for charity when she left.

Frank Bruni, former *New York Times* reviewer: In his memoir, *Born Round: The Secret History of a Full-time Eater,* Bruni said he had not used disguises many times. "I had concluded they were too unsettling and not effective enough, at least if they were anything less than seriously expert. And seriously expert disguises took too much time; they certainly weren't nightly options. Restaurant critics who touted their proficiency with disguises usually didn't mention that a night in costume was the exception, not the rule, and they either disregarded or truly didn't know that restaurateurs often recognized them anyway but were careful not to show it. Restaurateurs didn't want to spoil the disguised critic's fun."

Michael Bauer, the *San Francisco Chronicle:* "I'm always changing my look. I wear short or long hair, glasses, a goatee, or a beard. I darken my hair, mousse it so it's curly, or comb it back instead." He thinks wigs don't work because they're so seldom worn that they can always be picked out in a crowd. "Change a little bit so people won't recognize you," he advises. "You can't do a disguise if you feel uncomfortable, because you will draw attention to yourself." He advises not to engage waiters or look them in the eye, and not to gesture with your hands when you talk.

Restaurants want to identify him, though. "I was surprised when someone said they had a picture of me in the kitchen. I think, 'Why don't you just do the best job you can, treat everyone like they're the reviewer, and then you'll have no problems?'"

Mimi Sheraton, formerly of the *New York Times:* She had three wigs in different colors and wore them with innumerable glasses. "I had a friend in the eyeglass business." She also varied her face makeup by alternating heavy lipstick with no makeup at all.

Tom Sietsema of the *Washington Post* appeared on a panel I moderated wearing a wig, dark glasses, and a baseball hat. Many chefs in the audience were disappointed.

Many critics are surprised to learn how restaurants collaborated to identify them. Today, the Internet makes it that much more difficult to be anonymous. When Sam Sifton replaced Frank Bruni at the *Times*, Eatmedaily.com published doctored photos of Sifton to show how he'd look as Donald Trump and Groucho Marx. Some restaurant kitchens post photos of reviewers from their town and a reward to spot them.

Some people in the food community question whether disguises work. A colleague told me she waited for more than an hour while a professional makeup artist worked on Reichl to disguise her as an old woman. But when she and Reichl entered the restaurant, she could hear diners say, "There goes Ruth Reichl," as they walked by. A story in *San Francisco* magazine quoted chefs who contended that Bauer is not anonymous. I've talked to restaurant owners and chefs who say they can recognize reviewers based on how much food they order and whether they taste the food of others at their table.

In truth, many critics have been reviewing restaurants in the same city for several years, and perhaps they are recognized more than they would like. But the bottom line is that you won't be taken seriously by food writers, editors—and yes, restaurant owners and chefs—if you announce your presence at restaurants and demand or accept a free meal there, rather than trying to represent the consumer and pay for your meals. In her memoir, Sheraton, whose expenses ran about $95,000 in 1983—her last year at the *Times*—said regarding disguises that "The longer I reviewed restaurants, the more I became convinced that the unknown customer has a completely different experience from either a valued patron or a recognized food critic; for all practical purposes, they might as well be in different restaurants."

If you're writing a blog, you have the added complication of taking photos. Blogs are visual and most reviewers take photos of their dishes. It's almost impossible to remain anonymous if you've got a flash going off every few minutes in a darkened restaurant. In fact, the better restaurants don't allow flash photography. You've got to go early enough to capture available light, sitting by the window.

What About Top Ten Stories and the Like? Are They Reviews?

Yes. Articles such as "The Ten Best Places to Get a Cheesesteak in Philadelphia" qualify as reviews, because the author is critiquing and making decisions. These pieces are standards of many newspapers and magazines, and good ones to pitch. Usually roundups are positive. They are purely subject based and the point is to tell people about the best places you've discovered or about services they need, such as restaurants that stay open past ten at night.

What if you're doing a piece on the best barbecue joints in Kansas City, and Ken's Rib Joint is famous but the food is awful? It's best to say so, advises Sheridan. Otherwise readers will wonder why you didn't bring it up. "Negatives are invaluable in establishing credibility," Sheraton explains.

How Can You Get Started?

Now that you've absorbed the details of restaurant reviewing, you might be raring to go for a print publication. The first step is to be realistic. You're not going to break into a daily paper right away, where established reviewers fill the pages. Start small and either target neighborhood papers or start a blog (see chapter 4).

There's no disgrace in being published in small publications. "Editors notice who's writing for the free papers," says Grimes. "If you're any good, you will stick in their minds." Begin by collecting the local newspapers and magazines in your community. Find them at newsstands, cafés, clubs, coffeehouses, and libraries. Look online to find past reviews. Look through a few months of each publication to see what kind of articles they like. Make a pile of the ones that don't publish reviews and prioritize them, starting with the smallest. Maybe they'd start running reviews if they found someone good.

Let's look at *Time Out New York* as an example. A feature story written by an experienced reviewer runs in the front section. It might be a roundup of several restaurants, with a theme like Cheap Eats. That's not a likely place to start. Writers have to establish themselves as trustworthy beforehand to get an assignment like that. But the dining section has three restaurant opening announcements of 150 words each, tucked into the capsule reviews. Might these be doable? The publication uses new freelancers for these pieces because they are not critiques and are therefore less of a risk. The capsule reviews themselves aren't a good bet. They are pulled from the magazine's annual guidebook, which enlists close to 100 reviewers.

How do you get your foot in the door with an editor? You might call the paper, talk to an editor, and make a personal connection. The editor might give out tips about where to start. But that's unlikely. First, editors don't have time to chat with strangers, and few will encourage someone unknown to submit a review. Second, they don't know what kind of standards you apply to the food you review, and whether you've written false statements that make the publication liable for lawsuits. If they're going to give anyone a trial assignment, it's probably a person they know who has already demonstrated knowledge of food. It's not a great idea to cold-call an editor unless you're lucky and you know someone on the inside who can ask him or her to take your call, or talk with you in person for a few minutes.

The other way to go is to write one or two reviews for your target publication, emulating the paper's style, tone, and word count, just to see how you like the experience. Write to the publication's audience. That might mean avoiding a $100-per-plate restaurant if you don't think the publication's audience can afford it. If you wish, submit your work with a cover letter explaining your passion and qualifications. If you have already been published and can attach clips, you're one step ahead.

Sheraton says that since editors are unlikely to take critiques from an unknown writer, you'll do better to submit a related story. Try a piece about a tasting, a roundup of romantic places for dessert, or a funny article about a restaurant. Check other media around town for ideas, or brainstorm with a friend (see chapter 5 on freelancing). Use other kinds of pieces to prove that you know how to write and are knowledgeable about food.

If an editor eventually assigns you a review, it's time to ask practical questions. Find out if the paper will support you if the review is negative. Do they have an opinion about reviewing restaurants that also advertise in the publication?

WHOM TO SOLICIT FOR RESTAURANT REVIEWS

You don't have to review for your daily paper, and you probably can't start there anyway. Lots of alternatives exist that will pay for your work:

- weekly (alternative) and free newspapers
- regional magazines
- city magazines
- travel guidebooks
- city tourist information
- theater programs
- airline magazines
- some websites such as CitySearch (www.citysearch.com), Sally's Place (www.sallys-place.com) and Bay Area Bites (http://blogs .kqed.org/bayareabites), the Web site of public radio station KQED in San Francisco, pay nominal amounts for reviews
- (Eater, http://eater.com, with its lively gossip and mix of professional and amateur reviews, is an aggregate site. It collects previously published content through links.)

Study these sources to see how reviews are written in terms of style, structure, length, and content. Look at the publication's masthead to see if the critic is on staff or a freelancer. Contact the appropriate editor to find out how he or she acquires reviews. Perhaps they are assigned, or perhaps they will take written queries or writing samples.

If you want to write for citizen websites like Yelp, Chowhound, and Egullet, keep in mind that you'll be doing it as an amateur, for free. I can think of only two good reasons for doing so: you'd like to review as a hobby, and don't care if you get paid; or you'll use the electronic clips to pitch editors for paid reviews.

On Egullet (requires a paid membership at www.egullet.com), Yelp (www.yelp.com), and Hungry Monster (www.hungrymonster.com) forums and message boards, you'll find restaurant reviews of varying quality. Not everyone is a fan. Author Calvin Trillin jokes that the message is, "In a just world, I would be the restaurant critic of the *New York Times*. A bunch of phonies are actually doing this, but I am the one who knows."

~~~~~~

Or, write your own city guide. Seymour Britchky, Alan Richman's favorite critic, wrote *Restaurants of New York* in 1990. If you can find this guidebook you'll enjoy his hard-boiled writing style. More recently, Marcia Gagliardi started Tablehopper, a Web site and newsletter about San Francisco dining, which led to a book deal.

What About Money?

Ah yes, the eternal question of whether you can get paid for your work. This is an ongoing problem for freelance food writers. If an editor accepts your unsolicited piece, it's possible that the paper will not pay, or that they'll pay next to nothing, even if you get an assignment. If writing reviews for a guidebook for your city or an online restaurant guide, the pay might be a whopping $25 to $30 per restaurant. That's not nice, but it's okay because you need published work to trade up to the bigger newspapers and magazines, which should at least pay for your reviews.

Nothing is standard when it comes to reimbursement for meals, despite a Web site guideline from the Association of Food Journalists that reviewers should not have to resort to "personal funds to help pay the bill." That's a subtle way of saying you probably won't be paid enough to cover all expenses plus your writing, even from the dailies.

Time Out New York's annual dining guide reviewers get a flat rate for their write-ups. The company pays for two appetizers, two entrées, and two desserts, no drinks. Reviewers usually go to a restaurant only once because their pay will not cover more visits, and because of the volume of restaurants covered.

Larger newspapers pay more, if they use freelancers. They might pay one amount for the article and a budgeted amount for the meal. Ask lots of questions. Do they pay mileage, transportation fees, and parking? Are tips included in the meal reimbursement? How long will it take to get paid and/or reimbursed? This can be an issue if you get a credit card bill with fifteen restaurant meals on it, and you haven't received your check. Will the paper pay the late fee?

Moskowitz was initially paid $150 by an alternative weekly to write a 2,000-word feature on one restaurant each week. She paid for the food out of that budget. That structure lasted two years, until the paper got more advertising and she became better known.

Pack, who also reviews for an alternative weekly, the *Austin Chronicle,* says she is always reimbursed for her meals and visits a restaurant at least twice, maybe three times. She has also been reimbursed for parking when she has had to use a garage. Like many other papers, the *Chronicle* doesn't pay for alcohol. Pack points out that this policy is a little unfair if you're expected to critique the wine list.

My experiences are all over the place. One magazine paid me a $50 flat fee for reviews, including food. A newsletter paid nothing but gave me a free subscription. A guidebook paid $30 flat for two paragraphs per restaurant. A weekly paper paid $0.50 per word, which the editor said was higher than what they paid other writers. They gave a reimbursable budget of $160 for food that did not include alcohol, and paid my mileage. A daily paper paid a flat fee of a couple hundred dollars, from which I deducted the price of three meals. There wasn't much left.

J. P. Anderson, former restaurant editor at Chicago Citysearch (www.chicago.citysearch.com), said the amount he paid writers for expenses depended on the restaurant. "It could be as little as $15 for a hot dog joint or $250 for an upscale restaurant." Usually reviews are based on one visit, though follow-up visits are sometimes necessary.

So why would anyone in their right mind try to make a living reviewing restaurants? Most freelancers don't. They have other sources of income, such as a side job like catering, or better-paying writing jobs like creating marketing copy for corporations.

"There are fewer restaurant critics in this country than senators," asserts Moskowitz. "It's a luxury spot. Plus, there's no demand and nothing but competition. America needs nurses. Nobody needs more restaurant critics."

You have to be driven not by money, but by your passion for restaurants and your joy upon discovering great food. Besides the glamour and glory, there are advantages. If you're a great writer, you get noticed. You get better assignments. If you can show you've been published, you might get to deduct a percentage of the cost of a meal from your taxes, plus mileage, but only if it is not a hobby but a business.

Perhaps they're a dying breed, but the most respected restaurant reviewers are experienced journalists. Often they've worked as writers in other parts of the newspaper, or paid their dues for years in the food section. Other reviewers have English degrees and worked as chefs. But don't be intimidated. It really is possible to succeed. Now that you're privy to the secrets of restaurant reviewing, you're miles ahead of other people starting out. You have the insight and resources to get ahead.

HOW SOME CRITICS GOT THEIR START

Michael Bauer, executive food and wine editor of the *San Francisco Chronicle*, says he has always been in the food business. His father owned a meat market in Kansas. All through college he was a meat cutter in his father's store. Because his dad sold meat to most of the restaurants, he felt strongly about supporting them, so the family ate out every night. This was in the 1960s in a small town in Kansas. From there Bauer got his journalism degree and became a reporter and feature writer at the *Kansas City Star*. He moved on to food editor there and then became the restaurant critic and wine editor at the *Dallas Times Herald*. He joined the *San Francisco Chronicle* in 1986.

William Grimes was a copy editor at *Esquire* in New York, and freelanced on the side. After his reviews were published in the *Village Voice*, he drifted over to the *New York Times* as a full-time writer, working for the Sunday magazine and other parts of the paper. Later he moved into food writing and then restaurant reviewing, succeeding Ruth Reichl.

Ed Levine, author of the guidebook *New York Eats*, says he was a discriminating eater even as a child, but his family never had enough money to go to fancy restaurants. His book celebrates eating in New York, with lists of more than 300 take-out places serving a variety of foods, from hot doughnuts to mozzarella to Pad Thai. He said he used Patricia Wells' *Food Lover's Guide to Paris* as inspiration.

Dara Moskowitz, dining critic and senior editor of *Minnesota Monthly*, started working in kitchens when she was young, and always wanted to be a writer. She got her first break when an editor noticed the quality of her writing in a book review (she had worked on it for two weeks) and gave her more assignments. Eventually, Moskowitz made her way into food writing. She also worked for Microsoft Sidewalk when it launched, writing 50- to 100-word capsule reviews.

Tom Sietsema, head reviewer of the *Washington Post*, graduated from a foreign service school and interned with ABC news, where he fell in love with journalism. A friend at the *Washington Post* told him the food critic was looking for an assistant. Since Sietsema had always loved food, he manned phones, tested recipes, and did light research at first.

Gradually, he proved himself. "The *Post* was my cooking school," he says. He left his office at 2:00 or 3:00 P.M. to shop and cook. Within four years he had tested hundreds of recipes. His boss was critic Phyllis Richman, once identified by *Newsweek* as the most feared woman in Washington. His rise to replace her (after she retired) took a total of eighteen years from the time he started at the newspaper.

Patty Unterman, author of *Patricia Unterman's Food Lover's Guide to San Francisco*, had a graduate degree in journalism and was interested in criticism. "I opened a small restaurant in Berkeley and heard from a friend who had been in my class that *New West* magazine needed a restaurant critic. I wrote a sample review and they hired me." She went on to write reviews for the *San Francisco Chronicle*, and now writes a weekly column on food for the *San Francisco Examiner*.

Joan Zoloth, a reviewer for the *Oakland Tribune* for ten years, was a freelance writer when she met the paper's food editor at a social event.

After Zoloth bent the editor's ear about food passions and revealed she was a freelance writer, a former waitress, and had taken cooking school classes, the editor suggested she try her hand at a review.

As for **me,** in my 20s, after graduating from journalism school, I was the freelance editor of a city magazine, where I wrote a few short reviews, chef profiles, and feature articles about restaurants. Later I wrote reviews on the side for a regional magazine in California. When I became self-employed in the 1990s, I won a contest to write reviews for a weekly paper. For my test, the editor assigned me a review of a top restaurant I had never visited because it was so expensive. I took my husband and blew the entire budget of $160, without even buying a bottle of wine.

I keep the editor's follow-up email to read on days when I'm frustrated about my writing: "I really enjoyed reading your review, because it's obvious you did some research and also obvious that you're at home in good restaurants! To be perfectly honest, so far you're my leading candidate for lead reviewer."

Writing Exercises

1. Use adjectives: Write a 250-word review of the best restaurant meal you've eaten recently, using five descriptive words from the list on pages 161–162.
2. Overcoming your leanings: Recall a food you don't like that was prepared perfectly and served to you at a restaurant. Now write two paragraphs about your experience. The goal is to acknowledge your own prejudices and overcome them for the reader.
3. Do your research: Come up with an ethnic cuisine you've never had and review a restaurant that serves that cuisine. Research the country's dishes and their origins and ingredients before visiting the restaurant, and then write the review.

7

The Cookbook You've Always Wanted to Write

You love to entertain. Friends and co-workers compliment your cooking and ask for recipes. You've spent years traveling and learning about food and culture. You want to pass down heirloom recipes to your children. You've collected dozens of recipes and want to share them. Customers always ask for your recipes.

Everyone loves your stories about people and food. These are some of the many reasons to write a cookbook. Notice I didn't say, "You want to get famous and make a lot of money." If that's your motivation, forget it. Writing a cookbook is too difficult and time consuming to sustain such a notion. But if you're passionate and obsessed, chances are that your cookbook will succeed. Successful cookbook writers begin with an enthusiasm for food that keeps them going and fuels their ability to come up with ideas for future books. The hard part is coming up with a book that excites both you and the outside world.

It's easy to conjure up a first idea, but the first is not always the best. How to position or shape a book takes lots of pondering, research, and evaluating of pros and cons. You might change your opinion many times. Mulling it over is worthwhile. You can't write a worthwhile cookbook without a good idea, and you need to evaluate the competition to see if you have something new to say. This is true even if you want to self-publish.

This chapter will inspire you to shape your idea, think it through, and visualize the book you've always wanted to write, both in terms of subjects and eye appeal. It will tell you what kind of artwork is reasonable to expect. Since I can't squeeze all the details on how to write a cookbook into one chapter, the following chapter tells you how to write recipes, the bulk of your book. For more on the literary aspects of cookbook writing, see chapter 1.

Once you have the idea for a publishable book, use it to pitch articles to newspaper and magazine editors to float your idea. If they publish the articles, it's a great sign that your cookbook idea has promise. How to get an article published is covered in chapter 5. Once you've overcome that hurdle, you'll need to write a book proposal for an agent or editor, and with any luck, you'll get a contract. How to write a proposal, find an agent, and what to expect from a publisher are covered in chapter 11. But you can't write a proposal without a good idea and an understanding of which cookbooks work and why.

~~~~~~

HOW THEY GOT STARTED

Everyone has to start somewhere, even successful cookbook authors. Here's how some of them began:

- At a class on Chinese cooking, student **Julie Sahni** told fellow students how she used a *balti*—an Indian wok—to cook at home. The students asked her to show them. She began teaching cooking classes, and from the recipes she developed, had the beginnings of her first cookbook, *Classic Indian Cooking*.
- **Deborah Madison,** a student of Zen Buddhism, cooked at the San Francisco Zen Center and at Tassajara, a retreat in Big Sur. When the center opened Greens vegetarian restaurant, she became the first chef there. The impetus for her book, *The Greens Cookbook: Extraordinary Vegetarian Cuisine from the Celebrated Restaurant,* was to show customers who had requested recipes how to make the same quality dishes the restaurant served.
- **Anne Byrn,** a freelance food writer, became a working mom who wanted to make great cupcakes for her kids but didn't have much time. She wrote a newspaper story about doctoring cake mixes, and

based on the response, went on to publish *The Cake Mix Doctor*. The book has sold millions of copies.

- **Diana Kennedy** arrived in Mexico in 1957 to join her future husband, a foreign correspondent for the *New York Times*. In 1969, at the suggestion of *New York Times* writer Craig Claiborne, she began teaching classes in Mexican cooking and in 1972 published her first cookbook.

- **Martha Stewart** was a caterer in the Hamptons in Long Island, New York, before she became a lifestyle guru.

- **Ina Garten,** author of the bestselling *The Barefoot Contessa Cookbook*, also catered in the Hamptons, as did Julee Rosso and Sheila Lukins, authors of the Silver Palate series. (The three books in the Silver Palate series have sold several million copies.)

- **Paula Wolfert** went to Morocco because her husband found employment there. Over the years, she became passionate about Mediterranean cooking, watching cooks in their homes, and writing down their recipes. Today she's known as an authority on authentic Mediterranean food.

- After taking cooking classes in France, **Julia Child** opened a cooking school in Paris with two Frenchwomen. Many of the students were American, and soon Child decided to write a manual of French cooking for them. Her radical idea was that all ingredients should be available in the United States, and that readers should learn French cooking techniques. Her first book, *Mastering the Art of French Cooking*, took ten years to produce with her French co-authors.

What's a Good Cookbook Idea?

Agents and editors often give the same advice to someone who wants to write a cookbook: "You have to have something to say." That's true, but not very specific. They also say things like "Everyone reads but not everybody writes. Everyone cooks but not everyone can write a cookbook. It's harder than most people think." Agent Doe Coover told me that. Agents and editors are a tough group to impress, but hundreds of people have done it.

Let's get back to the good idea. Agent Lisa Ekus says she knows she's found one when she can't stop thinking about it. Typically, she reads incoming proposals once and puts them aside. "If I forget about it, it's not a book for me. If it lives with me and it excites me, I have to believe in the book, have a passion for the topic or writing, or think it's highly marketable."

Author Julie Sahni has more advice on what it takes to have a new idea: "A cookbook is more than a set of recipes. You have to have a message, a certain philosophy or technique or principle to pass on to the audience. It boils down to a simple concept. You know something more or something different than the reader. You have to inspire them."

What if you already have a cookbook idea? You've asked your friends and family if you should write your cookbook and they've said yes. Friends and family are not as hard to please as agents and editors. The very first thing to do, when considering a cookbook, is to make sure you have a workable idea. The second is to scope out the competition. Here are my tests:

You are passionate about the subject: As I've been saying, intense enthusiasm is the most powerful motivator. It's not enough to carry a book idea, but if you communicate excitement, intensity, and knowledge in your writing, it can be contagious. Suzanne Rafer, executive editor and director of cookbook publishing at Workman Publishing Company, said in a published interview that a potential author must ignite passion within her and successfully convey a creative spark and vision. Passion may be intangible, but editors and agents know it when they see it.

Martin Yan thrives on it. Now the author of twenty-seven cookbooks, he travels 250 days each year, teaching classes for consumers and chefs, taping television shows shown in fifty countries, and doing research for his cookbooks. "I love to capture some of the essence of individuals around the world and share my experience with people," he says. For one series and book, he targeted Chinatowns worldwide and interviewed chefs at the oldest and newest restaurants. He found families who had lived in each Chinatown for three to five generations, then asked the head of each household to walk with him and buy food for a meal. Yan went back to the family home, watched the cook in action, and shared the meal. "I see the entire picture of their life and heritage," he enthuses. "I am having a good time learning a lot of these things, which I may not experience again."

Laura Werlin was "seized by passion" when she decided to write her first book, *The New American Cheese*. She was a television assignment editor at a station in San Francisco who decided to take classes on food writing. Eventually she narrowed down her food obsessions to artisan cheese from Northern California. When researching her topic, she discovered a national trend of artisan cheese production. "From that moment, I never looked back," says Werlin. She wrote a sixty-page proposal, got an agent and contract, quit her job, and wrote the entire book in three months.

"I had a very steep learning curve, having not written a book or recipe before. I probably did many things the hard way because I knew no other way. I never left my house other than to buy ingredients. I would write until 10:00 P.M. On weekends, I sent my husband to a movie, and then I'd meet him at 10:00 P.M. for a late dinner. I had never been an A-type personality until then." Both this book and her second, *The All American Cheese and Wine Book*, won national awards.

The subject is timely: This is tricky, because few successful cookbook authors actually study trends before writing their books. It's more likely they have good timing because they read widely and talk with other people who love food. When freelance food writer Anne Byrn made a batch of doctored cake-mix cupcakes for her kids and wrote a story about it for a newspaper, the paper added a sentence asking readers to send in their own cake-mix recipes and received 500 responses in one week.

"The light bulb didn't go on instantly," Byrn admits. She wrote a follow-up story featuring six people who had sent in their favorite recipes. By then, Byrn had a hunch. Just to make sure it wasn't some kind of regional trend (Byrn lives in the South), she called six newspaper food editors across the country and asked whether readers requested cake mix recipes regularly. All said yes, particularly for favorites such as the Better than Sex cake. Byrn wrote her book and then wrote more. *The Cake Mix Doctor, Chocolate from the Cake Mix Doctor,* and *The Dinner Doctor* have sold several million copies.

This book was a departure for Byrn, a former newspaper editor who wrote restaurant reviews and traveled to Paris. "I have been such a food snob in my past," she admits. "But I live in a different world now and I have three children. Big deal if I use a Duncan Hines mix." There have been consequences. Certain newspapers will not interview her. Nevertheless, says Byrn, "I wrote this book for mass Middle America, which I feel very much a part of. I'm not ashamed of that and I do not live in Manhattan."

Alice Medrich capitalized on a trend as well. In her award-winning cookbook *Bittersweet: Recipes and Tales From a Life in Chocolate*, she addresses how to use today's varying grades of high-quality chocolates, which are identified by percentages. Purer chocolate has less sugar and more taste, and recipes need rules of thumb for substitutions and upgrades. An obsessive recipe developer, she writes of her desire to share tools she created for herself, so that readers can "experiment and convert recipes with ease and understanding."

Some authors do keep up with timely topics. "Developing salable ideas is not the same as just coming up with ideas," said author Nancy Baggett in a published interview. "Salability involves meshing what I'm interested in and capable of writing about with what I, and hopefully cookbook editors, think the public might buy." She keeps up by looking at bookstore shelves, reading food magazines and newspaper sections, and following trends and topics surfacing in the national media.

Agents and cookbook editors keep up with trends as well. The quick and easy trend, for example, is not going away. People still don't have a lot of time. Nor is the need for low-fat, low calorie books, or those with good nutrition.

The idea is about your area of expertise: Werlin and Byrn were not experts when they started their first book, but both became well versed on their subjects in a hurry. Medrich, by contrast, was already a chocolate expert and owner of a Berkeley chocolate store when an agent approached her to write a book. The best authors strive to develop in-depth knowledge of their subject. Even before they write books, they research extensively and write articles about their subject of expertise. They might also speak on the subject and hold cooking classes.

What, exactly, qualifies you as an expert? Let's say you have cooked Sicilian food for years. The recipes were handed down from your mother's side of the family. You might be an expert if, in addition to knowing family recipes, you devour all the information you can find about Sicilian cooking, speak decent Italian, travel to Sicily to watch people cook, write recipes on Sicilian food published in magazines, newspaper articles, or Web sites, or give talks about it. A cookbook would be your logical next step.

Steven Raichlen, whose barbecue and grill books have sold millions of copies, said in a newsletter interview that branding himself as a barbecue and grilling expert has helped make a name for himself and build his identity in the food world. "What I've done now that I hadn't done before is focus all my energies on a particular specialty. Of course, the trick is finding a sufficiently broad and deep topic to explore to keep you interested for many years and that has the potential to reach lots of other enthusiasts."

Paula Wolfert has been relentlessly passionate about authentic Mediterranean food since her first cookbook on Moroccan food was published in 1972. It calls for a dessert with hashish seeds. She justified the recipe to her editor by arguing none of the other Moroccan cookbooks had it. Wolfert is one of a handful of successful authors who takes an anthropological approach to further her expertise. She explores villages across the Mediterranean, meets with the women there, and asks them to introduce her to the best cooks. Sometimes she moves in with cooks so she can observe and take notes. "She has knocked on hundreds of back doors in obscure towns, searching for the cook who best executes a particular dish," wrote Peggy Knickerbocker in a profile of Wolfert in *Saveur.*

Wolfert even deals with recipes in languages she doesn't know by developing a network of people who translate recipes from abroad. She brings cookbooks in other languages to the United States and has people translate them for her.

Other cookbook writers who have tirelessly researched other cultures and traditions include:

- Carol Field, who documents the Italian lifestyle;
- Diana Kennedy, who traveled alone through Mexico to find authentic cuisine;

- Jeffrey Alford and Naomi Duguid, who travel in Asia for months at a time;
- Claudia Roden, who took eighteen years to write *The Book of Jewish Food: An Odyssey from Samarkand to New York.*

If you don't have an area of expertise, claim one. Start a blog about your particular passion. It worked for several bloggers, including Clotilde Dusoulier of Chocolate & Zucchini (http://chocolateand zucchini.com), and Shauna James Ahern of Gluten-Free Girl and the Chef (www.glutenfreegirl.blogspot.com). Once they gained an impressive audience, agents and editors were interested.

Freelance writer David Leite chose Portuguese cooking as his specialty. In *The New Portuguese Table*, he decided to write about food to chronicle the Portuguese dishes disappearing from his family's dinner tables as older family members passed on.

How long does it take to become an expert? That's up to you and how much time you spend thinking, blogging, researching, traveling, and testing recipes. W. W. Norton vice president and senior editor Maria Guarnaschelli, who edits cookbooks, takes the long-term approach. "Lynne Rossetto Kasper (*The Splendid Table*) and Rose Levy Beranbaum (*The Bread Bible*) were in their fifties when they wrote their books," she says. "Isn't an important work your life's work? In the end it will pay off."

Your idea is well focused: Lack of focus keeps many potential authors from moving forward. If you imagine a book that has to contain "everything," you might put off doing it forever. Writing about "everything" becomes an overwhelming topic. Because you're in love with it, it's hard to decide what to leave out and what to leave in. As a result, your book idea loses focus.

Examine your idea. Is it too general? Is it "all about" a topic? Think about how you would describe your cookbook to others. When you can form your description into a single sentence, you're much closer. Hone in on the most important subjects for readers, and make a list of points you wish to convey. Then whittle down the subject until it is specific and cohesive. Don't be afraid to discard. Throwing away can be liberating. Keep the ideas you've discarded in a file. You might want them someday for another book. (For example, a book on Mediterranean desserts might follow a book on Mediterranean main courses.)

You can be passionate about muffins, explains author Deborah Madison, but ask yourself why they're special to you, why muffins matter. "What is the story? Whom will it delight?" she asks. "Maybe it's stories about family, or maybe you add quick breads, and a book emerges." You could also narrow the idea and make it more specific, such as muffins that are fruit-only, sugar-free, or chocolate.

Madison's enormous reference work, *Vegetarian Cooking for Everyone*, needed lots of forethought on structure and content. The book idea came into Madison's consciousness after teaching a weeklong class on vegetarian cooking at Esalen in Big Sur, California. While there, she realized it was a shame that there was no vegetarian *Joy of Cooking* in which vegetarians could find everything they needed in one place. She decided to write that book.

Even so, it was not "all about" vegetarian cooking. "It took a year just to come up with the table of contents," she recalls. She had to define the scope of the book and make decisions. Should it include breakfast foods, or breads, or recipes already in the culture, such as hummus? She wondered what people would expect, whether to include sandwiches. "I had to become educated," she explains. "I was reading, thinking, and it changed as it went along." This new book was not personal like her prior cookbook, *The Savory Way*. "I wanted to make it a friendly guide for people I didn't know." It took six years to write, contains around 1,000 recipes, and won a national award.

Single-subject books are tightly written books about one ingredient, piece of equipment, or type of dish. Author James McNair developed a reputation as king of the single-subject cookbook. In 1984, he launched his first book, *Cold Pasta*, and followed it with about thirty more books on subjects such as cheese, chicken, fish, pie, corn, and custards, all with gorgeous full-color photos.

Focus becomes an issue when you research your competition. If you want to write a book on Asian noodles and five books already exist, you'll have to change or narrow your focus to succeed. For more on evaluating competition, see page 273.

You love to tell stories: While publishers once thought of cookbooks as strictly how-to books, today they find it likely that cookbooks will be read rather than used for cooking. Time limitations and changing eating habits mean that the average number of recipes readers try in a cookbook could be as low as two. Think of your own cookbook collection. You may not have made any recipes from many of them, but it doesn't make them any less valuable.

Many people read cookbooks in bed as though they were novels. They provide escape from daily life and a source of guiltless pleasure. With longer stories and full-color photography, cookbooks can take you on a travel adventure, allow you to enter a foreign land, whet your appetite for exotic ingredients, tell the history of a country, and let you imagine a pleasurable dinner party you'll give someday.

The literary aspects of food writing can bring new excitement to a book. Joan Nathan authored *Foods of Israel Today,* an ambitious look at the diverse cultural and culinary lineage of Israel. She said that after senior editor Judith Jones of Knopf edited her book, she asked Nathan to take her and her stepdaughter to the Holy Land. "I introduced her to my Israel," says Nathan. "It was about a week before the Intifada. I had written about a village of vegetarians I'd heard about but had never been to, and Judith was very taken with the idea. We took a cab. We could have been killed! Here we were, three women wandering around a Palestinian village." How's that for a testimony to skilled storytelling and writing? Your own editor is so fascinated by your work she wants to see the place.

You have a new approach: "If I hear there are too many books about Italy, yes, there are, but if you have something new to say about Italy, don't let it stop you," says editor Guarnaschelli. Americans are so in love with Italian cookbooks that they often command their own bookshelf in bookstores. Guarnaschelli worked with Lynne Rossetto Kasper on *The Splendid Table: Recipes from Emilia-Romagna, the Heartland of Northern Italian Food* in 1992. At that time, "no one thought anyone would be interested in the Emilia-Romagna area of Italy," she recalls. "They couldn't even pronounce it. Even I wasn't sure about using the name in the title." But they went with it. The book won awards, remains in print, and Kasper has a national radio show of the same name.

A Man, a Can, a Plan: 50 Great Guy Meals Even You Can Make takes an unusual twist on men's cooking. Printed on heavy stiff paper and coated like a children's book so it won't stain, this book gives the not-so-subtle hint that men are like children when it comes to cooking. Recipes have photos of actual cans with plus signs between them. Are the recipes in the book unusual? No. But its unique differentiation, or positioning, succeeds. The book has been particularly successful among college students, says author David Joachim.

Your idea has potential as a series: Agents and publishers like to envision a long stream of revenue from you over the years, and for that matter, so might you. A series sounds like an easy idea, but today's publishers are the ones producing most collections, such as the *Joy of Cooking* series or the *Williams-Sonoma* series. For these series, publishers might hire a different writer to write each book.

Chuck and Blanche Johnson took a different approach and self-published their Savor Cookbook series under Wilderness Adventures Press. Their full-color books feature independent restaurants' stories, histories, and recipes, and have been sold in Costco.

A large, well-defined audience will be interested in your book: Publishers want you to define exactly who will buy your book so they can sell to that audience. In the earlier example of a muffin book, you could slice your audience many ways. If the recipes have six ingredients or fewer and can be made in ten minutes, busy moms might snap up the book. If the muffins are gluten-free, vegan, sugar-free, low-fat, or low-cholesterol, you've targeted readers concerned about their health. If your idea is simply "All About Muffins," however, the audience is much harder to define. Who are these people who like muffins? Unless it's a major trend, it's impossible to know.

As mentioned earlier, if you have built up a large, well-defined audience for your blog, chances are good that an agent or publisher will be interested in a cookbook. If your blog is about gluten-free cooking, and you want to write a book about gardening, all bets are off. But if you're Ree Drummond, who has a huge, loyal blog readership (http://thepioneerwoman.com/cooking), you can write *The Pioneer Woman Cooks* and it will spend several weeks on the *New York Times* best-seller list.

Your idea is original: I'm talking about being a groundbreaker in the field. Back in 1969, a group of Berkeley, California, college students interested in Eastern religions and meditation gave up meat and created *Laurel's Kitchen,* a classic book on vegetarianism. Little information on meatless cooking and nutrition existed at that time. The group did its own nutrition research, and *Laurel's Kitchen* came out in 1976. "We weren't pushing tahini and weird mushrooms or seaweed, stuff that some of the other cookbooks that came along did a lot of," said co-author Laurel Robertson in an interview. "Mostly we just made normal things without meat." Total combined sales for her first and subsequent four cookbooks are in the millions.

The Whole Beast: Nose to Tail Eating by British chef Fergus Henderson captivated chefs all over the country because it advocates consuming the entire animal. The book includes recipes for pig spleens, duck necks, and whole birds. Eating this way is *de rigueur* for the poor, but Henderson, who serves offal in his renowned London restaurant, St. John, aimed his book at the carnivorous middle and upper classes.

You have exclusive access to information: Let's say you've inherited a box of papers from a well-known person in the food world who has just died. When you search through the box you discover his personal home cooking file for recipes, never before published. There's a good chance a publisher or agent will be all over it, and you. Another way involves doing so much research on a subject you become the expert by default, because no one else has amassed that volume of information, or cares to do so.

Your idea is not esoteric: Sure, your neighbor makes fabulous raw food dishes featuring seaweed, but the audience is too small to attract a publisher. Writing a book on a narrow subject is not the same thing, or entire books on grilled-cheese sandwiches would not exist. Agents and editors often evaluate a book idea by whether the story would be better as a magazine article. "I have to believe there's a large market for the book," says agent Carole Bidnick, who sold Werlin's book on grilled-cheese sandwiches and represents such cookbook authors as Janet Fletcher and Fran Gage. "I ask myself how many people would spend twenty-five dollars to read this. If I can't come up with a minimum 10,000 people, I don't believe I can sell the book. If the sales aren't there, publishers are not going to buy the project."

The title rocks: Your ability to convey the meaning of a book in the title is critical. You don't want agents and editor to scratch their heads. Straightforward is fine. One person I worked with came up with *Baking Basics and Beyond.* No confusion there. Strive for brevity, wit, and specificity. Restrain yourself from being cute. Avoid inside jokes or phrases no one but you will understand. If none of your friends gets your title, that's a large clue. Clever puns are acceptable only if truly relevant to your book content. Here are some compelling attributes:

- Titles or subtitles in which the reader benefit is clearly stated, as in *The Meatless Diabetic Cookbook: Over 100 Recipes Combining Great Taste with Great Nutrition.* Other good benefit-oriented words are "fast," "easy," and "foolproof."
- The use of numbers that suggest a wealth of information, such as *1,000 Vegetarian Recipes from Around the World* or *100 Best Hamburger Recipes.*
- The use of "greatest" or "best," as in *America's Best RV Cookbook: The Complete Guide to RV Cooking.*
- Labeling a book as "new," as in *A New Way to Cook.*
- Humor, as in *Help! My Apartment has a Kitchen Cookbook: 100+ Great Recipes with Foolproof Instructions,* which has sold more than 250,000 copies.
- Secrets, as in *Secrets of a New Orleans Chef: Recipes from Tom Cowman's Cookbook.*
- Words that suggest a book is comprehensive or definitive, such as *The Complete Meat Cookbook* or *The Wine Bible.*

If you're still stumped, look through your own cookbook collection for inspiration. Ask friends or family to brainstorm with you. No matter what title you choose, don't get too hung up on it, because the publisher has the final say and chances are good it will change.

It's an evergreen: This publishing term means your book will sell for a long time. That excites publishers. It might be a book on diet or self-improvement, for example, neither of which goes out of style. Or it might be a work so distinguished—like *Mediterranean Cooking*—that it's been in print since 1976.

Classic Indian Cooking is in its fortieth printing. How can you make your book sell for a long time? Author Julie Sahni says she modeled her ideas after Julia Child, choosing ingredients readily available in supermarkets. And like Child's cookbooks, hers is still in style. "I give the example of crossing a stream with slippery stones," she explains. "You have to make sure your back foot is firm. You have to give the reader simple ways of cooking dishes with supermarket ingredients. Otherwise a lot of people will be put off."

WHEN YOU'D RATHER NOT BE ALONE: COLLABORATING, CO-AUTHORING, AND GHOSTWRITING

If you're not ready to write a book by yourself, or feel you don't have the credentials, collaborating can be a great way to become published more quickly. Here are three ways to work with a partner.

Collaborate: Book collaborations work best if a writer works with a more knowledgeable or well-known person, such as a chef who wants to increase the visibility of his or her restaurant. The collaborator writes the proposal and the book and tests the recipes. You must have a good enough relationship with a chef to offer to collaborate on a book. Or sometimes agents find collaborators for a chef.

As the writer, you would take the chef's content, recipes, stories, and voice and translate them into a cookbook. You would change the recipes into those appropriate for the home cook, testing to make sure they work: eliminate terms home cooks wouldn't understand such as "flame off"; simplify elaborate or intimidating recipes; and cut down yields to servings of four to eight.

I did this kind of work when I co-authored *Grilled Pizzas & Piadinas* with Chicago private chef Craig Priebe. We had a great relationship, but even so, it takes sensitivity, as changing recipes can create a problem if chefs feel the integrity of the recipes will be sacrificed or lost. Many chefs cook without exact measurements, using technique and taste. They also use specialty ingredients not found in supermarkets. It's your job to measure, and to educate the chef on the target audience, usually home cooks.

In our case, Craig drafted the recipes and sent them to me. I edited them and sent them back, making suggestions to cut down the complexity or replace an ingredient. Once he signed off on the recipe, I would test it and make further adjustments. For the headnotes, I interviewed him or sometimes he sent me a rough draft. I wrote the book in his voice.

I know another collaborator where the chef came to her house to cook for her while she took notes and grabbed his hand to measure ingredients. For her latest project, she visits a restaurant and watches the chefs cook, then creates a recipe for their review.

Once you approach a chef or restaurateur about a book, start by discussing the scope and content. It gives you a chance to get to know the chef, test the waters, and see if you two click. You also have to decide whether you are passionate enough about the book's content to devote months to writing it, and whether you can translate the chef's voice and style successfully. Once you've made a good match, the two of you will sign a collaboration agreement, spelling out the responsibilities, deadlines, and compensation.

You must believe the money you receive will be enough to cover your time and effort. Collaborators get paid in many ways. Craig paid me a flat fee, called a work-for-hire, where I received no royalties. He also reimbursed me for groceries, both mine and for the testers I hired to make some of my recipes. Work-for-hire fees vary wildly—anywhere from $10,000 to $150,000. Other arrangements include a flat fee and a percentage of royalties, or a percentage of the advance plus royalties, with no payment up front. I was not enough of a gambler for that plan.

When writing the book, you'll interview the expert to get his or her thoughts, experience, and knowledge, and spend time in the kitchen observing him or her. The chef will approve your drafts, recipes, and other writing. If you have made a big contribution to the book, your name may appear on the cover, preceded by "with." That detail should be covered in your contract.

Successful collaborators have agents and can win awards, regardless of whether they co-author or ghostwrite. Mary Goodbody, who has worked with other writers on more than fifty books, received a James Beard Award for co-authoring *Taste Pure and Simple* with Michel Nischan.

Co-author: Co-authors do equal work for equal billing on the cover, where names are linked by "and." An example might be a recipe developer who hooks up with an expert in nutrition because she has less experience in that area. "You need two parties really willing to do their share," explains Nancy Baggett, who had a good experience co-writing books in a series based on *Skinny*. Each writer divides the work based on time, skill, or whatever criteria seem valid, and signs an agreement. "If one person underestimates and undervalues the time you put in, you're kind of doomed," she cautions.

Some husbands and wives partner on cookbooks. Naomi Duguid and Jeffrey Alford, photographers as well as writers, travel the globe searching for authentic food. Jane and Michael Stern travel around the United States looking for regional treasures.

Ghostwrite: Ghostwriters operate in much the same way as collaborators, but your job is to represent the chef and be invisible. Your name will not appear in the book, unless the author acknowledges you. Usually the more money you receive as the writer, the less credit you get on the book. Fees are similar to those I discussed for collaborators.

Writer Barry Estabrook worked with Jacques Pépin on his memoir, *The Apprentice: My Life in the Kitchen*. Estabrook recorded Pépin in long, detailed interviews, "goading him" into talking about and remembering his past. He captured Pépin's voice beautifully and accurately for the chef's dedicated following of fans.

What Kind of Cookbook?

If you're still not sure what kind of cookbook you'd like to write, look through your recipe collection and organize it into groups. See whether you have a surplus of one kind. Do you have more recipes for Greek food? Do most of the recipes fall into a certain category, such as salad, or does your biggest stack focus on a certain ingredient? Or group the recipes by degree of difficulty, or by whether they would appeal to certain groups of people, such as busy working people or singles dining alone.

Here are some of the most popular types of cookbooks:

- Thematic books based on events such as seasons and parties.
- Single-subject books focusing on a specific ingredient or type of dish.
- Appliance books based on tools like slow cookers or pressure cookers.
- Audience-intended books focusing on groups of people, such as diabetics, college students, campers, or the budget-minded. The writing style and recipes would be appropriate to the audience. A cookbook for campers, for example, would have quick, easy portable dishes with few ingredients, and steps that could be made ahead.
- Geographic books, distinguished by country or region. These might be travelogues, full of evocative dishes and photographs.
- Historical books, moving chronologically or covering a period.
- Hybrids. These books are crosses between two themes. Healthy cooking from Provence is two times more focused than a book on French cooking.
- Menu-based cookbooks arranged by meals, such as picnics or holiday dinners.
- General reference books with an encyclopedic, alphabetical approach. These can also specialize in a single subject, such as vegetables.
- Amusing or quirky specialty cookbooks. A romantic dinner cookbook might come with a CD of songs to set a mood, or a book about presidents might detail what they ate.

The most traditional structure, no matter what type of cookbook, is soup-to-nuts: appetizers, soups, salads, main dishes, and dessert. From there you could subtract or add other chapters, such as breads, eggs, side dishes, vegetables, pasta, cheese courses, and fruit. To help determine the order of chapters you'd like to use, look at some other cookbooks you admire.

Once you delineate the appropriate categories or chapters, fill out the book by adding titles of every recipe in your brain. A serious cookbook requires at least 100 recipes. Don't worry about finalizing the list at this point. You don't need finished recipes now either. Putting the names into categories helps you whittle down recipes that should not be included. You might be famous for your coq au vin, but if you're writing a book on Latin food, it doesn't apply unless you can tweak your recipe to give it a Latin spin. Set aside the recipes that don't fit for your next cookbook. Be ruthless to ensure your book is properly focused.

Which chapters or sections would you include, besides the lists of recipes? You might want to include one of the following:

- A shopping resource section to help readers find hard-to-locate ingredients on the Web or in specialty stores in their city.
- A glossary or primer, if you are writing an ethnic cookbook that uses unfamiliar foods.
- A list or chapter on fundamental techniques, such as how to poach or brine, if you plan to use these methods in many recipes.
- A list or chapter on pantry supplies, if your book calls for ready-made ingredients such as canned stocks, roasted peppers, olives, or canned fish.
- A chapter on basics like stocks and sauces. If your book calls for lots of recipes using homemade stocks and sauces like pesto and hollandaise, you might collect these "sub-recipes" in the front and refer to them later within more elaborate recipes. Although I personally don't like sub-recipes much, it makes no sense to keep repeating them as parts of many recipes.

- A section on pre-made mixes, such as pancake, rubs, and herb combinations.
- A bibliography, if you wish to direct readers to books for additional learning.

Also consider how much narrative you want in your cookbook. If you like to write, you might choose essay-length chapter openers, narrative boxes, or sidebars. Consider whether stories are a central part of your book. They might not be appropriate for beat-the-clock cooking, but if you're writing a book like Grace Young's *Wisdom of the Chinese Kitchen*, which covers her family's recipes, Chinese culture, and the Chinatown where she grew up, you'll want essay-length writing. Young included biographical stories, information about Chinese food and healing, personal memories, and culinary traditions.

When your book idea has jelled thoroughly, and you've written a proposal, you're ready to find a publisher. Chapter 11 explains how to get your book published, whether you're looking for a traditional publisher or want to be self-published, and how the publishing experience will play out.

How Artwork
Fits into Your Idea

Now that you see your book taking shape, you've probably thought about how it will look. Hardly anyone envisions a text-only book. Why bother, when you can have a gorgeous all-color hardcover with photos that illustrate the beauty of each dish, landscapes of rolling hillsides, or gleaming shots of just-picked produce? Not so fast. Color photos are expensive. They require heavier paper stock, glossier paper, and four colors instead of one. Even a text-based cookbook has extra steps for a color insert. Photos are printed on different paper and inserted into the book. Heavier stock means a book that costs more to ship, and a bigger book that costs more to shelve in a warehouse.

When editors review your book idea, they assess the risk of publishing it. Adding color to your book increases risk because it increases cost. Some cookbooks lend themselves to photography, such as those on the cuisine of other countries or regions. Sometimes the beauty of a chef's presentation makes color photos appropriate. If you are a first-time author, though, there's no guarantee.

Another choice is two-color printing. This works best when it's part of the design, such as illustrations, colored titles, or shaded boxes with type over them. If you want illustrations by a certain artist, state as much in your proposal, otherwise the publisher will choose the illustrator for you. Become more familiar with page design and design elements. Thumb through your own cookbook collection or go to a bookstore to discover details you may not have noticed before: the look of sidebars and tip boxes, the length of introductions and headnotes, and the use of pull-out quotes and other elements such as colored titles, boxes, and shading to enliven page design.

Sometimes a book just doesn't warrant color. As Leslie Stoker, president and publisher of Stewart, Tabori & Chang, said in an interview, "A prune cookbook wouldn't have a broad enough book-buying audience to support its production cost. And a meatloaf cookbook just wouldn't have the visual appeal."

Publishers such as Chronicle Books, Ten Speed Press, Artisan, Clarkson Potter, and Stewart, Tabori & Chang routinely print four-color cookbooks. Most of the time the author pays for the photographs one way or another. Three people I worked with on book proposals got different deals. One received a small advance and the publisher paid for a dozen color photographs. Another got a bigger advance but spent two-thirds of it on the photography. A third author wrote a historical book and provided all the photos herself.

A styled color photo costs anywhere from $500 to $1,000, depending on the prestige of the photographer. If you dream of twenty photos in your cookbook, it will cost between $10,000 to $20,000. Photographers often charge less per shot for big shoots of around 100 photos. Usually the editor determines how many photos the publisher can afford and hires the photographer, but sometimes the author has a photographer in mind and can negotiate.

Photographers like to shoot their food photos in studios so that they don't have to schlep lights and equipment to a location shot. They also shoot in restaurants, home kitchens, and the outdoors. Today most photographers use natural light to bring out the beauty of the food. Some do the food styling, too, but may also use some combination of food stylist, prop stylist, and assistants who move the lights around and other tasks. All these people must be paid, and their cost figures into the book's advance.

The food stylist prepares all the food for the photos and plays up the natural beauty of a dish. "We make it the way it would look for real," explains photographer Maren Caruso. "Not over-the-top perfect so people are intimidated and will never prepare it." You've probably heard about hairspray on salad greens and shellac on peas. That's more for advertising, explains Caruso, where "the milk splash has to happen in a certain place." I watched a food stylist use mashed potatoes in place of ice cream once. No one could blame her. When a photographer takes half an hour to get the shot exactly right while the ice cream melts under the bright lights, drastic measures become necessary. When I saw the finished photo, it looked like a creamy scoop of ice cream atop a fruit dessert. That's what matters.

A prop stylist provides all the plates, tablecloths, flowers, cutlery, and anything else needed in the shot. I attended a location shoot where the prop stylist drove up in a van and swung open its back doors to reveal a floor-to-ceiling cache. There were plates, platters, vases, flowers, tablecloths, napkins, cutlery, ribbon, and whatever else is necessary for beautiful photos. I couldn't imagine how she kept track of it all.

Do authors style their own food? Rarely, unless they're professional food stylists as well as writers. Usually the photo shoot takes place elsewhere, and the author's not part of it. Sometimes, if you have an artistic eye, you're successful, and the photographer trusts you, it can work. Deborah Madison has cooked and styled the food for all her books. "I don't mind when someone else is helping me, but I want the right to say when something is a jumble versus arranged, or to point out when the dish doesn't look like anything I've cooked," she explains. Madison makes some dishes that might be hard to visualize, such as vegetable ragout.

Another example of a book where the author had a hand in the photos is *Dessert University: More than 300 Spectacular Recipes and Essential Lessons from White House Pastry Chef Roland Mesnier.* Because of the complexity of the desserts and because the author had a strong vision of how they should look, he flew into town and stayed near Caruso's studio in Oakland, California. "He came in every day, worked in the studio kitchen in his chef's whites, and helped us create these over-the-top pastries when we needed direction," she says.

So that's a short explanation of how your book might look and what happens behind the curtain. Now, back to your book idea. As you've learned from this chapter, you have lots of thinking ahead. Keep working out the concept and details. Brainstorm with friends. Focus your idea. Look at other cookbooks for reference. Write the table of contents. Get your recipes in order. Next, it's time to start writing your cookbook, right? Yes, to some extent. The next part is to understand how to write most of what's in it: recipes.

Writing Exercises

1. Learn how to focus an idea by drilling down to specifics. Name a country you love and think of the particular region you like best. What are the food specialties of that region? Can you focus on a course? How else might you customize your idea to interest a publisher, based on title concepts I've listed?

2. If you've already chosen the subject of your cookbook, define your expertise. Write a one-paragraph biography. Doing so helps you feel more confident about the project, and might show you areas where you need more research. Perhaps you have taken cooking classes on the subject, traveled extensively, cooked a special diet, or grew up eating a particular cuisine. Have you written about the subject for a class, newsletter, blog, or newspaper? If you feel that you need more expertise, make a list of three steps you can take now to enhance your background.

3. When people have trouble describing their book idea to me, I ask them to get the idea down to one sentence. Doing so requires you to focus on the most important points. Ask a friend to help. Keep explaining the idea until you can get it down to one clear concept. Practice this sentence when you tell people you're going to write a cookbook.

8

The Art of Recipe Writing

My immigrant parents never used recipes. When they settled in Canada they had to reinvent the foods they knew—no easy task when neither had ever cooked before. Because no restaurants served their food, to eat it, they had to make it. Eventually they recreated most of the dishes, dairy products, pickles, sauces, and sweets they yearned for, tasting from memory and remembering how foods looked and smelled. An exception was the stuffed intestines my father smacked his lips over but my mother wouldn't allow in the house. (My parents were Iraqi Jews, born and raised in China.)

Both my parents are gone now, and ironically, they never taught me to cook. I have a few chicken scratchings on paper that hinted at a recipe, but when I tried to cook with them, I found instructions I didn't understand, shorthand for techniques I didn't know, or missing ingredients or steps that I didn't discover until it was too late. Nothing turned out right.

I kept trying. I cooked a few dishes repeatedly, refining the taste from memory, just as they did. Each time I cooked or baked, I wrote the recipe down, printed it out, and marked it up when I made the dish again. There was always something to improve: more or less of an ingredient, a little more simmering, figuring out how to make a pastry less tough or a step more clear. Today, I've got a handful of recipes I like, based on this process of experimentation and refinement.

And that's just one reason you might want to know how to create recipes. Perhaps you have a son leaving for college who wants to re-create his favorite dishes. Maybe your neighbor keeps asking you for your recipe for fried chicken. Perhaps you are a chef, caterer, or cooking school teacher who wants to hand out recipes to students or customers. Or maybe you have a child who needs allergy-free meals, and you want to record the dishes you've made that work well. No matter what your desire, if you want to write a cookbook, create a recipe-based blog, or write feature articles based on recipes, you need to write trustworthy and workable recipes for food that tastes good.

A well-written recipe is poetry, like beautiful writing. Agents and editors can see a good one a mile away. Sometimes they test them. Agent Lisa Ekus, who represents both new and established cookbook writers, says if she's found an unknown writer whose recipes look interesting, she will ask the writer or chef to cook for her. "If I can see them in action and taste their food, I can sell the book more passionately. If the book is restaurant based, I try to eat in the restaurant." Agent Doe Coover says she tests recipes from proposals "all the time," because if an editor tries them and they don't work, "it's going to come back on my head."

A badly written recipe is a disappointment. When I first cooked from published recipes I always blamed myself when the dish didn't turn out. I thought I had not followed a step properly or left something out. It's possible the recipe was not written well, not adequately developed, or not tested thoroughly. (I admit that I wasn't channeling Julia Child back then.) Today, when I read a recipe, I can judge whether it will work, or how to adjust it if I think it won't. You don't want readers to second-guess you, though. You want recipes that work the first time. Good recipe writers don't let go until they know their readers can reproduce the recipes faithfully and make dishes that look and taste as good as their own.

The best recipes are not only clearly written but include the personality of the writer. Consider the ending of Quick Cream of Chicken Soup, from my yellowed 1946 edition of *The Joy of Cooking*. After combining chicken bouillon and scalded cream, Irma Rombauer announces, "Add if you want to be luxurious: blanched almonds, ground (about 2 tablespoonfuls to 1 cup soup)." In just a few words, she reveals her playfulness, originality, and need to indulge.

If you are patient, exacting, and detail oriented, you can write a recipe. It's a form of systematic technical writing. In this chapter you'll learn how to write each part: the title, headnote, ingredients list, and method. You'll also learn how to develop, troubleshoot, compose, and test until you have a recipe anyone can follow and get the same results you did. Even if you've written recipes before—for yourself, a community cookbook, a neighbor, or a friend, even for publication—you'll learn tips here that will increase your skill level. You'll also find answers to many common questions, particularly those related to testing, attribution, and copyright.

If you wish to write a cookbook, I can't emphasize enough how critical it is that you write recipes well. Recipes must be precise, accurate, logical, consistent, clear, complete, doable, and satisfying. The best create visual images in the minds of readers as they imagine making the dish. In the best cases, they are sensuous, immediate, and evocative.

That's what readers want most, regardless of whether they are newspaper editors, your children, friends, or purchasers of your cookbook.

Developing a Recipe

You might think recipe writing is linear, where you create a seafood pasta dish, write the recipe, and send it to a friend to see if she can recreate it accurately. It sounds simple enough. But that's not how it works. Let's say you taste the pasta dish and decide it could use improvement, maybe some parsley and lemon juice. You add "$1/4$ cup parsley" and "1 tablespoon lemon juice" to the ingredients list and make the pasta again. Now it tastes better, but still needs more zing. You revise the ingredients list once more, this time changing it to "2 tablespoons lemon juice" and "2 tablespoons capers." You make the pasta again. Now you love it and you're satisfied. That's recipe development.

Three is not the magic number of times to make a dish. What if you realized, upon tasting the third version of the pasta dish, you should have kept the lemon juice to one tablespoon instead of two. Should you make the pasta again, just to be certain? The best recipe writers would say yes. Some have been known to develop a recipe up to twenty times, particularly bakers, where recipe writing is a more exact science because of the chemistry involved. "Those of us who write good recipes tend to be obsessors," admits Alice Medrich. "You have to fight it and go with it at the same time."

Sometimes it's all about ingredients. When she's developing a recipe for, say, a layered cake, she might change one of the cake layers to a different flavor, or change one of the fillings to custard, or take out nuts and substitute coconut. Other times she will start her development process with an ingredients and measurement grid. Let's say she wants a new chocolate cake recipe. She'll look through other bakers' recipes—those by writers she admires—and then fill in her grid with varying amounts of ingredients they specify. She'll put ingredients down one side and a list of measurements down the other. That way she knows which ingredients are basic and which are changeable. If all the recipes call for similar amounts of flour, Medrich knows the amount is standard, and she probably won't change it. She might test the recipe that calls for the most eggs to see how she likes the results. "It's like doing basic research before a history report," she explains. "It's about finickiness and curiosity, the teeny-weeny little details that make a difference."

Cookbook author Deborah Madison says she often gets inspiration from the garden and farmers' market when she's just "cooking freely in the kitchen. " If she makes a dish she likes, she wants to repeat it. "I cook as intuitively as I can, and make notes like 'needs more tang or sharpness,' and then I start correcting the dish. I go back and forth until I find something I like." She limits herself to making a recipe three or four times.

Recipes may also evolve from dishes Madison ate in restaurants where she noticed a flavor, unusual food presentation, or the texture of a silky soup. She makes notes on dishes she likes when she's away from the kitchen and refers to them when she's back. Some people have a good taste memory, she says, like her friend Clifford Wright. "He can remember the taste of foods he's eaten abroad. Somehow, he nails the taste." (Wright specializes in Mediterranean cookbooks.)

When tasting your work, savor the flavors and textures of each version or part of your dish, considering each separately and as a whole. For a dish with several components, evaluate each part separately before assembling to see how they complement each other. Take into account appearance, taste, texture, and appropriate serving size. Remember that this is *your* recipe. If your family loves it and you're not satisfied, keep refining or put it aside. If you publish a recipe on a blog and get a negative comment from a reader, replying with the defense of "my kids loved it" isn't very satisfying.

Philosophy of Recipe Writing for a Cookbook

You want the right list of recipes to include in your book. How do you think about creating the recipes? "Choose dishes that best reflect your strength," advises Medrich. "You want the best results possible for [the] least time and work spent. Minimize drudgery. Streamline activities, increase convenience." Creating dishes with appearance in mind is particularly important for baking books, which often include color photos.

Many people aren't sure what level of instruction to give. I'm on the side that says not to make assumptions about what readers know. Most cooking magazines hold readers' hands and will expect you to do the same, if you're writing for them. Most of their readers didn't grow up cooking with their mothers, and lack basic knowledge.

Julia Child took beginning cooks seriously. When she lived in France and studied French cooking, she noticed that most of the cookbooks for serious students were chef's shorthand notes, with not much instruction for such techniques as how to fix a broken sauce or how to poach. Child wanted a "real teaching book" with clear reasoning and every step and technique thoroughly explained. In her first book, *Mastering the Art of French Cooking*, she described how a dish should look at each stage of preparation and told readers what could go wrong with the process, along with corrective measures. Her recipes are long, but they always work. And that is a big reason why readers appreciate her.

Back in the 1950s, Judith Jones was an editor at Knopf (now she's a vice president, and still edits cookbooks). She tried some of the recipes when she received Child's manuscript. She found the book revolutionary because it was "like having a teacher right there beside you in the kitchen, and everything really worked," she told the *New Yorker*. Today Jones is still an admirer. "She told us what to expect, how to achieve it, how to taste, how to correct our mistakes, and how to work out our own variations," she says.

Your first task is to accept that not all readers are probably not exactly like you. They may not prepare ingredients before they start or have the same equipment. They might not understand the meaning of words like "blanch" or read your recipe all the way through first. They might not be as excited as you are about making several time consuming dishes for a dinner party.

Madison acknowledges that real life intervenes in the kitchen. "Cooking is a dynamic and complex process and I'm always trying to look at the whole picture," she explains. "Where in a recipe is there a gap where you can start something for the next day, set the table, or simply sit down and have a glass of wine with your partner? If you think of recipes only in terms of the final dish rather than a process, a meal, or an experience, then it's a rather limited way to see cooking."

Bearing these thoughts in mind, in the next section I detail each part of a recipe, how to think about recipes, and how to write them.

Recipe Titles

Recipe titles should be simple, descriptive, informative, and inviting. You don't want them to read like a menu item in a restaurant. And you don't want them to be vague, so readers can't envision the dish.

Like good writers, good recipe writers have their own styles. I like an accurate, specific title I can understand. Marion Cunningham takes a straightforward approach in *Lost Recipes: Meals to Share with Friends and Family*. Titles are as simple as Southern Green Beans, Stuffed Cabbage Rolls, or Raised Waffles. She wouldn't consider Green Bean Surprise, Organic Cabbage Rolls Stuffed with Long-Grain Rice and Corn-Fed Ground Beef, or Judy's Famous Raised Waffles. Any dish called a "surprise" will be a mystery to your readers because they can't envision the dish. The second title belongs on a menu. The third won't mean anything to readers, since they don't know Judy. It's best to credit Judy and explain her significance in the headnote.

It's easy to write a confusing title. You might think Stone Fruit Ice Cream is perfectly fine. But now you've asked readers to work. "Which fruits have stones in them?" they might wonder. "Does she mean plums? That doesn't sound good." And then they turn the page. If peaches make the best and most appealing ice cream, call it Peach Ice Cream, and list other stone fruit types as variations.

Readers want to be enticed. Even something as simple as James Villas' Creamed Leeks with Italian Sausage sounds good, because he added "creamed" and "Italian" as descriptors. Leeks with Sausage wouldn't do it for me. "Easy" or "quick" are always inviting if they fit the style of book. Avoid adjectives like "the best" or "sublime." You probably think almost all of your recipes are the best or sublime. Let the title speak for itself.

For recipes from world cuisines, some authors go for the recipe title in its original language first, followed by an explanation in English, and some the other way around. The style of the book is a factor, as is the readers' sophistication level and the style sheet followed by the publisher. In *The Book of Jewish Food*, Claudia Roden names Chicken Soup with Rice in Arabic first: *Shorba bi Djaj*. Julia Child titles a recipe *Choux Brocoli Blancis*, followed by (Blanched Broccoli—Plain Boiled Broccoli). Grace Young, however, in *The Wisdom of the Chinese Kitchen*, calls my favorite dim sum dessert Sesame Balls, then *Zeen Doy* in smaller type, perhaps placing the original phrase afterward because people are unfamiliar with Mandarin and Cantonese. If you are writing a cookbook, compile a list of titles for each chapter. To ensure variety and liveliness, alternate their styles, wording, and length.

The Headnote or Introduction

Here's your second chance to draw readers into the recipe. Headnotes set a mood, give the recipe a personality, or tell a story. You need headnotes for several reasons. One is because without them, the first thing readers will see after the title is "2 pounds pork butt, well trimmed." That's not terribly inviting.

These days, headnotes in books and often on websites contain narrative and read like novels. They tell stories or entertain. They're written in a conversational style. You might have a funny story about a kitchen disaster, or a particular memory or occasion you'd like to share. Blogger and cookbook author David Lebovitz will write unusual headnotes such as, "I tried to flush this ice cream down the toilet." "Is that going to turn people off or is that funny?" he asks. "I write that way on my Web site, and people read it, so they must like it. That's the good thing about having a Web site: you get immediate feedback."

If you have no story, don't feel you have to fill a void or make one up. Instead, write about the connection of food to history, dining rituals, and celebrations. Or encourage readers to make the dish. Inventive sales pitches are fine, such as "This is one soup I make all winter long which has the double virtue of being scrumptious and effortless" (Laurie Colwin); or, "My favorite chicken dish was the ring mold with wild-mushroom sauce served on a beautiful Sunday afternoon in late spring when the doors could be left open and the warm rays of the sun streaked across the dining table, saluting my mother for her efforts in presenting a beautiful meal gathered from field, forest, garden and barnyard." (Edna Lewis)

When you read a good headnote, you appreciate it. Your readers will want to do the same. Give them context for the larger issues. Janet Theophano, author of *Eat My Words: Reading Women's Lives Through the Cookbooks They Wrote*, explains: "As cooks, we must first taste a dish in our imaginations, see it on the table, share it with guests—sometimes more fanciful than real—and then actually reproduce it from a text. A longing for the pleasures of the table reflects a concern for balance and harmony and an integration of the physical and spiritual nature of our existence. In this way, cookbooks are a meditation. Preparing a dish or a meal is not merely an effort to satisfy physical hunger but often a quest for the good life."

John T. Edge, author of *Southern Belly: The Ultimate Food Lover's Guide to the South*, says there are five kinds of headnotes. Here are his examples:

- **Cultural:** In this neck of the woods, we eat hominy when . . .
- **Historical:** The Hot Brown sandwich was first concocted by Chef . . .
- **Personal:** I remember the night Aunt Minnie slipped on that banana peel . . .
- **Instructional:** Only soft winter wheat will do for this . . .
- **Sensual:** This cake rises so high that it looks like an Eisenhower-era bouffant.

Most of all, headnotes are practical, particularly in magazines, where they tend to be shorter than in books. They tell readers what to expect. They state benefits such as saving time or using up leftovers.

Simplicity can be beautiful. Sometimes headnotes are no more than a set of brief, descriptive instructions. Here's an example from *Feasts for All Seasons,* by Roy Andries de Groot, a book on seasonal cooking that came out ahead of its time in 1966: "We like to serve asparagus as a separate course, before the main dish. The problem of cooking asparagus is simple. The tips are tender and should never be in contact with boiling water. The stems, on the other hand, must be boiled." At a minimum, your job is to consider readers' needs, explain the recipe, and establish trust. For example:

- If the recipe looks long and complicated, or is made in stages, reassure readers that it's worth their trouble, that they can make parts in advance, or that the dish comes together quickly.
- If the recipe calls for advance preparation, let them know.
- If the method uses a new technique critical to the recipe's success, say so here so readers can prepare for and focus on the task.
- If the recipe includes an unfamiliar ingredient, explain where to procure it and why it's worthwhile. If the recipe calls for several unfamiliar ingredients, you're on thin ice, unless you're writing a book on a relatively unexplored ethnic cuisine and want to be accurate. A cookbook with lots of recipes calling for obscure ingredients makes agents and editors very nervous. Reassure readers that if they can't find the exact ingredient, a substitute will work. For example, in her recipe for Zinfandel of Beef, Julia Child declares, "If you are out of zinfandel, use another good young red wine and call it simply Beef Stew in Red Wine." You can bet that Child, a responsible recipe developer, tested this variation.
- If the dish can be made with variations, explain how adding or changing an ingredient works as an alternative.
- If the dish is hard to imagine, describe it with specific words—not by saying delicious, wonderful, or great, but instead something like, "this sharp, refreshing sauce."
- If the dish is traditionally served during certain holidays, or goes well with other recipes in the book, let readers know.

- If you think it would taste best with certain wines or beers, you might make suggestions.
- If the recipe needs a hint, help readers out. In *The Way to Cook,* Julia Child suggests soaking one cup of beans in ten cups of water to get rid of "the rooti-toots" they bring on.

I would be remiss if I did not include my pet peeves here. Please do not state in the headnote, "Add a green salad and a crusty loaf of country bread for a complete meal." You could say this about any Western or European entrée. Or that a dish is the best thing you've ever tasted. You'll make readers suspicious. Instead, show the reader how good it is with description.

At the end of the headnote, state the number of servings. Sometimes servings are based on precise measurements, such as "makes four half-cup servings," and sometimes you might have different sizes based on whether the item is an appetizer or main course. List cookies by the dozen.

Attribution and Copyright

Now we get to attribution, an issue usually discussed in the headnote. How do you address using a recipe with an unknown origin—such as a handwritten recipe from an aunt who got it from a friend? It might be an heirloom, from a restaurant, or taken from a cookbook. It's best to find the origin, even if you changed the recipe in at least three major ways. When in doubt, give credit, and you'll create fewer problems. Even if you have no idea, you can still say your best friend's mother gave it to you in the 1980s on a handwritten card. Or that it was adapted from, inspired by, or based on another recipe. Even if you've completely reworded the recipe, to be safe, say where it came from.

As to the question of copyright, most publishers register cookbook copyrights in the author's name. The commonly held industry belief, however, is that only the headnote and method can be protected, not the ingredients list. You can't copyright "1 cup flour," and other ingredients in the list, because they are too generic.

To the question, "How do I protect my recipes?" the US government answers: A mere listing of ingredients is not protected under copyright law. However, where a recipe or formula is accompanied by substantial literary expression in the form of an explanation or directions, or when there is a collection of recipes as in a cookbook, there may be a basis for copyright protection. See this Web site for more information: www.copyright.gov/fls/fl122.html.

If you are self-publishing, you may request forms from the United States Copyright Office at the Library of Congress, (202) 707-9100 or www.copyright.gov. If you want to reproduce a published recipe for a freelance article or for a Web site, you must contact the publisher and ask for permission.

RECIPE WRITING FOR CHEFS AND CATERERS

If you're a food professional who wants to write recipes for home cooks, you have challenges other cookbook writers do not. Most chefs and caterers create recipes to feed crowds. It's different to make a dish for four. You might also make assumptions about reader knowledge and experience. My favorite example of a chef trying to write a recipe for home cooks is an opening sentence a friend read to me: "Roast a duck as you would for any occasion." If you don't understand why this is funny, you won't be successful writing for a home cook.

My friend had that recipe because she was rewriting a chef's recipes for home cooks. For best results, take your best shot at a recipe and hire a recipe developer or experienced cookbook writer to rework it for you. Have someone who represents your reader test it, not a professional cook. For more details, see "When You'd Rather Not Be Alone: Collaborating, Co-authoring, and Ghostwriting," on pages 192–194.

Ingredients List

Think of the ingredients list and the directions that follow as a formula. The most important rule of this formula is to list ingredients in the order they will be used in the directions or method. That way, if some ingredients require preparation, as in toasted nuts or thawed berries, readers see it right away. Or if they lose their place in the method, it's easy to scan the list to see which ingredient comes next.

The other rule about listing ingredients is that it's good to be specific. Instead of oil, say olive oil. State whether the butter is salted or unsalted. Specify onions and potatoes by size, such as "1 large onion, chopped." Sizes of cut vegetables range from smallest to largest: minced, diced, or chopped. And you'll want to put the largest quantity first, such as in a group of spices: 2 tablespoons oregano, 1 teaspoon salt, $\frac{1}{2}$ teaspoon pepper.

Measurements can be tricky. Some recipe writers like to say "2 carrots, peeled and chopped." Since carrot sizes vary, you could also say "1 cup chopped carrots (about 2)." Readers like to know the exact amount for the recipe and the number of carrots, in case they have to shop.

Some writers prefer to state the weight, as in "$\frac{1}{2}$ pound carrots." Since most cooks don't have a scale at home, how would they know if the carrots they already have on hand are enough? If a food is sold by weight, however, give reader both measurements, such as "1 cup strawberries (about 8 ounces)."

When using canned foods, state the size, as in "1 (14-ounce) can whole tomatoes." If possible, use the whole can of broth to make life easier for readers. In the "making life easier" department, canned stock is acceptable in most cookbooks, and canned beans don't have to be soaked overnight. State your preference for dried beans, but also acknowledge that canned beans will work. If you only tell readers the amount required for dried beans soaked overnight, however, they won't know how many cans of cooked beans to buy instead. (By the way, one pound dried beans equals five-and-a-half to six cups cooked.)

In baking, know the difference between liquid and dry measure. Do not use a scale to measure ingredients, even if you think it's more accurate. I know some chefs feel strongly about using weights for dry ingredients, but American home cooks do not use scales to measure flour. They do not use metrics either, so keep measurements in cups, tablespoons, and teaspoons. If you are converting a foreign recipe, make these conversions. Use large eggs, the standard size. If it matters whether water is ice cold, rather than cold, say so.

Consider whether a food should be measured before or after use. Distinguish between "1 cup almonds, chopped," or "1 cup chopped almonds." Similarly, "1 cup sifted flour" is different from "1 cup flour, sifted." Make sure you figure this out, as imprecise measurements drive recipe editors crazy.

Many people get stuck on how to refer to ingredients used twice in a recipe. Avoid double listing. Write "½ cup plus 2 tablespoon olive oil," for example. In the oil's first mention in the method, tell readers to add the "1 tablespoon olive oil," not "the oil." Later tell them to add "the remaining 2 tablespoons olive oil." You could also say "½ cup olive oil plus oil for greasing the pan." Some writers use the term "divided" to follow a single amount, but often readers can't figure out what it means until they read the method. If you call for flour in two parts of a recipe that has different components, such as a pie, separate the ingredients with subheadings and groups, such as "For the piecrust" and "For the berry filling." Write one method for the overall recipe, not a method for each sub-recipe, unless the sub-recipe can stand alone and will be referred to elsewhere in the book, such as for piecrust.

Recipes with parts need subgroups with subheadings. Irene Kuo's Beef in Blackbean Sauce [*sic*] has a recipe for the "slippery coating," followed by a general recipe for the dish, and a third recipe for the sauce. I like this method because it's clear immediately to marinate the beef, stir fry it, and add sauce. Breaking up the recipe is particularly important with a lengthy recipe. If your recipe calls for a sub-recipe on another page—such as stock or a sauce—cross-reference the dish. Too many sub-recipes make readers turn to another page elsewhere in the book. Most don't like flipping from one page to another, or seeing that they have to prepare three parts first before assembling them all in the final fourth. Even on a blog, put the whole recipe in one place, not carved up in links.

When it comes to type of ingredient, call for the most commonly available whenever possible. This is particularly important for recipe writers who present food from other countries or particular regions of the United States. "We like to do things in authentic ways, but authentic ways are not necessarily the way to make things accessible," said Mark Bittman, *New York Times* columnist and author of *How to Cook Everything*. If you really want readers to use the hard-to-find ingredient because it's essential to the dish, or because the dish won't taste as good with a substitute, say so in the headnote. Give readers an incentive and enough information to search for it. The same is true with brand names. Avoid them unless you think a dish will be diminished by not using a particular brand. Name it in the headnote, not in the ingredients list. If you list an optional ingredient, a substitution, or a variation test each recipe that way to evaluate whether the change worked.

Method or Directions

The method is where you tell readers how to make the dish. At its most basic, it is systematic technical writing, written in a lively voice. At its best, method writing has personality. Editor Jones advocates writing directions that sound like you're standing next to a friend in the kitchen, helping that person cook. "You want to give the impression you have done it many times and can cook with confidence," she explains.

When Jones reviews recipes, she looks at the quality of the writing and use of language. "It's not that the recipe per se is striking and new," she says. "It's what the writer does with it." One of her authors, Lydia Bastianich, wrote "a whole meditation on what you're doing while stirring risotto," she explains, "what you listen for, see, and smell. Writing like this comes from something within."

Put each step in a separate paragraph. Sometime they are numbered, but most often not. I like recipes that start with a verb, such as rinse, chop, or beat. If you're writing for a magazine or a publisher that has a recipe style sheet, you'll refer to it for guidance.

Often the first direction is to heat the oven, but this is not necessarily correct. Make sure readers do so at the right time. If you ask them to "marinate meat for 20 minutes," or "put cookie dough in the fridge for 1 hour," you'll want them to turn on the oven later.

Specify the size of commonly available pots and pans by small, medium, and large. Don't make readers guess what size they need and pick the wrong one. Baking, particularly, requires specific pan sizes.

I'm not a fan of the term "set aside." As Jones is likely to say, "What else are you going to do with it? Throw it away?" Instead, give specific instructions only when necessary, such as "cover and refrigerate for at least 1 hour."

Jones, as you may have guessed, has strong opinions on recipe writing. She tries to undo formulaic writing. The word she likes least is mixture. "You mix milk with bit of salt, now it's called the milk mixture," she says incredulously. She suggests specific language instead, such as batter, dough, custard, dry ingredients, and liquid ingredients. Jones also likes Child's mastery of visceral action words, such as toss, dump, pour, plop, and scrape. Another term she dislikes is "in a bowl, combine." "Recipe writing has become very sterile," she says. "People think you take the bowl out first. You don't always do it in a bowl, and why do you have to use six bowls?"

As you write your method, watch the length. There is such a thing as too much explanation. If the method becomes too long, simplify instructions or put preparation into the ingredients list, such as "1 cup cooked rice," or "2 red peppers, roasted and cut into thin strips."

When you state a time on how long to cook, stir, or bake, use a timer to ensure the times are accurate. Give a second visual description for doneness, such as "bake until the custard is set, or until the top becomes golden brown." Or "sauté butter until it turns to a nutty brown." Watch food as you cook and come up with accurate language, such as "stir until sauce thickens, hardens, or reduces."

Try not to use expensive or specialized tools readers might not have in their kitchens. Not everyone has a standing mixer or a food processor. Don't refer to appliances by brand names, such as the Cuisinart.

~~~~~~

ACTIONS WORTH EXPLAINING

People cook less and less. You don't want to intimidate them by using a term they don't understand. Doing so makes people feel stupid, then mad at themselves because they don't know the word.

The following words are some you should either avoid or, if using, explain exactly:

Blanch	Dice	Julienne
Blend	Deglaze	Pan-broil
Braise	Dredge	Poach
Combine	Flame off	Reduce
Cream	Fold	Sweat
Cube		

I'm holding out on sauté, although many writers now explain that too. And some people don't know what "separate the eggs" means. Move them further apart? I'm not kidding. A cookbook author told me someone just asked him that.

~~~~~~

Some terms require complex explanation and may bog down your method. Greg Patent, author of *Baking in America*, suggests that, because describing how to fold can take several sentences, you include a technique section where you can describe it once.

Sidebars or Notes

Sidebars come into play when you want to give miscellaneous information in more detail. The information is never essential to the recipe, and can be read if desired. They are often presented as part of the design, and might have a shaded background, lines around the text to create a box, or colored text. Subjects include:

- tips for preparation or technique (e.g., how to roast a pepper);
- serving suggestions or variations if you have a long list;
- how to choose a particular ingredient (e.g., look for clams that are tightly closed);
- additional details about ingredients;
- history or customs related to a dish.

Notes often serve the same purpose but go at the end of the recipe.

As you develop a recipe, keep track of the most current version by numbering and dating your various drafts and files. Keep all drafts. When you think you have a winner, review your recipe with a critical eye:

- Ask yourself whether your readers would make this dish. Does it meet their needs? Is it too complicated? Have you written a headnote that would draw them in?
- Make sure ingredients are listed specifically.
- Look for opportunities to explain a step more clearly.
- Look for missed steps, or steps in the wrong order.

- Check the ingredients list against the method.
- Check temperature times, yields, and pan sizes.
- Check that you have specified low, medium, or high heat and pan size when cooking on the stove.
- Check whether you handled all foods according to food-safety techniques.
- Look for wordiness or illogical reasoning.
- Examine earlier drafts to ensure you purposely changed the amounts.
- Banish typos.

Joan Nathan says that even when she thinks she is done, she will spot test a few recipes at random to ensure there are no mistakes.

When you start writing recipes you'll notice a certain amount of duplication in phrases and directions. Create a style sheet to ensure your recipe language is consistent. Use it to record unusual spellings and as a check on whether to use articles (a, an, the) in the method. This practice helped me enormously when I wrote *Grilled Pizzas & Piadinas*. I wanted to give instructions the same way for each pizza. They're still burned into my brain. "Brush the grilled side of the pizza crust with the Herbed Grill Oil. Dust with the Parmesan and sprinkle with the mozzarella."

Some styles have become standard: figures always come first in an ingredients list; and tablespoon, teaspoon, pound, and cup are spelled out. When you get a book contract, publishers usually give you their own recipe style guide to follow. Magazines and newspapers have certain styles as well. If you're uncertain, read the publication's published recipes to see what style they prefer.

Testing, the Final Frontier

I know this book is about writing, but you are not done with recipes until you or someone else tests them and successfully reproduces the dishes. I'm a fan of having mere mortals—or whomever best represents your potential readers—test your recipes. Otherwise you run the risk of making assumptions about what readers know or of leaving errors they might find.

On the other hand, I've interviewed experienced recipe writers who rely on their own judgment, since they are ultimately responsible for their own recipes. Mark Bittman says emphatically, "I develop and test. I don't hire testers. I don't really trust anyone else anyway." He adds, "My *Times* column is read by one million people per week. I probably get two or three mistakes a year, such as calling something Turkish when it should be Greek." Deborah Madison has written thousands of recipes and feels confident about the process. Sometimes she sends recipes to family, friends, and readers to try, but most often, she relies on herself. Paula Wolfert had not used testers until recently, when she met food enthusiasts from all over the world on email through Egullet.com and used them to test her recipes. "It was incredibly eye-opening," she says.

Joan Nathan says she likes to test everything in her book and still finds things she takes for granted. "I gave my daughter a recipe that asked for one pound of carrots. She gets everything from farmers' markets. She said she doesn't know what a pound is. So I decided it was about seven carrots." Nathan likes to keep in touch with readers. She finds that their result is not always the same as hers, even when they tell her they have made the recipe exactly. Readers also give her ideas. Someone who was allergic to coconut milk suggested using soymilk with coconut flavoring as a substitute, and Nathan says she would never have thought of that.

Nathan spends a day making six or seven recipes, hosts a dinner party for twelve, and then asks guests for their honest opinions. "My social life surrounds my cookbooks," she explains. Many other writers I've interviewed use this technique instead of recipe testers. Some feel recipe testers are not always trustworthy, as they might make unauthorized substitutions that will influence whether the dish succeeds, such as canned chilies instead of fresh ones, or kidney beans instead of pinto beans.

Some authors have testers come to their homes and cook. The authors watch the tester make a recipe. Like many authors, Nathan uses an assistant to help her test. She uses college interns three days per week, with one day set aside for cooking. Other writers might have assistants shop for them or prepare ingredients.

When testing your recipes, it's best not to give them to family members and friends. Chances are they will not be entirely honest in response, even if you give them a test sheet (see Test Sheet Sample Questions below) and tell them to be brutal. They may decide not to bring up something they don't like because they think their opinion isn't as valid as yours, or because they don't want to hurt your feelings. I also wouldn't give a recipe to a culinary school student or a professional recipe developer, unless they are your target readers. You want people you know slightly, who like to cook.

Many recipe writers don't pay testers. Others have found drawbacks to that system. Unpaid testers take forever and are less likely to provide thorough feedback, said cookbook author David Lebovitz (www.davidlebovitz.com) in an interview. "When money is involved, people take it more seriously." He has paid home testers fifty dollars to test three recipes. Others reimburse testers for ingredients. Regardless of how or whether you pay, acknowledge testers in your book.

If you have an online presence, you have testers built in. For Jaden Hair's first cookbook, she recruited testers on her Steamy Kitchen blog and got more than 200 testers. She asked them to test three recipes and provide honest feedback on specifics of the recipe and final dish, and to submit a photo of each dish. She found a volunteer to help manage the testers and testing feedback. She set up a private blog where they could respond, and as a reward, promised to name the testers in her book. After testing each recipe three times, David Leite of Leite's Culinaria (www.leitesculinaria.com) turned to 14 recipes testers, all of whom volunteer on his site, to test each dish in his cookbook, *The New Portuguese Table*. Paula Wolfert used members of Egullet to test recipes for *The Slow Mediterranean Kitchen*.

Nancy Baggett, author of *The All-American Cookie Book*, saved her developing and testing notes so she could show documentation if anyone asked. "Just for curiosity's sake," she adds, "I totaled up the testing and found I had made 38,000 cookies."

ADDING NUTRITIONAL DATA

If you want nutritional data for your recipes, such as calories and fat per serving, you have a few options: buy software, use professional services, or enter the info into free online calculators. Some software and recipe writing programs (see page 296) offer nutritional analysis and are less expensive than professional versions, which cost around $800. Keep in mind that the resulting information has room for error based on what you feed it. A "serving size," for example, determines the result, but there are no standards on what determines a size.

Some recipe developers hire dieticians or nutritionists who own their own software programs. "There are so many nuances to correctly entering data for specific ingredients that I prefer to leave it to someone who does it regularly, knows the standards, and preferably is a dietician," says Rosemary Mark, a recipe developer with clients including Haagen Dazs. "Someone who owns software should also be continuously updating with new ingredients and nutrition data."

If Mark needs approximate data, she uses free online software (such as www.nutritiondata.com or http://recipes.sparkpeople.com recipe-calculator.asp), but says they often don't have data for more unique ingredients. There's also the old-fashioned way of calculating each ingredient then adding them up using www.nal.usda.gov/fnic/food comp/search, but that's "very tedious," she adds.

By the end of this system of developing, writing, and testing, you should have a batch of well-written, accurate, consistent recipes. Look at all the benefits: If you've always wanted to create a lasting chronicle of your cooking, you will have succeeded. Great recipes mean editors will take you seriously. Readers who need explicit instructions will be grateful. And those who fantasized about making a dish like yours will get it right the first time.

TEST SHEET SAMPLE QUESTIONS

Whenever possible, ask questions that avoid a simple yes or no answer. Here are examples:

- Did you use the ingredients in the order listed?
- What kind of questions did you have about the directions?
- Did the ingredient quantities seem to work, or would you have added or subtracted anything? Were any ingredients difficult to find? What

was your substitution, if any, and how do you think it may have affected the dish?

- How would you evaluate the time it took to prepare the dish?
- Was there anything confusing about the recipe steps?
- How did you choose which utensils, cookware, or equipment to use? Would you prefer that be specified?
- How were your results? What did you like or dislike about the flavors, textures, and tastes of the dish?
- What was visually appealing about the dish?
- How would you evaluate portion sizes, preparation times, and level of difficulty, on a scale of one to ten for each? Please elaborate on your answer. Say if anything was too hard or too time consuming.
- How does this dish taste to you, on a scale of one to ten?
- How likely would you be to make this dish again? Why or why not?
- How did this recipe compare with similar ones you have tried before?
- Overall comments?

~~~~~~

REFERENCE BOOKS

- *Food Lover's Companion,* by Sharon Herbst. Definitions of culinary terms, origins of foods, and explanations of techniques.
- *The Recipe Writer's Handbook,* by Barbara Gibbs Ostmann and Jane Baker. Much more detail than I could ever include here.
- *Recipes Into Type: A Handbook for Cookbook Writers and Editors,* by Joan Whitman and Dolores Simon. A good complementary book to the above, as they have different content and organization.
- *The Oxford Companion to Food.* Useful for clarifications on ingredients and for writing headnotes.
- *On Food and Cooking: The Science and Lore of the Kitchen,* by Harold McGee. Scientific explanation, culinary lore, and food history in a fascinating compendium.
- *Cookwise: The Secrets of Cooking Revealed,* by Shirley Corriher. Explanations of how certain outcomes of cooking occur and will help you understand how to make changes.
- Your own cookbook collection. When words fail me on how to explain a technique, write a headnote, or describe an ingredient, I often turn to trusted authors to see how they do it. Aside from the ones

mentioned in this chapter, other outstanding recipe writers are Richard Olney, Craig Claiborne, Rose Levy Beranbaum, Madeleine Kamman, and Flo Braker.

- For historic recipes, consider the work of Escoffier, Caréme, and Pomaine.
- Other styles: Edouard de Pomaine, an early twentieth-century food writer, often wrote the method in the second person, telling you what you see and smell. Elizabeth David writes recipes in narrative style rather than listing the ingredients first. Instead she specified them within the method, and the method is all that appears. James Beard used this style as well in *Delights and Prejudices.*

~~~~~~

Writing Exercises

1. Write a recipe for your favorite sandwich. Include a headnote at least three sentences long. Now check your ability to be specific. Did you ask for a certain type of bread, or for slices of a certain thickness? Did you specify the type of mustard (not the brand name)? If you called for an exotic mayonnaise like aioli, did you include the recipe? Did you specify special equipment, such as a panini maker? If so, describe how readers can make the sandwich without it.

2. Find origins. In your files, find a half-dozen handwritten recipes given to you by others, with no credit listed. Contact each person to find out where the recipe originated. If they can't remember, consider how you would alter each recipe to make it your own, or what you would write in the headnote to explain the situation.

3. Determine the sophistication level of your readers. If you plan to write a cookbook, look in your cupboards and refrigerator, and list foods and spices you think your target reader probably will not have. Decide which will be essential to your cookbook, and which you could leave out or use substitutions.

9

Memoir
and Nonfiction
Food Writing

In the last decade or so, hundreds of books on every possible subject related to food have flooded the shelves. Fueled by the success of Ruth Reichl's best-seller memoir *Tender at the Bone: Growing Up at the Table*, they picked up steam. Food history books, once thought obscure and esoteric, entered the mainstream with books like *Cod: A Biography of the Fish that Changed the World* and *Salt: A World History*. Single-subject books on topics such as chocolate, oranges, and vanilla abound. Guidebooks on food and travel, biographies, and exposés such as *Fast Food Nation: The Dark Side of the American Meal* have crossed over into other categories of the bookstore. Reference books demystifying foods, their origins, and uses are plentiful.

The growth of the non-cookbook food-writing world makes me wonder if the cookbook section of bookstores will be renamed. So if you prefer not to write a cookbook, or if you've already written a cookbook and want to try another form, consider food-based books. To succeed at narrative or reference food writing, you have to be a great detective and researcher rather than an expert. After all, what is the appropriate background of someone who wants to write a book on, say, the history of barbecue?

Take Andrew Smith, author of several books including the *Oxford Encyclopedia of Food and Drink in America*, who had no expertise in food when he started writing for publication. In fact, his field is international relations. Smith entered the food-writing world after using a candy bar to explain complicated international topics to fourth graders. He pointed to a map of the world to show where chocolate comes from, where it's manufactured, and where the money from candy bar sales goes. He realized that talking about food is a great way to get people interested in "all the things they wouldn't normally care about," such as history, culture, and science.

This chapter talks mostly about memoir, the largest category of non-cookbooks, and the closest to a traditional cookbook, since it usually includes recipes. From there you'll find lots of other possibilities that will help you with your own ideas of what to write, whether on history, cultural anthropology and philosophy, reference, guidebooks, biographies, food and health, adventures, and politics. The door's wide open for food-based books.

Food-based Memoir

Many of my coaching clients and students want to write memoirs. Why are we attracted to this genre? We use our love of food to access family, culture, and emotions. First-person books based on food memory are usually joyous, even when the memories evoked are bittersweet. Some are filled with intimate memories of life, love, and food, particularly the memoir-like *The Gastronomical Me* by M. F. K. Fisher.

One of Fisher's disciples, Ruth Reichl, the former editor of *Gourmet*, came out with her first memoir in 1986. She single-handedly fired up a new generation of food memoirists with the best-selling *Tender at the Bone: Growing Up at the Table*, a sensuous coming-of-age tale of a career spent following her appetite.

"It had been a forgotten genre," recalls Reichl. "M. F. K. Fisher had done it, then nobody had done it again until 50 years later. I didn't understand it was going to be a game-changing book. It touched a nerve. I feel like my whole career, my timing is based on that I was interested in food when almost no one in America was. Then suddenly everyone was interested and I was the person already there."

Her sequel, *Comfort Me with Apples: More Adventures at the Table*, gave further credibility to food-based memoir as a category. Her third memoir, *Garlic and Sapphires: The Secret Life of a Critic in Disguise*, about her adventures as a restaurant reviewer, is being made into a movie. Other food-based memoirs made into movies are Julie Powell's *Julie & Julia: My Year of Cooking Dangerously*; Kathleen Flinn's *The Sharper the Knife, the More You Cry: Love, Laughter and Tears in Paris at the World's Most Famous Cooking School*; and Ree Drummond's memoir, *Black Heels to Tractor Wheels*.

One year after Reichl's first memoir debuted, Frances Mayes caused a sensation with *Under the Tuscan Sun: At Home in Italy*, a memoir about fixing up a rural Italian villa, living with her husband, and cooking. It also included recipes. In 2000, Anthony Bourdain's classic, *Kitchen Confidential: Adventures in the Culinary Underbelly*, became a *New York Times* bestseller. More recently, another blog-to-book memoirs arrived, headed by Molly Wizenberg's *A Homemade Life: Stories and Recipes from My Kitchen Table*, a coming-of-age memoir based on her blog, Orangette.

These memoirs aren't just about food, and that is why they succeed. Adept storytellers write about people and relationships, where conflict between characters is as important as stellar meals. The most successful food-based memoirs combine extraordinary stories with beautiful writing. "It seems to me that any good memoir is about relationships and telling events so it doesn't matter if it's about food or not," says Amanda Hesser, author of the memoir *Cooking for Mr. Latte: A Food Lover's Courtship, with Recipes*. "Food can provide an organizing principle to the book or can serve as a sensual element or symbolism, but if the core narrative isn't there, it's not going to be a very interesting memoir."

"What makes good food writing is an exploration of the way that food shapes our lives, the way we interact with food, the way that food is a part of our relationships and the shape of our lives," agrees Wizenberg. "Not everyone thinks about food the way you and I do, but food gives their lives a certain shape, and they all have emotions and strong opinions about it."

Food-based memoir has its own characteristics. It may sound obvious, but the stories must center on food. "This is both limiting and liberating," explains Shoba Narayan, author of *Monsoon Diary: A Memoir with Recipes*. "Limiting because you don't include aspects of your life story that are not food related. Liberating because this gives it a tight structure and therefore one less thing the writer has to obsess about."

While many excellent books can guide you through the general topic of memoir writing (see Great Books on Memoir Writing, page 228), they do not cover the specifics of this particular genre. Here are the most important characteristics:

Food memories: Reconstruct meals and dialogue around the table, cooking events, and how you learned about food and food traditions. Describe the sights, tastes, sounds, and smells of the kitchen and who was there. Tell people about what they couldn't possibly have tasted or known by themselves.

Focus on the senses: Most of your scenes will take place in locations where food and eating are at the forefront, whether it's in the kitchen, dining room, garden, restaurant, market, cooking school, cafeteria, picnic area, or the woods. Put the reader there with you, experiencing all the sensations. Here's an example from *Comfort Me with Apples*, where Reichl watches a chef at work in the kitchen: "Mr. Chen told me to taste it and then asked if I could guess the secret ingredient. I felt as if it was a test, so I tried really hard. There was an indefinable richness to the dish, and I thought of that golden liquid, and guessed chicken fat. Mr. Chen was delighted with me."

Sophisticated storyteller Isabelle Allende's *Aphrodite: A Memoir of the Senses*, her lusty celebration of sex and food, takes a different approach by combining more than 100 recipes with poems, stories, photos and drawings, and discussions on the sensual art of food, attracting your mate, and the effect of smell on libido.

Recipes: Just about every food memoir I've read includes recipes, except for those by restaurant critics and the memoirs of farmer Mas Masumoto such as *Epitaph of a Peach: Four Seasons on My Family Farm*.

The number of recipes to include seems to be up to you. Some books contain just one or two at the end of each chapter. Some have dozens. Reichl has said that in her first book the story drove the recipes, while in her second the recipes drove the story. Hesser's book contained more than 100 recipes, on the other hand. Says Hesser, "I included recipes because I'm a cook and I wanted readers to be able to taste what I was talking about—if they were motivated, that is."

Decide whether recipes are fundamental to your book's story, whether they deepen it and add texture and context. In Hesser's book about her relationship with a man who later became her husband, she detailed the meal her future mother-in-law made, the first meal Hesser made for Mr. Latte, and the first meal he made for her. These events are critical to the book's story line.

Memoir has characteristics particular to its genre as well. The first is that it covers a certain period of time, perhaps a single aspect of your life. It's not your life story, or you would call it an autobiography. Memoir tells of an emotional, physical, or psychological journey you experienced over a certain time, such as going to culinary school, or moving to Japan to learn a tea ceremony. The best memoirs read like novels. This style is called literary nonfiction, or narrative non-fiction, in which the quality of writing is as important as the story. Here are the elements of memoir:

- Insights are critical. The story is not just about what you did, but how what you did changed or affected you. Without these insights, the book will be a recounting, with little liveliness and depth.
- The story evokes emotion from the reader.
- Strong characters come alive on the page. Even more minor characters need vitality. Describe the person's appearance in specific detail to create a picture for the reader. One writer who excels at character study is Ludwig Bemelmans. His hilarious memoir *Hotel Bemelmans,* a behind-the-scenes tell-all about a New York hotel in the 1920s, was recently reissued.
- The dialogue of your characters rings true. In writing *Kitchen Confidential: Adventures in the Culinary Underbelly,* author Anthony Bourdain said in an interview that he "did not want real working cooks and restaurant people to read the thing and say, 'What the hell is this? I don't know any chefs who talk like this! This is not my life!'"
- You tell the truth. "If you're not honest, it's boring," says Hesser. "It's the texture of relationships that's interesting, and if you smooth it all out, it's going to be insipid."

- You use plot devices from fiction, such as conflict, suspense, and tension, by creating desire. "All storytelling from the beginning of recorded time is based on somebody wanting something, facing obstacles, not getting it, trying to get it, trying to overcome obstacles, and finally getting or not getting what he wanted," writes Sol Stein in *Stein on Writing*.
- Your book has a story arc. This is the critical point in a novel, where tension is at its highest, and you have used suspense to build up to this moment. "The biggest thing was finding my way to a story with a narrative arc," says Wizenberg. "It required diving in. I didn't know what the arc was going to be until it was there."
- Your conclusion shows how your life and impressions have changed, and the consequences of that change upon you.

You might start by figuring out the reason you want to write a memoir in the first place. Does it fill a powerful need? Do you have an unusual story or a life-changing experience? Was it the first time you did something? Did you overcome adversity in a way that will inspire others? Do you want to record an event from the past, your accomplishments, family history, meals you ate, or recipes?

If you're worried your life might be too boring, you're not alone. Hesser said as much in an interview. Even though she was a full-time *New York Times* writer, she said she was afraid she wouldn't be able to find or gather stories. "I didn't want it to be just self-involved blather about my life," she admitted. Even though it's hard, keep your inner critic at bay. Hesser knew she had a good story. She probably felt vulnerable by publishing such personal aspects of her life. You must believe you have a good story, too, particularly if you have told it and people respond positively.

GREAT BOOKS ON MEMOIR WRITING

- *Writing Life Stories*, by Bill Roorbach
- *Inventing the Truth: The Art and Craft of Memoir*, by William Zinsser
- *Writing About Your Life: A Journey Into the Past*, by William Zinsser

- *Old Friend from Far Away: How to Write a Memoir,* by Natalie Goldberg
- *Unreliable Truth,* by Maureen Murdock

When thinking about your topic, consider how your experiences relate to readers and their lives. Sometimes things that fascinate you will not translate well to your readers. If you deal with universal themes of accomplishment, such as graduating from culinary school, taking a fantasy trip abroad, or leaving home and forging your own life and cooking style, you are more likely to succeed. Make readers feel as though they are experiencing your story, help them learn, or give them inspiration to duplicate your experience for themselves. Show them how the world works. To do so, you'll have to get out of the way. Otherwise readers will be passive, reading about you and what you did, and not experiencing your story directly. Be part of the scene without dominating it.

Here's an example from A. J. Liebling, who pays for his feasts in Paris with money wired from his parents. He writes in *Between Meals: An Appetite for Paris,* "At the Credit, I would be received with scornful solemnity, like a suitor for the hand of a miser's daughter. I was made to sit on a bare wooden bench with the other wretches come to claim money from the bank, all feeling more like culprits by the minute. A French bank, by the somber intensity of its addiction to money, establishes an emotional claim on funds in transit. The client feels in the moral position of a wayward mother who has left her babe on a doorstep and later comes back to claim it from the foster parents, who now consider it their own."

Can't you imagine Liebling at the bank, seething? You share his disgust and discomfort, right down to how it feels to sit on a hard surface. You agree that the bank is unreasonable to treat him this way, because things like this have happened to you. And you're having fun reading his diatribe because it's witty. On the other hand, he could have written, "I really hate going to the bank. I don't like the way they treat me. I feel like I've done something wrong. They have no right to keep me from my money." Now, it's all about him, not about the scene. You don't know where he is, you feel no compassion or outrage, and there's no humor to provide levity. You watch him have a tantrum, from a distance. That's boring.

Your story must seem real to readers, and you must have enough distance to make realistic assessments of where you were emotionally at the time. If readers are not convinced, it doesn't really matter what happened or how it unfolded. Many people use memoirs as a form of therapy. It's fine to do so, but your story may not be publishable if you are the only one who understands the course of events, or if there is no action or dialogue. You must be capable of objectivity about that period in your life. If not, turn it into fiction.

In memoir as in fiction writing, your character and tone are essential to the book. As Amanda Hesser said earlier in this book, she had to make herself into a character as well, even one that wasn't exactly true to life. I like memoirs that show a writer's excitement about that fascinating part of his or her life and the wonder of it. Victoria Riccardi, author of *Untangling My Chopsticks: A Culinary Sojourn in Kyoto,* said in an interview that her approach was, "What a gift to be here." Another way to show character is to use humor and self-denigration in your writing.

Be an expert on you. If you want to write a memoir about summers you spent on tourist farms in Umbria, you're the expert about your experience. You don't have to be an expert on farming or food. Those subjects are secondary to the story. Do enough research on these subjects to put your tale in perspective and provide enough context.

In food-based memoirs, nostalgia can be boring. No one wants to read about a perfect past of discovering food during childhood, where a loving mother and grandmother were ingenious cooks who made complicated meals by hand. Avoid sentimentality as your main theme. Be willing to write about something mundane or imperfect. Write about how the person across from you at the restaurant ate lunch. It will train you not to be so emotionally attached, and your writing will change for the better.

Memoir writing includes extensive research so that you can choose which details to include. If your memoir captures your family's past, look for documents other than recipes that give clues about that time, such as marriage and death certificates, letters, maps, family trees, photos, music, movies, and magazines from that era to give you a sense of the times. If you plan to write about an adventure while you are living it, such as cooking on a houseboat in France, collect and save the things around you to unlock memories later. Take photos. Write in a daily journal. Save menus, tickets, and relevant newspaper stories.

If certain people are critical characters in your story, interview them now. You think they'll always be around and there's time, but you can't be certain. I conducted oral histories with my aunt and mother before they died. Now I have a transcript of their memories. I can listen to the tapes to add texture and credibility to my characters. On the tape, I hear how my auntie paused to take long drags on her cigarette, for example, and the raspy quality of her voice.

Know how the story ends. A big part of defining your memoir is to determine where it stops. You have to be over the experience to put it into perspective. When you write your story, you will lead up to the end, foreshadowing it throughout the book, and you must know what to conclude. Your book must have a definable beginning, middle, and end. In *Animal, Vegetable, Miracle*, by Barbara Kingsolver, the subtitle says it all: *A Year of Food Life*.

The structure of a memoir can be a series of anecdotes, vignettes, or essays strung together into a larger, overarching narrative. It can be chronological or written as diary entries. A memoir is not about every event, or even the most important ones during that time, unless they are relevant to the central story of your book. Organizing a long project like this requires vigilance. You will continuously distill and discard, and it may take you some time to get to the exact theme to pursue. You may write a list of points you wish to make, or a skeleton or outline, and change it several times. That means you're making progress because you're thinking it through.

If you feel apprehensive about exposing certain thoughts or incidents, there are ways to create boundaries between yourself and readers. Just as you want to be careful not to overdo the emotional aspects of your past, you must be prepared to live with whatever you disclose about yourself. Reichl said she "didn't talk about the really bad stuff in the first book. I didn't want to hurt people's memories." At the same time, your duty is to tell the essential emotional truth, and not get lost in what you think you should be feeling. You don't have to reveal everything about yourself. Choose what's essential to the story, and reveal these secrets throughout the book.

To play it safe, some writers employ false names for individuals they want to protect, those who might be hurt or upset by the way they are portrayed. Because I was trained as a reporter, I'm not fond of this technique, where emphasis is on telling the literal truth. Since no two people remember an event or individual exactly the same way, however, writers can take license, as long as the point is to bring out the inherent truthfulness of the story. Some authors also merge characters or alter the setting or timing. That sounds like fiction to me, but you have to decide what you can live with. If you're afraid you can't accurately reconstruct a conversation, put a disclaimer in the front of the book saying you did your best to get the essence of what people said.

Typically, you shouldn't let the people mentioned in your book read your manuscript before it's published, because they will find things they don't like. Find ways to reassure them without getting specific about their role in the book. If you're afraid you'll hurt or embarrass a loved one, make that person less identifiable in the book. If you write something potentially damaging, a publisher might ask for a written consent form from that person.

Reichl got permission from Colman Andrews, co-founder of *Saveur*, to write about their affair. She didn't send him the manuscript. Andrews told me the story: "She took me to lunch at Fleur de Sel in Manhattan and told me she had written about me and our relationship in the book, then asked my permission to use my real name and the actual circumstances. If I was uncomfortable with that, she said, she would be willing to give me a pseudonym and change some identifying details. She added that she didn't think I'd mind anything she had written.

"On the principle that one probably shouldn't do anything in life that one wouldn't be willing to read about later, I told her to go ahead and use the 'real' me. And as I told her later, it turned out I did mind some of what she had written, not because it made me seem like a cad (which I probably was), but because it made me sound so humorless about food and wine, which I'd like to think I wasn't. But ultimately, I can't complain. She did a good job of capturing the spirit of the times (and of our relationship), even if she played a bit fast and loose—as she readily admits—with the facts."

For more on writing memoir, read some of the books I listed or take classes to jumpstart your writing. Now, let's go on to all the other kinds of books that are neither cookbooks nor memoirs. Below are several other genres of food-based books to choose from. Many of these categories cross over each other, so there's no need to feel limited.

Food History

Do you wonder about the history of foods, cooking, food preparation, and food etiquette? Consider writing about food from the past and providing new insights. Many forms of food-based books include history. For memoir, you'll want to find your own culinary history and family information about who cooked where and what they made. For a book about travels in Mexico, you might want to investigate the origin of tortillas, if that's part of the adventure. Researching origins and significance of foods in history make the material come alive.

If you are passionate about a subject that requires delving into history, your book can bring fresh perspectives to old stories, says food historian Sandy Oliver. So many questions need answers. She's curious about so many things, such as "What did the pilgrims eat for the first Thanksgiving? Was the Italian Catherine de Médici responsible for French haute cuisine? Is it true that people spiced meat highly in past times to hide the bad taste of spoilage?"

While many food history books languish in obscurity, some make their way into the mainstream, as demonstrated by Mark Kurlansky's *Cod* and David Camp's *The United States of Arugula: The Sun-Dried, Cold-Pressed, Extra-Virgin Story of the American Food Revolution*. Most historians wouldn't think of food as an appropriate category, says author Andy Smith. The field was wide open when he entered it twenty years ago. He believes it still is. "Anybody can pick a topic," he says. "The secret is to talk to people about things they know but have never thought about before, and are shocked and surprised when you start giving them context."

What all good food history books have in common is the hundreds of hours of careful research authors put into them. Accuracy is paramount. "If you're working from your own memory [as in a memoir], no big deal, but in a historical context, you have to be right," says Oliver, author of the award-winning book, *Saltwater Foodways*. To research historical cooking, you must go past theorizing and recreate the food as accurately as possible, she says. If you're interested in fireplace cooking, for example, "Go find a fireplace and cook something in it. Or take a vacation. Or visit house museums. Living History museums sponsor all kinds of weekends," Oliver advises.

To get started, she suggests you "go to the library and read everything you can lay your hands on for a week or more. Or do library research on the Internet. Use Google. Find out what the standards are." Rather than work in isolation, get to know other food historians who can advise you on how to write food history well. She lists culinary history groups across the country on www.foodhistorynews.com.

For general information on writing food history, and for a lively discussion as food history is being made, go to http://food-culture .org/listserv.php and join the Association of the Study of Food and Society's listserv, where academics and historians exchange information about everything from cannibalism to vegan diets. A listserve allows you to broadcast a message to a group without knowing the addresses of each member.

How long does it take to write a history book? Oliver estimates that writing a one-subject book can be covered in a year or two. "Grab something out of your life experience that interests you terribly," she advises. That's good advice for any kind of book.

Cultural Anthropology and Philosophy

These books study the social, symbolic, political, and economic roles of food and cultures. Often written by academics, they may require peer review and are often published by university presses. Some emerge from masters' theses or doctoral dissertations.

These books have a hard time getting into the mainstream, partly because they are written in a scholarly tone for a specialized audience, and are often expensive to purchase. Many cite previous works and are heavily footnoted, perhaps intimidating the casual reader. Plus, they are not as accessible as books in the cookbook section of bookstores. Instead, search for them in the history, philosophy, or anthropology sections. For example, my paperback edition of *No Foreign Food: The American Diet in Time and Place,* by geography professor Richard Pillsbury, suggests on its back cover that it be placed in "American/cultural studies."

Some books in this category cross over. *Much Depends on Dinner: The Extraordinary History and Mythology, Allure and Obsessions, Perils and Taboo of an Ordinary Meal,* by Margaret Visser, tells the story behind ordinary items found on the American dinner table, such as butter, salt, and roast chicken. *USA Today* reviewed *We Are What We Eat: Ethnic Food and the Making of Americans,* by Donna R. Gabaccia, and said, "Today's multiethnic American diet offers intriguing insight into the character of the nation. . . . Gabaccia explores the journey of these ethnic foods from pushcarts to the national marketplace and how . . . ethnic cuisines have retained their essential and often ritualized role in American life."

Another respected book is the anthology *Food and Culture: A Reader,* edited by anthropology professors Carole Counihan and Penny Van Esterik. It examines the social, symbolic, and political-economic roles of what—and how—we eat. While M. F. K. Fisher and Frances Moore Lappé (*Diet for a Small Planet*) penned two of the essays, academics, historians, cultural anthropologists, and researchers wrote the rest. Topics in this kind of food writing can be challenging to the general reader. Take this opening sentence from the essay "Food as a Cultural Construction," by Anna Meigs, an associate professor of anthropology: "Eating for the Hua people of the Eastern Highlands of Papua New Guinea is one of several ways in which physical properties and 'vital essence' are transferred between objects and organisms." I'm sure she wrote a distinguished work, having made it into this anthology, but the subject matter caters to a narrow audience.

Reference

These books are structured as a series of listings, like dictionaries, where you look up something to do with food. Sharon Tyler Herbst spent years refining and updating various versions of the *Food Lover's Companion.* Her book has sold more than one million copies. Another book I love and use regularly in my kitchen is David Joachim's *Food Substitution Bible*, which tells me exactly what and how much to use when I don't have the required recipe ingredient on hand.

Smaller reference works on the subject of your passion might be a bit less ambitious and more doable. Former *New York Times* restaurant critic William Grimes wrote *Eating Your Words: 2,000 Words to Tease Your Taste Buds*, as the kind of book he could have used on the job. It includes a long list of types of mushrooms from agaric to yellow-foot, a definition of court bouillon, and short essays on such topics as defining a hoagie. If general topics seem too enormous, tackle a narrower subject that serves as more of a guide. Some of these books do quite well. Ben Schott's quirky *Schott's Food & Drink Miscellany* contains an addictive blend of oddities, such as how to cook a swan, how Hemingway liked his martinis, and why asparagus makes your urine smell. *Newsweek* called it "as hilarious as it is addictive," and *Vanity Fair* reviewed it as "utterly indispensable."

Even the big reference books don't take forever. Editor Andy Smith told me his *Oxford Encyclopedia of Food and Drink in America* was published three years after he got the contract. He hired dozens of freelance writers who wrote entries and indexes. Like other big reference books on food, the *Encyclopedia* is an invaluable research tool. If you don't want to buy these huge books, go to a library large enough to keep them. The best known are:

- *The Cambridge World History of Food*
- *The Oxford Companion to Food*
- *The Encyclopedia of Food and Culture* (part of Scribner Library of Daily Life)
- *The Oxford Encyclopedia of Food and Drink in America*

Literary lists are another form of food reference. If you enjoy searching publications for pithy quotes, you could collect your findings in a compendium of witty one-liners and quotes about food. Some books trace the history of words and explain their usage. Lists of historical cookbooks or food-based poems, bibliographies by people who collect cookbooks, and books with meal suggestions for reading groups are just a few of the book ideas that might inspire you.

If you like essays, anthologies are a good way to get your first book or essay published. Get permission to collect essays, book excerpts, or other writing forms and write an introduction. Holly Hughes created an instant annual work when she compiled the first *Best Food Writing* in 2000. She guaranteed her success with a foreword by Alice Waters, and the series is still going strong annually.

Guidebooks, Both Local and Abroad

If you like to travel—even locally—and you've devoted yourself to finding insider information, you could write a guidebook. Packed with useful, practical information, these books are written by those who pick an area and become experts on it, guiding the reader with careful research. These days, they compete with the Internet for in-depth, up-to-date information, which makes them more challenging to publish.

Laura Taxel spent two years writing *Cleveland Ethnic Eats,* a profitable guidebook. If you're considering writing one of your own, here is her advice:

- Look for an unmet need, a lack of organized, easy-to-use, easy-to-access information on a topic people want to discover.
- Define a specific geographic area to cover.
- The yellow pages already exists, so don't think all you have to do is gather names, addresses, and phone numbers. A guidebook's value is in the personalized, value-added information a knowledgeable author provides.
- Invest time and legwork in gathering a significant sample of your listings, and put together a meaningful representation of the book's content before you take your idea to a publisher.
- A guidebook requires a big investment of time and out-of-pocket expense up front. You'll have to pay for your own transportation costs, food bills, and telephone calls.
- View your guidebook as an ongoing project. Regular updates require a steady infusion of new and corrected information.

If you've written a book that sells, you'll have to keep it up to date. Taxel revises hers annually. "You won't make big bucks fast, but it can become a steady source of revenue and make you a recognized expert in a particular market, which leads to many other writing and speaking opportunities," says Taxel. "That's what *Cleveland Ethnic Eats* has done for me."

Take the same kind of guidelines and go abroad to your most beloved tourist destination. You may want to pitch a book idea to a travel based publisher, such as the *Eat Smart* culinary travel guides from Gingko Press, which published such books as *Eat Smart in Poland: How to Decipher the Menu, Know the Market Foods & Embark on a Tasting Adventure.* What you decide to write depends on your area of interest, your ability to find information meaningful to other visitors, and whether you have the means to travel and pay your own bills.

Biographies

Fascinated by a certain figure in the food world? Write a biography. Laura Shapiro, an accomplished author of two historical books, *Perfection Salad: Women and Cooking at the Turn of the Century* and *Something from the Oven: Reinventing Dinner in 1950s America,* turned to a biography of Julia Child after Child's death. She calls the book "an extended essay about Child and her impact on the culture, who she was and what she meant. I could only do it after her death. It's more of an appreciative analysis," she explains.

How do you come up with the right person to profile? It can be anyone who strikes a chord. "You have to want to lose yourself in that person. That person has to be big and interesting enough, or small and interesting enough, with depth you can throw yourself into," says Shapiro.

Two other examples of biographies publishers found worthwhile are *Stand Facing the Stove: The Story of the Women Who Gave America the* Joy of Cooking, which chronicles the lives of *Joy of Cooking* author Irma Rombauer and her daughter; and *Cooking for Kings: The Life of Antonin Careme, the First Celebrity Chef,* which examines the life of Europe's most famous chef.

Shapiro says the biographies she used as guides are two about James Beard: *Epicurean Delight: The Life and Times of James Beard,* by Evan Jones, and *James Beard: A Biography,* by Robert Clark.

Food and Health

Health writing uses food as a vehicle to help readers feel better. Most are advice-based cookbooks, written by doctors, nutritionists, and dietitians, with a few chapters of advice in the front.

Your decision about what to write will be fueled by your enthusiasm, interest, experience, and ability to find credible information. If you feel you need expertise, team up with an expert and co-write the book. Ask experts for access to their information and credit them in the book. Or interview experts and quote them to give more credibility to your project.

Kitchen Science

The best-known book on kitchen science is *On Food and Cooking: The Science and Lore of the Kitchen,* by Harold McGee, a reference book that explains everything from lactose intolerance to the composition of a corn kernel. He wrote it as a companion guide to cookbooks in which readers could discover more in-depth information about cooking, particularly the chemistry, history, and uses of foods.

McGee taught English and writing at Yale University, and trained as a physicist and astronomer. Recently he updated and expanded the book into a more general food reference book. His biggest problem was knowing where to stop. "Writing half a page about coffee isn't going to cut it anymore," he admits. He thought ten pages would be better, but "each subject is fascinating and could be a book." When I asked him how he could verify the accuracy of hundreds of entries, he said, "You do the best you can, then the world decides whether you did a good job. It has to do with personal standards. If you skim the subject, you are most likely to make mistakes. I try to burrow down a few stages and then I feel confident about the material." This is excellent advice for researching any kind of book, but then again, it took him ten years to write the second edition.

If you want to write about how to become a better cook by under-standing science, this category might be for you. To see what's re-quired, research a few books that have done well. These books include lots of recipes, while McGee's book does not. They cover similar top-ics but have their own personalities. Here are some examples:

- *What Einstein Told His Cook: Kitchen Science Explained* an-swers more than 100 questions on such topics as why water boils and freezers burn, and which frying pan is best. Author Robert Wolke is a retired chemistry professor and food columnist for the *Washington Post.*
- Biochemist Shirley Corriher wrote *Cookwise: The Secrets of Cooking Revealed,* and *Bakewise*: *The Hows and Whys of Suc-cessful Baking,* about the way food works in a recipe, to enable cooks to get the results they want. Her books explains such things as why cookies made with butter turn out flat and crisp, while cookies made with some shortening are soft and puffy.
- *I'm Just Here for the Food: Food + Heat = Cooking,* by the Food Network's Alton Brown, explains cooking principles to peo-ple in their twenties and thirties.
- Russ Parsons' *How to Read a French Fry: And Other Stories of Intriguing Kitchen Science* focuses on scientific principles as well.

Adventures, Journalism, and Essays

Many of the categories in this chapter overlap, particularly here, where adventure-based, journalistic books are likely to include memoir, food politics, and food history.

If you're interested in chronicling a hands-on experience, such as at-tending cooking school or working in a restaurant, you've come upon a topic publishers like. Bill Buford, a staff writer for the *New Yorker,* wrote *Heat: An Amateur Cook's Adventures as a Kitchen Slave, Pasta Maker, and Apprentice to a Dante-Quoting Butcher on a Hilltop in Tus-cany.* That's the longest subtitle I've ever read. In *The Making of a Chef: Mastering Heat at the Culinary Institute,* Michael Ruhlman explains how the most prominent cooking school in the country trains chefs, and included his own thoughts as he went through the process. Both books are also memoirs, capturing a slice of time in the authors' lives.

Speaking of culinary adventures, *A Cook's Tour,* chef Anthony Bourdain's politically incorrect world tour, chews up and spits out the usual food/travel journalism where a writer might typically discuss more rarified meals such as a long, luxurious dinner at three-star Taillevent in Paris. (Not that there's anything wrong with it. *A Meal Observed,* by Andrew Todhunter, does just that.) Bourdain, a first-rate chef and now host of his own television show, *No Reservations*, took what was then a new approach. Here's his first sentence, in the form of a letter to his wife: "I'm about as far away from you as I've ever been—a hotel (*the* hotel, actually) in Pailin, a miserable one-horse dunghole in northwest Cambodia, home to those not-so-adorable scamps, the Khmer Rouge."

If you have a reporting background and don't mind causing trouble, you might investigate a part of the food industry. *The Jungle,* a novel by Upton Sinclair, set the standard in 1905 when Lewis exposed the inhumane conditions of Chicago's stockyards. Most investigative reporting is nonfiction, however. Eric Schlosser's *Fast Food Nation: The Dark Side of the All-American Meal* enjoyed a deservingly long ride on the best-seller lists because of his prescient timing, excellent journalism, and passionate writing. *Food Politics: How the Food Industry Influences Nutrition and Health,* by Marion Nestle, takes an insider's perspective. It's an eye-opening read as well.

UC Berkeley Journalism Professor and Science Writer Michael Pollan eclipsed them all, however, with *The Omnivore's Dilemma,* which examines America's "national eating disorder" by tracing four meals, and subsequent books *In Defense of Food* and *Food Rules*, each with several weeks on bestseller lists.

"More people feel that food is the solution. That is, they see food as the way to change the world around them," explained Brian Halwell on Edible Manhattan. "As a result, food writers carry the weight of the world on their shoulders. People don't learn how to eat from doctors and nutritionists anymore, they learn from Michael Pollan and Barbara Kingsolver.

"In this sense, food writers today have more in common with Upton Sinclair than with Maureen Dowd, or with restaurant reviewers, for that matter. That is, food writers are required to keep the bigger context in mind; are required to shine a light not just on a restaurant's service or noise level, but on how the foods got to the plate. Weaving in issues of sustainability and ethics must be done tactfully and artfully, but it must be done."

If you're not into issues of sustainability, company profiles are popular ways to write about food and who controls the food industry. *The Emperors of Chocolate: Inside the Secret World of Hershey and Mars* looks at the chocolate wars between the two industry giants. A background as a reporter would be particularly useful here, as this is not a vanity book, where the company approves the book before it can be published and often controls its content. But that's not out of the question either, if you want a work-for-hire position where you are retained to write a company's history. A related book, *Candyfreak: A Journey Through the Chocolate Underbelly of America,* takes more of a travel memoir approach from the perspective of the candy-obsessed author, Steve Almond.

Another type of nonfiction book combines self-contained stories written in essay form. Most often, these books comprise stories previously published in a magazine. The writing can be literary, entertaining, or educational—or all three—and often combines reporting and adventure. My favorite witty, hilarious essayists are Jeffrey Steingarten of *Vogue* magazine and Calvin Trillin, a freelancer for the *New Yorker.*

Fran Gage's first book, *Bread and Chocolate: My Food Life In and Around San Francisco,* began as a book about nuts. Her book proposal included a fervent, long essay on chestnuts. When her agent showed her proposal to an editor, he liked the chestnut piece so much he asked Gage to write more for a book about the Bay Area food scene, with recipes. At that point, the sum of Gage's published writing experience was a newsletter about her defunct bakery. "I just started writing and it sort of worked out somehow," she says modestly.

To come up with topics for her essays, she made a list of foods divided by those she felt passionate about, those she knew could become a story, or those for which she could visit the people who made or grew the foods. When she found crayfish in a farmers' market, for example, she figured she could write about the crayfish itself and going fishing with her children when they were little. Gage asked the crayfish vendor to accompany her on her fishing boat, and "There I had an essay in three parts." Gage thought up an essay based on a trip to the market, a memory, a conclusion that research would be doable, and a fishing trip with a vendor. Sometimes great ideas can be serendipitous in the way they come together.

In conclusion, I hope this chapter made you as excited as I am by this expanding category of nonfiction food writing. The variety shows how mainstream the subject of food has become and how it can be translated into many styles of nonfiction writing. If several book ideas popped into your head as you read, capture that list. Book ideas have to come from somewhere, and one of my goals in writing this book is to help you generate yours.

Writing Exercises

1. Generate food-based memories for your memoir. Map out the street where you lived as a child and write about the food you tasted from other homes. Draw the street where you grew up on a sheet of paper. Add a drawing or X marking the spot of each house. Add the names of families you knew or kids you played with. Now draw upon your memory of eating foods for the first time. Write about three or four times when playmates or their parents presented you with a food you had never eaten before. Create the scene. Remember your apprehension or excitement. Recall the taste on your tongue. Once you have documented a few strong images, weave them together in a story. Write about how you felt eating those new foods, how they changed you, and whether you eat any of them today.

2. Flex your research skills with an essay on food history. Name your favorite spice. Now write 500 words about it. Discover the country of origin and how the spice is harvested, processed, and sold. Find out whether it was used in a famous historical dish or prized by certain people. See whether traders took it on trade routes to another country, and how that country used the spice. Say how it's used today and how you cook or bake with it. If you like, conclude by developing a recipe using the spice.

10

Writing About Food in Fiction

S o far this book has been about nonfiction, the biggest category of
food writing by far. But writing fiction, it turns out, is not that different from nonfiction. In both cases, your job is to tell a story, convey
passion, put the reader in the scene, and let the food play the leading
role. Both fiction and nonfiction include suspense and tension to drive
the narrative. Both use food to establish the place, time, culture, and
mood. If you've read the other chapters, you've spent your time well
preparing for fiction.

Fiction writing is fun. You get to make up characters, plot, and
dialogue. Your story can take place anywhere in the world, during any
period. You get to merge people you know into a single person and
take revenge on people you don't like—as long as they won't know it.
If some events haven't turned out well in your life, they can turn out
well in your fiction. If you've always hated your mother's cooking, a
character can have a mother who's a celebrated chef.

In fiction, food is a device that helps you develop characters based
on how they cook, which foods they like, and how they eat. It also
creates a mood or sets a scene, and establishes the time. "Food is everything," says Phyllis Richman, author of *The Butter Did It: A Gastronomic Tale of Love and Murder, Murder on the Gravy Train,* and *Who's
Afraid of Virginia Ham?* "It's part of the relationship between Chas
[Richman's main character] and her lover, Chas and her daughter, and

it's the murder weapon. While they're having an argument, the daughter cooks and Chas sets the table. Food is what occupies them. It facilitates working out problems among characters, explains characters to one another, and identifies people."

In that vein, a skilled writer might shape a character's personality based on how the character handles food and how and when he eats. In *The Garden of Eden*, Ernest Hemingway writes: "He went out to the empty kitchen and found a tin of Maquereau Vin Blanc Capitaine Cook and opened it and took it, perilous with edge-level juice, with a cold bottle of the Tuborg beer out to the bar. He opened the beer, took the bottle top between his right thumb and the first joint of his right forefinger and bent it in until it was flattened together, put it in his pocket since he saw no container to toss it into, raised the bottle that was still cold to his hand and now beaded wet in his fingers and, smelling the aroma from the opened tin of spiced and marinated mackerel, he took a long drink of the cold beer."

Wow. I've read that paragraph at least two dozen times and it still slays me with its muscular sensuousness. Hemingway is not the kind of guy who would just write, "The man went to the kitchen, found some fish and drank some beer." Look at the specific language, how he slowed down the moment. Now, what do you know about this character? He's strong, masculine, sexual, and deliberate. He takes great pleasure in food. He doesn't litter.

In some fiction, food itself becomes a character. In *Five Quarters of the Orange*, by Joanne Harris, an orange becomes the villain by taking on evil powers. The smell of oranges brings on a woman's crippling headaches. She will not permit them in her house. Her daughter steals an orange and uses it to control her by placing it on her mother's pillow, triggering migraines. Other negative roles food can play include dismay, disgust, detachment, disillusion, destruction, danger, or even death—the all-important D-words.

The assent to eat—sitting down to dinner, taking a cup of tea—can become the catalyst for action. In *Anna Karenina* by Leo Tolstoy, Levin, the main character, drinks an awful lot of tea, often at the start of a paragraph as a way to begin a scene. He might order tea sent to his study, signaling the beginning of work. Or he might sit with others and have tea, as in "Levin was sitting beside his hostess at the teatable and had to keep up a conversation with her and her sister, who was sitting opposite him."

By default, much of the dialogue in novels with food themes takes place over food at parties, cafés, and particularly at dinner tables. Edith Wharton's *The Age of Innocence* uses food to advance the plot, eventually: "After a velvety oyster soup came shad and cucumbers, then a young broiled turkey with corn fritters, followed by a canvas-back with currant jelly and a celery mayonnaise. Mr. Letterblair, who lunched on a sandwich and tea, dined deliberately and deeply, and insisted on his guests doing the same. Finally, when the closing rites had been accomplished, the cloth was removed, cigars were lit, and Mr. Letterblair, leaning back in his chair and pushing the port westward, said, spreading his back agreeably to the coal fire behind him, 'The whole family is against a divorce. And I think rightly.'"

Sometimes the plot relies on the elaborate meals the main character makes and the dialogue that results. In *Serving Crazy with Curry* by Amulya Malladi, a woman gets fired from her job and suffers a miscarriage. Feeling shame for abandoning her traditional Indian family, she attempts suicide. Her mother saves her life. She moves in with her parents but refuses to speak, taking up cooking instead, and prompting her family to engage in conversations over meals that draw them closer.

There are all types of culinary fiction, from murder mysteries to children's books to novels based on food to joint themes of food and sex. While many classic writers are never thought of as food writers, they write beautifully on the topic, as illustrated above by Hemingway, Tolstoy, and Wharton. Even children's books with food themes present a satisfying challenge. This chapter explores all types of food writing in book-length fiction. Its goal is not to teach you how to write fiction, but to generate story ideas by giving you examples of successful titles and plot lines, and to help you shape your individual voice, style, and view of the world.

Culinary Crime Capers

Great dining has often been a part of mystery novels. In the 1960s, Nero Wolfe, Rex Stout's sleuth, had a rule that no one could interrupt a meal, including those prepared by his personal chef, Fritz. Meals were an integral part of the plot in Agatha Christie books, from arsenic in the food to the way the murderer stalked his victim at a dinner party to exposing the murderer at tea. More modern examples of culinary crime are Nan Lyons's *Someone is Killing the Great Chefs of Europe,* and television personality Anthony Bourdain's thrillers set in the restaurant industry and seasoned with culinary detail: *Gone Bamboo* and *Bone in the Throat.*

Some writers create food-based murder mysteries based on ordinary characters. They have moved the genre away from stories about hardboiled detectives who never eat, to cozies, books that focus more on character and relationships. Joyce and Jim Levine, who have written more than forty books together, describe the genre:

> Cozies are light mysteries depicting real-life people solving mysteries in unusual ways. The genre is steadily broadening as their popularity increases. Traditionally, the cozy was a British novel featuring sweet elderly women and other harmless protagonists. Probably the best known is Agatha Christie with her *Miss Marpole* series.
>
> Today's cozies occur in every place and time with men and women as sleuths. They have an amateur detective, although there is often a police officer in a supporting role. The amateur sleuth gathers clues by listening to gossip and by paying attention to surroundings. The cozy sleuth attracts murder. Murders happen everywhere around him or her. The sleuth has access to a large number of people, usually through a career.
>
> The cozy is heavy on dialogue, light on gritty depictions of death and the murder itself. They are full of suspense and dark corners of intrigue. But cozy murder mysteries are tamer than their thriller counterparts. Descriptions of the crime scene are toned down. Sex is never graphic. The stories are thoughtful rather than thriller. The books generally have strong, quirky characters and are set in interesting places. Cozy sleuths come from many different occupations and from any time or place.

That means the main character could be a food journalist, baker, caterer, innkeeper, chocolate maker, or coffeehouse owner, as they are in the books I've discovered. Here, the plot ideas are often campy and the titles full of puns and double entendres. Recipes are always part of the form, although the amount varies.

Phyllis Richman, the top restaurant reviewer of the *Washington Post* until her retirement, wrote her three cozies while working full time. "I had been doing my job for so long I needed some freshening," she explains. "I had been thinking for decades about doing mysteries. I also thought if I wanted to get published, it would be easier to do so from the *Post* than from retirement." She stayed home one day a week to write, and after fifty-two weeks, her first book was ready.

Richman used her insider knowledge of the restaurant business as a theme for three books, as cozies are usually written as a series. In *Murder on the Gravy Train,* Chas Wheatley, restaurant critic for the fictional *Washington Examiner,* flies to Paris with her chef lover for a benefit gala. When her lover dies of an apparent heart attack from soaring cholesterol, Wheatley knows better. She continues writing her reviews and recipes while investigating his death. In *The Butter Did It,* Wheatley finds something rotten with the food at one of Washington's most popular new restaurants. The head chef is missing. Wheatley tracks down the dead chef, eating her way from one restaurant to the next and giving readers an inside look at the restaurant business. In *Who's Afraid of Virginia Ham?* a new reporter, angling for Wheatley's job as food editor, dies by eating lethal Virginia ham at a work function.

At first Richman had to get used to new tools of plot, character development, point of view, and dialogue. But there's nothing that different about fiction, she decided. "It's just another form of restaurant reviews and travel writing."

Probably the most famous of the food-themed cozy writers is Diane Mott Davidson. Some of her mysteries have appeared on the *New York Times* and *USA Today* best seller lists. When starting out, Davidson wrote two regular mysteries before selling her third, *Catering to Nobody,* to St. Martin's Press at age 41. An avid cook and fan of Julia Child, she convinced the publisher to include four recipes.

Davidson's writing group suggested she focus her murder mystery on Goldy Korman, a caterer, who was then a minor character. "For Goldy, cooking heals," said Davidson in an interview. "If she can cook, she can get a feeling of control over the world. Cooking is more than just comfort food, it's about nurturing oneself while nurturing others." Davidson's recipes come from food ideas suggested by friends, colleagues, restaurant dishes, or sometimes right out of her head, featuring ingredients she thinks would taste good together.

Like Richman, she has a good time while writing her books. Some of Davidson's culinary capers are:

- *Dying for Chocolate.* Korman, a divorced culinary artist, starts Goldilocks Catering in Aspen Meadows, Colorado, to support herself and her teenage son.
- *Killer Pancake.* While Korman caters a cosmetics firm's low-fat luncheon, a sales associate dies in a hit-and-run while animal-rights people demonstrate in front of her store.
- *The Last Suppers.* On Korman's wedding day, her husband gets arrested for a homicide.

While Davidson started out as a mystery writer, Joanne Fluke wrote psychological thrillers before moving to culinary capers. Now all of her murders have to do with baked goods. In some of her books, the pastries provide a clue. In *Lemon Meringue Pie Murder,* the protagonist, Hannah Swensen, discovers one of her pies at a crime scene and finds out how it got there. Baked goodies win friends and get people to talk, says Fluke, particularly at Swensen's own bakery and coffee shop in Lake Eden, Minnesota. There she hears local gossip and private conversations as she refills coffee cups. Food is also a facilitator, says Fluke, where Swensen uses her cookies and desserts to soothe pain and calm nervous people, thus disarming them and prompting them to talk.

Fluke catered in college to make extra money, but the author traces her passion for baking back to childhood. Her grandmother was an assistant pastry girl for a wealthy family. "Gammie used to bake every winter morning to warm up the kitchen, and all it took was a whiff of vanilla, chocolate, or cinnamon to get me out of bed in plenty of time for school," recalls Fluke. "When I was old enough to reach the table, Gammie and Mom taught me how to bake. It was something we all did together and I'm sure that's why the kitchen is still my favorite room in the house."

Fluke wrote her first culinary mystery, the *Chocolate Chip Cookie Murder,* in 2001. Swensen returns home upon the death of her father and opens the Cookie Jar bakery. She becomes an amateur sleuth when she finds a dead delivery truck driver still holding a chocolate chip crunch cookie in his hand. A few of Fluke's other books are:

- *Strawberry Shortcake Murder.* Swensen judges a dessert bake-off. Someone finds one of the judges face down in Swensen's own strawberry shortcake.
- *Blueberry Muffin Murder.* The baker finds the dead body of a cookbook author and tracks down the killer.
- *Sugar Cookie Murder.* The baker compiles a cookbook of the locals' favorite recipes for the Christmas party at the community center. Swensen finds her mother's silver cake knife stuck in the chest of one of the guests, who is lying dead in the parking lot.

A CULINARY MYSTERY WRITER TELLS YOU HOW

I asked Joanne Fluke to pass on some simple ways to get ideas and writing going for your upcoming food-themed book. Her three-notebook idea, which follows, is particularly good. I've learned from experience that when I go back to notes I've taken at the scene or soon thereafter they're so much more detailed than if I wait. I always carry a little notebook around to jot down ideas as they come up.

Her advice about honing your skills is something you've read before in this book, but it can't be said enough. Here are her suggestions:

- Buy three notebooks. Use one to jot down all your favorite dishes, especially if you're going out to dinner and trying something new. Write down the name and your impressions. You may think you'll remember the great meal you had at that little French bistro, but you won't. Use the second notebook to take notes while you read everything you can get your hands on in the genre you've chosen. Write down what the authors do that you like. Use the third notebook to note what the authors do that you don't like.
- Start writing. Try the techniques from the second notebook to see if they work for you. Avoid the things in the third notebook like the plague.

- Hone your skills. Take a writing class or join a critique group if you think it'll help you. Get a copy of the *Writer's Market* and study it for practical advice and information.
- When thinking about your story, jot down little notes about the characters. When the story and characters are clear in your mind, outline it so that you won't forget.
- Begin writing your book. If that first paragraph eludes you, try writing the last chapter first. Then, when you write the first chapter, you'll know where you're going.
- Write every day. Work hard. Be optimistic, but don't give up your day job.

Two other writers who write culinary capers are Mary Daheim and Joanna Carl. Daheim crossed over from a career as a historical romance writer. Her Bed and Breakfast series includes *Just Desserts,* where an innkeeper solves the mystery of a murdered visitor. Other titles I love are *Nutty as a Fruitcake* and *Legs Benedict.* In *The Chocolate Frog Frame-Up,* part of the Chocolate Chocoholic mystery series by Carl, small-town chocolatiers debut their chocolate frog at a Fourth of July party. The first customer to buy it dies and a chocolate clue leads to solving the murder.

Certainly, you can read these books for fun. While you do so, notice how authors advance the plot, throw in plot twists, and create suspense and tension. Without suspense, there's not much of a mystery at the end, when you reveal the culprit. You need narrative drive, or the promise that something's going to happen. These authors know how to build events and suspicions to a crescendo. If you're interested in learning how to write mysteries, see Useful Reference Books for Fiction Writers on page 253.

I love how these writers don't take themselves so seriously. I can't resist telling you about a few more ways writers create funny titles and plots:

- In *On What Grounds,* by Cleo Coyle, the manager of a historic coffeehouse arrives to find her assistant manager dead. In *Through the Grinder,* business is booming but customers seem to be dying after drinking her house coffee blend.

- In *Too Many Crooks Spoil the Broth,* by Tamar Myers, a mean-spirited innkeeper solves the murder of a dead guest. *Eat, Drink and Be Wary: A Pennsylvania Dutch Mystery with Recipes,* and *Parsley, Sage, Rosemary and Crime* are two more titles I love.
- *Death by the Glass: A Sunny McCoskey Napa Valley Mystery,* by Nadia Gordon, investigates the seamy side of the restaurant and wine world. Wine professionals, cooks, and gourmet friends help a chef-owner of a Napa Valley restaurant solve a crime.
- In *A Catered Murder,* the best-selling author of vampire fiction drops dead at an affair the main character caters. Isis Crawford, a caterer and travel writer, wrote the book.

When your characters are caterers, bakers, innkeepers, restaurant critics, chefs, and candy makers, you can live vicariously by fictionalizing their lives. Take a moment to imagine one of these characters, the hero of your book, coming upon a dead body. In your mind you've already constructed the scene, imagined your hero physically, and identified the body. These details could be the start of your own mystery book. Write down the scene while it's still fresh.

~~~~~~

USEFUL REFERENCE BOOKS FOR FICTION WRITERS

This chapter offers just a taste of fiction writing. For more, try these books:

- *Stein on Writing: A Master Editor of Some of the Most Successful Writers of Our Century Shares His Craft Techniques and Strategies,* by Sol Stein. Well written, useful advice on how to fix flawed writing, improve good writing, and create excellent writing.
- *How to Write a Damn Good Novel: A Step-by-Step No Nonsense Guide to Dramatic Storytelling,* by James Frey. Detailed descriptions of common pitfalls and how to avoid them.
- *Write Away: One Novelist's Approach to Fiction and the Writing Life,* by Elizabeth George. A personal approach to mastering the tools and techniques necessary to writing the novel.
- *Description,* by Monica Wood. Includes advice on how to use description to awaken readers' senses. Part of the Elements of Fiction series.

If you're interested in mysteries, you'll find around a dozen books on how to write them, many written by successful mystery writers, including:

- *How to Write a Mystery*, by Larry Beinhart. Advice on narrative drive, the promise that something will happen. Not systematic, but useful advice on how to approach plot, character development, and other writing techniques.
- *How to Write Killer Fiction: The Funhouse of Mystery & the Roller Coaster of Success*, by Carolyn Wheat. Lots of useful tips and insights on such things as the difference between mystery and suspense and how to plant clues.

Main Characters in the Food Business

Like culinary capers, lots of novels have main characters in the food business as well. Cookbook author and novelist Bharti Kirchner was traveling in Japan and stayed in a hotel that had a bakery nearby. When she visited the bakery she was surprised to find it full of beautiful French pastries. She kept turning the scene over in her mind, she says, picturing a Japanese man with a passion for French baking. Kirchner wrote *Pastries: A Novel of Desserts and Discoveries*, about a bakery owner who struggles when a competitor opens a bakery down the street. For research, she read industry trade magazines to learn about running a business, interviewed several bakers, and hung out in their kitchens. Over time, she understood the life, character, challenges, and work of a baker, and the atmosphere of a bakery.

Good Grief, by Lolly Winston, has a different baking theme. A woman quits her job and discovers her talent as a baker. She opens her own bakery, and the town paper describes her porcini and Brie cheesecake as "sure to be a hit." Winston's book is also a laugh-out-loud funny and poignant story about surviving the loss of a spouse.

Here are more sample characters and plots based on the food business, to give you ideas for your own story:

Food writer: The best-selling *Heartburn*, by Nora Ephron, tells the story of a food writer whose husband cheats on her. Ephron makes a convincing case of how her heroine got into food writing, starting out as a journalist (how Ephron got started in real life), then writing a food column for a newspaper. Recipes are included.

In *Cooking for Love*, by Sharon Boorstin, a Beverly Hills cookbook author dreams about food and the man who got away. She finds him on Google twenty-five years later, leading to a culinary adventure halfway around the world with her girlfriend.

Restaurant owner, chef, waiter, or reviewer: If you've ever worked in a restaurant, owned one, or have been a reviewer, you must have lots of material for a good yarn. If you haven't and would love to imagine this lifestyle, consider these plotlines:

- *Crawfish Dreams: A Novel*, by Nancy Rawles. A Creole who moved her family from Louisiana to South Central Los Angeles opens Camille's Creole Kitchen and recruits her family to help her get the restaurant on its feet.
- *Crescent*, by Diana Abu-Jaber. A chef in a Lebanese restaurant has her passions aroused only by the preparation of food, until a handsome Arabic literature professor starts dropping by for a little home cooking. Falling in love brings Sirene's heart to a boil, stirring up questions about her identity as an Arab American. The author worked as a cook throughout college and for a few years after.
- *Eating Crow*, by Jay Rayner. A London restaurant critic attempts to redeem himself after a chef commits suicide because of a bad review.
- *Liquor: A Novel*, by Poppy Z. Brite. A New Orleans alcohol-themed restaurant's bumbling owners close the place down. The author's husband was a chef at Commander's Palace.
- *Love and Meatballs*. A daughter works in a family restaurant and becomes torn between two men. Author Susan Volland is a classically trained chef who had written freelance articles and recipes for magazines and cookbooks.
- *How I Gave My Heart to the Restaurant Business: A Novel*, by Karen Hubert Allison. A woman and her boyfriend open a successful restaurant in Manhattan and give up their outside lives.

- *The Food of Love,* by Anthony Capella. Based on Edmond Rostand's *Cyrano de Bergerac,* but set in Rome, an Italian Casanova falls in love with an American art student and tells her he's a chef. He can't cook, but his less attractive friend can, so he uses his friend's skills for a culinary seduction.
- *High Bonnet: A Novel of Epicurean Adventures,* by Idwal Jones. Written in 1945, this book reveals a restaurant world in Paris entirely devoted to food. Anthony Bourdain called it "porn for cooks."

Chocolate shop or sweetshop owner: In *Chocolat,* by Joanne Harris, a woman opens a chocolate shop in a rustic French village and angers the church by appealing to pleasure-starved parishioners. Taste the chocolates in your mouth as you read.

Cheesemaker: In *The Mammoth Cheese,* by Sheri Holman, an artisan cheese maker and his daughter go on a historic journey to recreate a huge Cheshire cheese once given to Jefferson, presenting it to the president.

Television producer: *My Year of Meats,* by Ruth L. Ozeki, features a Japanese-American documentary filmmaker invited to work on a Japanese television show meant to encourage beef consumption. She becomes increasingly aware of the beef industry's practice of using synthetic estrogens on cattle and plans to sabotage the program.

Some novels focus on the dual pleasures of food and sex, filling the senses to near overflowing. Why do food and sex go together so well? "Food is our most public sensual pleasure," explains Richmond. "It's second only to sex in terms of sensuality, and since you can't really do sex in public, reading about it fulfills a basic need."

Perhaps the best-known book in this category is *Like Water for Chocolate: A Novel in Monthly Installments with Recipes, Romances, and Home Remedies,* by Laura Esquivel. The daughter of a rancher falls in love and uses magical realism to pour her emotions into her cooking. Each chapter opens with a recipe. Another example is *In La Cucina:*

A Novel of Rapture, by Lily Prior, which tells the story of a girl growing up on a Sicilian farm who spends most of her time in the kitchen. She meets an Englishman in Palermo, and together, they explore their culinary and sexual passions.

What About Recipes?

Some culinary fiction authors swear by including recipes in their works. Others put them in grudgingly, and some don't do it at all.

"If I didn't include recipes, my house would get egged, people would call to yell at me on the phone, and I'd receive a slew of angry emails and letters," says Fluke. Twice now, she's written in passing about a cookie and a cake without including their recipes. She mentioned Lisa's White Chocolate Supreme Cookies in the *Chocolate Chip Cookie Murder.* "I got so many letters and email messages I had to create a recipe and put it in *Blueberry Muffin Murder,*" says Fluke. "I also got in trouble when I wrote about Rose's Famous Coconut Cake in *Lemon Meringue Pie Murder.* I didn't have a recipe for that either, but hundreds of people asked for it in emails so I had to come up with one and put it in *Sugar Cookie Murder.*"

Other fiction writers dislike the switch from writing narrative to writing the instructions that recipes require. "Recipes destroy the flow of the story," says Kirchner. "They take away from the literary quality of the novel." She prefers to write about cooking in more general terms, such as how someone baked a cake. Richman's restaurant-based mysteries include a recipe at the back of each book. In the narrative, she makes a point of writing about dishes in enough detail that they're workable; some chef-readers have tried them out and told her about their efforts. Ephron uses a similar technique in *Heartburn,* but with more specific measurements and instruction, so they read more like recipes. Twenty recipes appear in the book, inserted conversationally as part of the story. It's an effective way to keep the narration going, but the style makes these recipes harder to read than those in a more traditional structure.

As you can see, there's no one right way to add recipes. I prefer them at the end of each chapter, in traditional recipe format, with an index by title in the back so readers can look them up alphabetically.

Food in Classic Literature

I'm not the type who thinks you shouldn't read while writing or you might write in the style of the author you're reading. I don't know how you can become a good writer without reading great writing. Earlier I provided examples to show how classic writers inserted descriptions of food or meals to move a story along or to depict emotion. Once you start looking at classic literature, you'll find useful examples everywhere.

Marcel Proust's wistful passage about a madeleine in *Swann's Way* introduces the relationship between food and memory: "But when from a long-distant past nothing subsists, after the people are dead, after the things are broken and scattered, taste and smell alone, more fragile but more enduring, more unsubstantial, more persistent, more faithful, remain poised a long time, like souls, remembering, waiting, hoping, amid the ruins of all the rest; and bear unflinchingly, in the tiny and almost impalpable drop of their essence, the vast structure of recollection."

Henry Fielding's witty eighteenth-century *The History of Tom Jones, A Foundling* has a narrator who says literature is like a meal, in which the paying customer expects to be entertained and satisfied.

F. Scott Fitzgerald's *The Great Gatsby* details summer parties out on the famous lawn: "On buffet tables, garnished with glistening hors-d'oeuvre, spiced baked hams crowded against salads of harlequin designs and pastry pigs and turkeys bewitched to a dark gold."

In Edith Wharton's *The Age of Innocence*, a man engaged to a society girl longs for a life of passion with someone else, set against a New York backdrop of grand dinners and parties. And *Down and Out in Paris and London*, by George Orwell, includes his experiences in the unpleasant hotel and restaurant world in which he worked in the 1930s. Even *Moby Dick*, by Herman Melville, describes foods of the times as a way to show authenticity and detail. Here's a picture of seafood chowder: "It was made of small juicy clams, scarcely bigger than hazelnuts, mixed with pounded ship biscuits, and salted port cut up into little flakes; the whole enriched with butter, and plentifully seasoned with pepper and salt."

For a taste of many writers and their love of food, read *Feast of Words: For Lovers of Food and Fiction*, by Anna Shapiro. She pairs inventive menus and recipes with passages of fiction by authors such as Dickens, Lessing, and Hardy. Her book is instructive because it is organized by themes found in classic novels, such as "Starved Love," "Penitential Meals," and "Eating the Social Index."

Children's Books

If you've always wanted to write young adult or children's books, why not combine your passions and write about food? Food in children's literature can serve several purposes, no matter what your intention. Primarily, of course, it tells a good story, just like adult fiction. *Stone Soup* (there are various versions by multiple authors) tells an old French tale of three hungry soldiers who convince inhabitants of a village to make them a soup that starts with boiled rocks. In *Blueberries for Sal*, by Robert McCloskey, two sets of mother and child, one a momma bear and cub, go on a hunt for blueberries and end up intermixed. In Maurice Sendak's *In the Night Kitchen*, a boy stumbles into a night kitchen where bakers prepare cakes for the morning.

Food is not only a source of entertainment for kids, but it's also an educational and experiential tool. Here are some other ways writers employ it in children's fiction:

It can make eating look enticing: *Eating the Alphabet*, by Lois Ehlert, shows fruits and vegetables so enticing that even finicky kids will want to eat them. *The Seven Silly Eaters*, by Mary Ann Hoberman, comprises rhymes about how a mother accommodates picky children who will only eat certain foods such as applesauce or eggs.

Aids you can't use in adult novels can help younger readers indulge their senses. *The Wiggles: Yummy, Yummy Fruit Salad*, published by Grossett and Dunlap, has fourteen scratch-and-sniff stickers in flavors like apple, banana, watermelon, and grape.

It can introduce foreign foods: Some authors build songlike lyrics around food. Amy Wilson Sanger's *World Snacks* series explains sushi, dim sum, Mexican food, Jewish "nosh," and soul food. Here's a line from *Soul Food:* "When I wake up I smell biscuits / and gravy for our grits. / I say thanks for smoky ham / cut into little itty bits."

It helps children understand other cultures: In *Henner's Lydia,* by Marguerite De Angeli, readers see how a Pennsylvania Dutch community makes cider in the backyard and what kinds of food the community members eat, such as apple butter and half-moon pies. Artist and poet Grace Lin's *Dim Sum for Everyone* describes the pleasures of a Chinese dining tradition. For children ages eight to twelve, Joanne Rocklin's *Strudel Stories* weaves a tender tale about seven generations of family members who bake apple strudel, from Odessa to Brooklyn to the Pacific.

Food can be a learning tool: In *Chicken Soup with Rice: A Book of Months,* by Maurice Sendak, children learn activities they can do during different months and seasons while sipping this soup. In January they eat it while slipping and sliding on the ice, while in July they find a turtle selling it at the bottom of the ocean.

Whether you write a mystery about a cook, a novel with food-based theme, or a children's book, all the fiction writers I've interviewed share similar advice. They suggest joining a critique group with regular meetings and producing work to share with the other members. They recommend reading books on how to write novels, and reading novels to understand how authors use food to craft scenes, plot, and character. They suggest you take classes. And most of all, if you want to be a writer: Writers write. Do it every day.

Writing Exercises

1. People in your book or short story must seem believable to your readers. Build up characteristics by writing a sketch. Go to a restaurant with a pad of paper and take notes about your waiter. Describe the person visually, then get inside his head and imagine his life in the workplace and at home. Does he work fourteen-hour days, ending with drinks at bars at three in the morning? Does he spend tips on heavy-metal music? Describe his home, how he cooks, what he likes to eat, and whether he is a food snob.

2. Write a dramatic dialogue between you and the waiter, based on the food. This is a next step in developing the waiter's character, where you imagine a conversation based on your personality and

what you know about him. Write several lines of dialogue suggesting the beginning of a relationship that may continue later in your story. You can choose to create conflict and tension (you hated the food; he was snippy), but not all drama is negative. In the previous example, perhaps he stalks you later for revenge. If it's positive, maybe he's a flirt and you build suspense that the two of you will meet elsewhere.

3. Choose a food, then write a story that is set in a particular historical period. If you chose baked beans, for example, you could write about cowboys hunched over a fire, camped out at night while driving a herd of cattle. Next, write a dialogue between two people who are consuming your chosen food. Incorporate action related to the food in the scene, such as how one cowboy slurps the beans from a tin cup, or how another tears bread and leaves crumbs in his mustache. Try writing three paragraphs.

11

How to Get
Your Book Published

Writing a nonfiction book will make you better known, but there's a problem: publishers prefer authors who are already known, since it's less risky for them. Lots of people rush to get their book proposals out the door before they have the credentials to interest a publisher. When I suggest they write a few articles, teach a class, or speak on the subject, they resist. "I just want to write the book proposal," they say.

Yes, but without the necessary credentials, a finished book proposal won't do you any good. An agent or publisher will want to see your "platform," industry-speak for your ability to establish a base of interested readers who are likely to buy your book. A blogger with thousands of readers per day, a newspaper or magazine columnist, a cooking teacher who does fifty classes per year, a television show host, a well-known restaurateur, chef, or caterer, or a consultant who speaks all over the country are examples of people with platforms. Potential purchasers of their books know them, and they can get in front of their readers with regularity.

Working on your reputation before you write your book will dramatically increase your chances of success. And here's a great side effect: once you establish your credentials, your self-confidence goes way up, and you'll write a stronger and more convincing book proposal.

The best and easiest way to beef up your credibility is to get published. Stories with your byline show that someone else thought your writing was good enough to publish and make you more desirable. If you don't believe me, consider this quote from Rux Martin, executive editor of Houghton Mifflin, who has edited cookbooks by *Gourmet* magazine and Jacques Pépin. "It would be virtually impossible for someone to have a proposal that would excite me and be worthy of consideration who had never written for publication."

Some agents and editors read food blogs or count on scouts or colleagues to direct them to someone who's hot. It may be enough for them if you blog and have never been published in print, if your page views are high enough. Sydny Minor, now executive editor at Crown Books, was an early reader of food blogs and that's how she found Molly Wizenberg of Orangette. But the field of food blogging is much more crowded now, and for many editors and agents, print is still king. They want to see your byline in a daily paper or national magazine.

Regardless of the topic of your blog or freelance writing, you're more likely to succeed with a book proposal if your book is based on it. Write on the subject of your book as a way to test the idea and confirm its value. It also shows publishers that readers are interested in the subject. A restaurant review and a recipe for grilled salmon are better than nothing but won't get you very far if you want to write a cookbook on birthday party desserts. Why not start a blog on the subject? (If you have not begun writing for publication or blogging, read chapters 4 and 5.)

Do you need prior publication or a book proposal if you are writing a novel, a memoir, or plan to self-publish your book? As a novelist, you will be more attractive if you get short stories published first, but this may not be essential. To approach agents and publishers with fiction, you don't need a proposal. You write the whole book first and send agents or editors a cover letter with a few sample chapters. If you're writing memoir, write the proposal after you complete your manuscript. If you plan to self-publish and sell your book, you don't need a proposal, although it will help you to flesh out the table of contents, the competition, and the promotion plan. Readers may be more likely to buy your book if you have credentials as a previously published writer, although it's not essential. The exception is if your book is only for yourself or family members, or you are compiling a community book or recipes to raise money. If so, you might want to skip ahead to the self-publishing section on page 295.

But if you are hoping to have a nonfiction book traditionally published and you've already written the manuscript, you have to back up. I'm sure you're not happy that I'm telling you to do more work. You'd rather submit your book to a publisher; maybe not even bother with an agent. Unfortunately, that's not much of a strategy, and it rarely works. Editors hardly ever accept manuscripts as a first step to working with an author. Many big publishing companies don't accept unsolicited manuscripts at all, let alone read them. In fact, the rejection rate just for book proposals from both agents and publishers is the same, around 90 to 95 percent. Why not get into the 5 to 10 percent that succeeds?

On first contact, agents and editors will want to know who you are, how you came up with your idea, how you will promote your book, who you know in the media, whether you have a built-in audience, and if you've ever been published. If you send your finished book with a cover letter that says, "Please publish this," you're not answering any of these questions. You're not selling yourself. Selling is a big part of the game, as is understanding where your book fits into the landscape and having something new and fresh to say.

The document that answers editors' and agents' questions is called a book proposal. Not only does it discuss your book, it sells you as the author. This chapter shows you how to write a killer proposal. You'll also learn whether you need an agent, how to find one, and how to query prospective agents. The section on contracts explains what happens when a publisher wants to buy your book. Finally, you'll find a section on self-publishing, which is of increasing interest to more and more of my students and clients.

The Landscape

Around the world, around 26,000 food and wine titles are published each year, according to Edoard Cointreau, founder of the Gourmand World Cookbook Awards. While publishers keep churning out cookbooks, the market is getting tougher, says agent Jane Dystel, head of Dystel and Goderich Literary Management. There are too many cookbooks, and some publishers have cut back or cut out publishing them, she says. But on the other hand, "There are always going to be new cooks and new consumers who want to do fresh things." And perhaps the rise of non-cookbook-based food books shows there are lots of opportunities outside the cookbook world.

The competition will be intense. "We get around 250 proposals a year and publish twenty books, and we're a big cookbook publisher. Probably five are our idea to begin with, so only fifteen cookbooks come from outside," explains Bill LeBlond, editorial director of food and drink for Chronicle Books. By "our idea" he means that an editor suggested a book idea to a previously published author, perhaps as her next book. Or the editor has invited someone, such as a chef, to write a book.

Even though it's a tough market, you can succeed. You have to know what agents and editors want, which can be elusive. "It really boils down from personal taste," explains agent Doe Coover, who represents such authors as Jacques Pépin, Rick Bayless, and Deborah Madison. "Some decisions stem from what I think is salable. I have to feel passionate about it. I have to know I'm not going to be daunted if the first two publishers turn it down, or the first six. I have to know I'm in it for the long haul." Coover has represented first-time authors as well as the stars, but obviously she's picky. If you follow the advice in this chapter, you'll have a much better shot at getting an agent at her level or a good editor and publisher.

Writing the Book Proposal

When you have a solid non-fiction book idea, it's time to write the book proposal.

A book proposal is a document you send to agents and editors. It introduces you and tells them why they should be interested in both you and your book. It includes your bio, a table of contents for the book, sample recipes if you're writing a cookbook, and samples of your writing. It explains the target market, the potential competition and how your book differs from it, and how you will promote the book. Regardless of whether you want an agent or plan to submit directly to a publisher, you need a proposal. It's normal to spend at least six months writing it.

You might have heard that you can send a one-page query letter instead of a proposal. That's true, and it's a lot less work. But if agents or editors like it, they will say, "Yes, this sounds interesting. Please send the book proposal." Now what? You haven't written it. Six months or a year from now, when you finish the proposal, your cover letter will say, "Remember when I sent you that query and you liked the idea." Write the query letter after writing the proposal, so the proposal's ready to go if you get a green light.

Think of a book proposal as a sales pitch that provides vital details about your idea and shows your voice and writing style. It might be as long as fifty pages double-spaced. Remember that you're writing it to agents and editors, not readers, so keep your audience in mind. Think about what an editor and agent want to know. The only sections you write directly to readers are the writing samples and recipes, because they are samples of what will appear in your book. A book proposal must answer these questions: Why you, why now, and who cares? Here are the main elements:

Title page: Create a cover page with the title of book, subtitle, and all of your contact information.

Table of contents for the proposal: If your proposal is long, it needs a table of contents listing sections by page number.

Summary or concept: Agents and editors are busy. Aaron Wehner, publisher of Ten Speed Press, says he spends about thirty-three percent of his time acquiring 25 to 30 manuscripts annually, ten to fifteen percent editing, and the rest of the time running the business. He's responsible for about 105 books per year, including those from high-end restaurants such as A16 in San Francisco and Alinea in Chicago.

A summary gives someone like Wehner an immediate understanding of the book, as soon as he begins reading the proposal. Craft two or three dynamite paragraphs that sum up the book, the market, and you. Here's the proposal summary for *My Nepenthe: Bohemian Tales of Food, Family, and Big Sur,* by Nani Steele:

> *My Nepenthe: Recipes and Tales from the Legendary Big Sur Restaurant* (the subtitle she envisioned) weaves together stories and tales of the famous California restaurant. It celebrates the magic and history of a place through its food and the family that started it. In 2009 Nepenthe

will commemorate sixty years of bringing writers, artists, dancers, travelers, actors, and cooks together around the table, including author Henry Miller, who used it as his favorite watering hole. Today about 200,000 people visit Nepenthe per year.

A lyrical feast written by the owner's granddaughter, who grew up at the restaurant, *My Nepenthe* covers the food, the unconventional family, the colorful people, and the art and architecture that were the genesis of this legendary restaurant. The book includes 60 favorite recipes culled from the restaurant, the café, and the family's archives.

I am a freelance food writer, food stylist, and recipe developer. I opened Café Kevah, named after my maternal great grandmother, at Nepenthe when I was 26 years old and later became a pastry chef. I now live in Oakland, CA with my two children."

You probably do not know enough to write the consummate summary right now. Write a draft summary and leave it as a placeholder. Go back when you've finished the proposal and punch it up. By then you'll have a stronger and more focused notion of what it should say.

Overview: This is the proposal's introduction. It tells the agent or editor what kind of book you plan to write and why. The overview is like a mini-proposal that sums up all the points you will make. Even though it comes first, write it at the end, because it's hard to sum up the proposal and the book idea at first. Writing the proposal forces you to think through the book's structure and content. Often you're still fleshing out and refining the book as you write. The overview:

- must engage the agent or editor immediately, in the first few sentences. They may stop by the bottom of the page if you have not dazzled them or made them curious or excited;
- establishes your idea as solid and salable;
- describes the book's main points, scope and breadth, material to be covered, your writing style, and the book's special features;
- tells how readers will benefit from reading your book;
- makes a case for why the market needs a book on this subject now;

- explains how your book is different or unique;
- explains why you are qualified to write this book;
- tells the reader the size of the manuscript or how many recipes it contains, and how long it will take you to complete it.

To begin your overview, pull readers in. Former cookbook agent Martha Casselman has said she likes an overview that reads like a novel or news story, pulling readers along, involving and exciting them, creating sensual images in their heads. An anecdote might work at the beginning—even statistics, if they grab attention.

Once you hook your readers, summarize the elements listed above in a few compelling paragraphs. Help them visualize your book by outlining the material you will cover, the main points, the philosophy behind the book, its unique conception, and its organization. Explain what you will include, such as the number and types of recipes, special sections, or sidebars. Be as specific as possible without resorting to a list of chapters (that comes later). If appropriate, use anecdotes or name a few dishes and describe them, using all the senses. Think of this section as the book jacket copy. If you're not sure how to word it, read a dozen or so jackets of books you have at home.

If you're writing a cookbook, explain how this book will be better than a database of free recipes readers can find online easily. Tell agents and editors your strengths when it comes to writing this type of material. Are you a terrific recipe developer, with a gaggle of people who test for you? "Can you write about food traditions and cooking practices in a serious way? Or can you write about regional and cultural background in an enlightening and fun way?" asks Miner.

Talk about yourself and why "you are the ideal person for the job because of passion, experience and expertise. Tell us how you still will be involved with the subject two years from now, when the book appears. Publicity interviews will be as much about you as they are about the book," advises Miner.

Describe your voice. Will it be friendly, knowledgeable, or witty? Will you attempt to break down complex concepts? If you've described your book as humorous, do you know how to use humor? It's not enough to say, "The book will be funny." Demonstrate humor within the proposal. Tell how the book benefits your readers, what's in it for them. Close the overview with a strong statement that reinforces your most important point.

Do not insist that the book must look a certain way. The publisher determines the design. If you think photos or illustrations are critical to your book's success, explain why. A guidebook on identifying oysters, for example, would be harder to use without visual images. If you plan to provide your own artwork, such as illustrations, historical photographs, or old letters, say so here. For more on the visual aspects, see page 197 in chapter 7.

Target audience and market: Agents and publishers want to know if a definable market exists for your book. This is part of what constitutes your platform. The target audience identifies who will buy the book and why.

Even though you'd like it to be so, your book is not for everyone. Saying so implies you have not thought through who will buy it. Look for definable populations. Quantify the groups by finding statistics or other identifying information. Identify your readers in as many ways as possible, such as income level, gender, or frequency of visits to fine restaurants.

It's okay to identify more than one kind of reader, as long as you build a solid case for each. When Andrew F. Smith began compiling the audience for his book *The Tomato in America: Early History, Culture, and Cookery*, he found tomato-lover societies, huge tomato festivals with 25,000 attendees, and tomato-growing contests attended by tomato lovers. When he wrote *Pure Ketchup: A History of America's National Condiment, With Recipes*, Heinz bought 5,000 copies. For *Peanuts: The Illustrious History of the Goober Pea*, he found a peanut-lovers' association with 41,000 members.

Say whether you have a built-in strategy to reach potential readers, such as targeting customers at your restaurant or students in your cooking classes, or creating a newsletter or Web site dedicated to potential readers. Describe any strong contacts or connections in the culinary field or media who might help promote your book.

Establish that your topic interests the media. Perhaps magazines or television shows have covered the subject recently. Knowing your reader base will help you choose which publications, Web sites, televisions shows, and other media might have articles or content that applies.

Identifying your target audience will make your book more focused. The more you know about your readers, the more you know what they desire, what they need to know, or what will benefit them. When you write your sample chapters or recipes, you will be able to visualize your target readers sitting across the desk from you. When you write directly to them, you make a connection that comes through in your book.

Promotion plan: Unfortunately, you can't count on publishers to promote your book very much. Often they have paid large advances to authors whose books are coming out the same time as yours, and those books get the bulk of the marketing money budget. Publishers want to know how *you* will help them sell the book. That means getting in front of your target audience and promoting it. While this section of your proposal will be based on a theoretical plan, it must be realistic. If you say you plan to appear on *Oprah* and get your own television show, unless you can state how you plan to do it or demonstrate that you have made inroads, agents and editors probably won't believe you.

Write your promotion plan based on what will happen when the book is published, not based on what you are doing now. If there are events where you could promote your book, list them, and contact organizers in advance to get actual commitments. Let's say you ask your local bookstore, for example, if you could give a talk when your book comes out. If the owner expresses interest, that's more valuable than saying you plan to approach the store.

The best ways to promote your book may be on a television show, in articles you write or on your blog or Web site, in a cooking class, in a restaurant, or at a speaking event. If none of these apply, you'll need a platform, as discussed earlier. Hold a class on the topic of your book now. If it's successful, the venue will be more likely to commit to another event when your book comes out, and you can put that in the proposal. Do you have a Web site where you can promote the book? Can you write articles for publications on the subject of the book? If so, which ones? Will you do demonstrations at department stores? Will you try to get interviewed on radio stations, and if so, for which shows? Make contacts and state them in your proposal.

You might benefit if a significant figure in the food world or media writes an endorsement—called a blurb—on the back cover or a foreword to the book. If so, it's best to ask that person to commit now, so you can say so in this section. You may be nervous about sending a letter or email asking for a commitment to read the book, but often people are honored.

Describe outlets other than bookstores, mega-stores, and culinary stores that might sell your book, such as wineries, home-design stores, or specialty stores for products such as cheeses and chocolate. If you're writing a book for a restaurant or retailer, you have a special sales opportunity that will make editors' and agents' eyes light up. Publishers will sell discounted copies in bulk to companies who commit to buying say, 2,000 to 5,000 copies. It will make your proposal look that much more attractive, and for publishers, it boosts first printings and amortizes production costs. If you have endorsement deals with companies, put them in as well.

About the author: Here's where the agent or editor gets to know you. Don't write your life story, beginning with how you started cooking as a child. Leave out how you've always wanted to write this book, or how people keep telling you to write one. Instead, create a bio highlighting the experiences most related to your book. Many people I've worked with say they had no idea their bio could be so long until they thought it through. When you've never compiled your accomplishments in one place, it can be very satisfying to do so.

If you are already a published author, particularly if related to the subject of your book, that's your best credential. The same is true if you can show you are an expert on the subject of your book.

Otherwise, look deeply into your past. Publicity, experience, jobs, volunteer work, research, awards, travel, and special skills might qualify. Maybe you've had a life experience that provided a valuable lesson and material for your book. Brainstorm lots of ideas, but pare them down to the ones that apply most. Even if you are proud of all the quilts you've made and belong to a quilting group, leave this information out unless it somehow relates to your topic.

Join organizations and take classes to punch up your bio. If you become an officer of one of these associations, your bio will look even stronger. See if you can speak or do a demonstration on the topic of your book.

Analysis of the competition: Choose three to five books that either you or your target readers would find competitive because of the subject or approach. A book with a similar title and completely different content may still be a competitor if it would appear next to yours on the bookshelf. List all information about each book, including title, author, price, whether it's a hardcover or paperback, and publication date. In a paragraph or two, describe each book's contents briefly and compare it to yours. End by stating how your book will be different. Do not be disrespectful. You never know whether the recipient of your proposal sold that book, published it, or is best friends with the author.

"Tell us why your project is different, not why it is better," advises Sydny Miner, executive editor of Crown Books. "'Better' is a subjective judgment and ultimately the consumer is your judge. Do not tell us that there has never been anything like your book, that there is simply no competition. If that's the case, there may be a good reason. Instead, tell us that there have been successful books kind of like yours, but that yours will be different."

Table of contents: There are two. The first is a short list of chapter titles that fits on one page so agents and editors can grasp the book's concept, content, and structure. On the next page, start a chapter-by-chapter outline that describes the book in more detail, from introduction to index. Write up to a one-page description of each chapter, describing what it will cover, its purpose, and how it benefits the reader. Follow with a list of all recipes, if you're writing a cookbook. Include sidebar names, if known. Other parts of the book to list might include a glossary, pantry list, resources list and buying guide, and bibliography.

Ten to twelve chapters are common. The structure usually starts with the simplest elements and flows to the more advanced aspects. Make sure the chapters flow in some logical way. For more details on cookbook organization see page 195.

Sample recipes and/or sample chapter: This section shows that you not only have a well-thought-out understanding of your book, but you can deliver. It must be substantial, and it must be your best writing. If your book is primarily recipe-based, submit up to one dozen recipes, each on a separate page. Recipes must be foolproof and flawless, showcasing the range of your skills and knowledge. You must have tested every recipe before submitting it, because agents and editors can tell whether recipes work just by reading them, and they might even test them. Each recipe should be complete. If it includes tip boxes or a sidebar, include them with the recipe. If your book is recipe based but contains lots of narrative writing, submit a few chapter openings or other text as examples.

If your book is not a cookbook, submit at least one complete chapter. Do not submit the introduction, because much of its content is already covered in your overview. Review your table of contents and choose a meaty chapter in the middle somewhere, one that is also not too long, perhaps 6,000 words at most.

Supporting materials: This is information that promotes your book idea or you, such as recent articles you've written on the subject. Here it gets a little complicated, depending on whether your proposal will be printed or mailed. If printed, you need a separate stack of feature articles, Web site content, blog postings, and other material relevant to your book idea. Start the section with a list of the supporting materials in the order readers will see them. Choose pieces that appeared in prestigious publications or websites, show the variety of your work (if appropriate), and are samples of your best writing. Include any stories written about you, and a video clip if you appeared on television.

If you're emailing your proposal, link to all online material whenever it comes up in the proposal, and create a separate PDF file of other print material. If you have video clips, such as of you in a cooking show or on television, put it on a Web site like YouTube so you can link to it.

Format: Double-space your proposal with 1- to 1.5-inch margins all around. Include page numbers, beginning with the table of contents, with either the title of the book or your name. This is not a design project. Do not make the proposal hard to read by using all caps, which looks like shouting. Do not use colors or other gimmicks that detract from the substance of your text. Boldface and italics are acceptable for headings. Clean text in one font and size lets readers see the quality of your writing. Bulleted lists are easy on the eyes. Do not print on both sides of a page. Do not bind the proposal in any way. You may staple a set of supporting materials together if you have many.

Regarding photography, if you are photogenic, you may include a mug shot at the top of the bio page, or on the front page of the proposal, if it is small. Make sure it looks like a professional photo. Do not include other photos, such as of finished dishes, in your proposal, unless you are proposing partnering with a professional photographer and showing examples of his or her photography and your dishes. Ten Speed's Wehner says he's seeing more and more proposals from agents where they bundle the photographer with the writer.

Cover letter: Whether you're writing fiction or nonfiction, introduce your proposal or sample fiction chapters with a short cover letter written specifically to your target editor or agent. Spell the person's name correctly. Get the title right. These sound like small details, but agents and editors always complain about them when they're not done right.

Overall: No typos, punctuation, or grammatical errors. I cannot overstate the importance of proofing, proofing, and proofing again. You are selling yourself. Copy with errors reduces your credibility, even if there are just a few typos. Print out your proposal and read it several times. Have other people read it for mistakes you did not catch. You may have to do this a half-dozen times. It's worth it.

HELPFUL BOOKS ON GETTING PUBLISHED

While there's only so much I can say in one chapter, these books are devoted entirely to getting published. I recommend them highly and bring most of them to classes when I teach food writing.

- *How to Write a Book Proposal,* by Michael Larsen. A clear, thorough, nuts-and-bolts guide from an agent dedicated to helping writers succeed.
- *The Fast Track Course on How to Write a Non-Fiction Book Proposal,* by Stephen Blake Mettee. A short but well-focused book from a seasoned editor. It includes a sample proposal, sample contract, and glossary.
- *Nonfiction Book Proposals Anyone Can Write: How to Get a Contract and Advance Before Writing Your Book,* by Elizabeth Lyon. A solid, detailed book with a proposal template and models for success.
- *Thinking Like Your Editor: How to Write Great Serious Non-fiction and Get it Published,* by Susan Rabiner and Alfred Fortunato. An agent and her husband, a freelance editor and writer, offer useful advice on how books succeed and why.
- *The Shortest Distance Between You and a Published Book: 20 Steps to Success,* by Susan Page. Advice and strategies all the way from goals for the book to getting a contract to writing it to dealing with doubt and procrastination.
- *Literary Agents: What They Do, How They Do It, and How to Find and Work with the Right One for You,* by Michael Larsen. How to launch your career as a writer, with an unexpected plus: it helps deal with rejection.
- *Be Your Own Literary Agent: The Ultimate Insider's Guide to Getting Published,* by Martin P. Levin. If you want to do it on your own, try this book.

Do You Need an Agent?

If you want to be published, rather than self-published, you probably need an agent. The exception is if you plan to pursue small publishers, such as university presses and regional presses. Your chances of being published are exponentially better with a good agent. If you don't believe me, look at the *Writer's Market,* which lists information on book publishers every year. Each listing gives the percentage of books a publisher accepts from agents versus authors. You'll notice that:

- The number of books publishers accept from agents (versus unrepresented authors) is usually higher, frequently much higher.
- Typically, the larger the publisher, the more books it publishes from agents. At HarperCollins, only 5 percent of its books come directly from writers.
- The smaller the advance ($10,000 and under), the more writers the publisher accepts directly. Rutgers University Press accepts 70 percent of its books from authors without agents and offers a $1,000–$10,000 advance.

If you're thinking you just want to get published and you don't care about the advance or quality of the publisher, snap out of it. You will "live, sleep, and breathe that subject, 24/7, for two or more years, and it will take money away from your other jobs," says agent Carole Bidnick, who represents such authors as Peggy Knickerbocker and Fran Gage.

For such hard work, you deserve a good deal. Aim high with a good agent who will be your advocate and guide. Author Mark Bittman once wrote in a newsletter, "An agent will change your career. If your idea is a good one and you're capable of delivering on it, an agent can recognize that and convince an editor you're worth a gamble. Yes, you might be able to do it yourself, but the process will work better, faster, and more profitably with an agent. Most experienced authors agree that doing it yourself is a complete waste of time and money."

Harriet Bell, former vice president and editorial director of William Morrow Cookbooks, says she'd hire an agent if she wanted to get published. "If I ever wrote a book—and I have no intention of doing so—I'd hire an agent even with twenty-five years in the business," she says. "An agent allows the author/editor relationship to be about the work, not the business or money, and an agent is there for contingency purposes. If anything goes wrong, authors need someone on their side to navigate the waters." She's talking about after you get the contract. Contrary to what people believe, agents do lots more than just get you in the door.

The agent's job: Agents understand the industry and can evaluate your book's chances. If they take you on as a client, they should review your proposal and give suggestions on how to improve it. You will sign a contract in which you agree that the agent receives a 15 to 20 percent commission of all money due you. You may also be charged for office expenses relevant to your proposal, such as phone calls and shipping. Agents will target the most appropriate publishers for your book and send out your proposal with a cover letter. Right there, you've got a huge advantage. Editors drown in proposals and query letters. Most take boxes of mail home at night to keep up. They pay attention to cover letters from agents. Rux Martin, executive editor at Houghton Mifflin, says 95 percent of the proposals she sees come from agents.

Regardless of whether the agent contacts the editor or you send the proposal yourself, here's how the process of reviewing a proposal might work at a publishing house. An assistant sorts the proposals into piles. The top priority pile could come from a previously published author, someone with name recognition or someone recommended by a friend of the house, such as an author, agent, or employee. Or it might capitalize on a trend or appear to be well written. The second pile might represent books more modest in scope but with commercial appeal, well written but not referred. The third pile does not fit with what the publisher wants.

Many publishers put unsolicited, unagented queries, proposals, and manuscripts into what's called the "slush pile." It's a derisive moniker for low-priority reading. That shows you how much editors rely on referrals, authors they've already published, and agents. On the other hand, all proposals get read, regardless of how they come in over the transom.

If you've managed to work with an agent who specializes in cookbooks and food-based books, you'll be in the top pile. Agent Coover explains, "We have a more intimate relationship with editors because editors, like agents, specialize. It's our job to know the editors' tastes, what they're looking for, and what's on their lists (which books they publish)."

Not only do agents know editors' tastes, they often know the editors personally, keeping track of who just had a baby, who got married, and who got promoted. Some can reel off memorized phone numbers. Most agents arrange to see editors regularly, regardless of where the editor or agent lives, meeting to gage interest in upcoming book projects.

When it's time to send out the proposal, agents decide whether to send it to just one editor or make multiple submissions. Sometimes they think a certain editor would love your book and call that one editor first. Or they might ship out the proposal to ten or twelve editors and wait for replies.

Some agents spend up to three years trying to sell a book, but it usually takes less time. If every appropriate editor turns it down, that's the end. If editors say they would buy your book if it were different, you and the agent will decide whether to change it. If an editor makes an offer, the agent evaluates it and negotiates it on your behalf. This is another advantage, as contracts are often ponderous documents with small type and obscure language. Agents know the terminology and which items to pursue. "An agent is your buffer, but also your advocate, always looking for more: more advance money, more public relations and marketing, more design input, more photographs, and so on. Your agent is also your reality check as to what's reasonable and possible," says agent Lisa Ekus.

Finding and Getting an Agent

Agents can be elusive. Since they reject at least 95 percent of all book ideas, many limit their visibility. At the same time, they sincerely want to discover fresh talent, so many others have websites and attend writers' conferences. To contact them, avoid a phone call, unless you've been referred and know they want to have a conversation. If they don't know you, go through traditional channels by sending them queries and proposals.

You'll have lots of competition. Like editors, agents also drown in queries and proposals, and most represent all kinds of non-fiction, not just cookbooks and food-based books. Coover says she gets 25 to 30 cookbook proposals per month, not counting other kinds of non-fiction. Jane Dystel of Dystel & Goderich Literary Management represents such authors as the Food Network's Ellie Krieger. She says she sees around 40 proposals per month, with food-based books making up only 10 percent of the books her agency represents.

Like editors, agents want to be contacted a certain way. Some like email, some want regular mail; some want just the query, some want the whole proposal. Call the office or look at their Web sites to find out how and what to submit before doing so.

All agents say they want new writers and new voices, but most don't take on writers who will attract low advances, such as $5,000. Because they get 15 percent of the advance, it's not worth their time. When Lisa Ekus started her agenting business, she dedicated half of her list to first-time writers. "I felt it was critical to give new voices a platform," she says. "Publishers are more resistant to an unknown first-time writer. I sold about 80 percent. Almost all are working on a second and sometimes a third book." Today, however, her business has matured, and she will turn down writers with good credentials and book ideas if she feels she can't give them the time they deserve. Ekus also has businesses that teach media training and offer public relations services to writers.

To find agents, try these tactics:

Look in the acknowledgments section of a book: When authors thank their agents, they do so in the acknowledgments section.

Join the International Association of Culinary Professionals: If you are a member of the food industry, a cooking teacher, restaurateur, or a published food writer, membership entitles you to go to the annual conference that agents attend and to review the online directory, which contains contact listings for agents who specialize in food-based books (www.iacp.com).

Join other food-based associations: Agents might be members or attend events. Members might know agents and be willing to help you. Associations include:

- The American Culinary Federation: www.acfchefs.org
- The American Institute of Wine & Food: www.aiwf.org
- Les Dames d'Escoffier: www.ldei.org
- The Research Chefs Association: www.researchchefs.org

- Slow Food: www.slowfood.com
- Women Chefs and Restaurateurs: www.womenchefs.org.

Go to writing conferences: Agents often speak at conferences, teach classes, lurk in the audience and sign up for pitch meetings that are like speed dating. Sometimes you can pay extra and have an agent evaluate a few pages of your proposal.

Take a writing class or join a writing group: The instructor might know an agent and refer you, or someone in the group might know an agent.

Someone you know, or a friend of a friend, must have written a book: That person might have an agent—ask.

Go to book signings: Agents might attend to support their clients.

Research online databases: At Publishers Marketplace, http://publishersmarketplace.com, look under agents who specialize in cookbooks. Literary Marketplacc, www.literarymarketplace.com, lists agents in alphabetical order by name, with limited contact information. Agent Query is a newer database that also lists agents, www.agentquery.com.

When you find an agent who wants to represent you, make sure you have good chemistry and that you trust the agent. You want an agent who returns your calls and keeps you up to date, someone who is truly excited about your book. You'll probably sign a short contract, and you might pay for their expenses in mailing out proposals.

What If You Still Don't Want or Need an Agent?

Not everyone wants an agent, and not everyone needs one, particularly if you're targeting a smaller publisher such as Pequot, Running Press, Robert Rose, Sasquatch, and Storey Publishing. Smaller publishers, and some of the larger ones, will read your query letter or proposal, regardless of whether you have an agent. Few larger publishers read unsolicited manuscripts, however, so don't start there.

"Editors read unsolicited material because some good stuff comes in that way. You may be surprised by a proposal with an unusual take on something. You can't take anything for granted," says Bill LeBlond of Chronicle Books. San Francisco caterers and twins Sara Whiteford Corpening and Mary Corpening Barber came to him without an agent, with an idea for a smoothies book that sold 300,000 copies.

If you decide to target a small publisher, a regional publisher, or a university press, agents may not be interested in your book anyway because the advances are much lower than from traditional publishers, and the 15 percent of your royalty will not be worth their time. That's fine. Andrew F. Smith, a prolific author of food history books, says he's been successful by networking and getting to know editors at small publishers without the help of an agent.

Before you send off your proposal, do your homework. Find out which publishers would be most likely to publish a book like yours by looking for similar books in the library or bookstore. Don't send a proposal on regional foods of Kentucky to Random House, a national publisher, for example.

Most publishers have Web sites with submissions guidelines. Read them before submitting your query or proposal, and submit what they ask for. If all they want is a table of contents, don't send the whole proposal.

If you want to target particular editors, find out how each likes to be approached by calling a junior person in the editorial department of that publishing house. Some editors want an email query first, some only want proposals, and some want snail-mailed query letters. Do not send a generic letter that says "Dear Editor."

If an editor expresses interest in your book, you might want an agent to negotiate for you and deal with the contract. Agents often take a reduced commission for this work. If not, and an editor makes an offer on your book, hire an attorney who specializes in publishing to review the contract. Don't have your regular attorney, who specializes in trusts or tax law, review the contract. His or her unfamiliarity with standard publishing practices will drive your editor crazy.

Reasons for Rejection

When you've compiled your list of agents or editors, send out your proposals or queries all at once, and follow up if you don't hear back. Unless you have a connection, waiting for a response takes forever because agents and editors take weeks, often months, to answer. Be prepared for rejection, but also realize that it only takes one agent to like your book idea. Agents and editors reject projects for several reasons, not necessarily because they don't like you or your book idea, such as when:

- An agent has already sold a similar book, or it conflicts with a current project in the pipeline at a publishing house.
- They find the material well written and well presented, but are not interested in the subject.
- They think the idea is too narrow and will attract too few readers.
- The subject has been done to death.
- The trend has already passed. (Most books at big houses take two to three years from first contact to publication, so trend-based books can be dangerous there. Smaller publishers often can turn around a book more quickly.)
- Your idea is too trendy or not substantive or interesting enough for a whole book. It might be best for a magazine article instead.
- They don't like your writing.

Most often, however, agents reject queries and proposals because the author has not done a professional job. "It's amazing how many people can't be bothered to do the simplest things when they submit proposals," says LeBlond. "If you're going to the trouble of submitting it, why not get it right? We get badly copied proposals that were tossed into one envelope, rejected, and then stuck into another envelope with a photocopied letter that says 'Dear editor.' They look shabby and worn." Ekus has had similar experiences. "Often I receive proposals that are incomplete, poorly researched, about a subject that's been done to death, or even illiterate."

Sometimes publishers think your book has the germ of an idea and may suggest how they'd like to see it. Lori Longbotham wanted to write an unillustrated cookbook of lemon recipes, both savory and sweet, says LeBlond. Chronicle recast it as a book on lemon desserts, with only sixty recipes and beautiful photography. It was so successful that Chronicle had Longbotham follow with *Luscious Chocolate Desserts* in 2004, *Luscious Berry Desserts* in 2006, and *Luscious Coconut Desserts* in 2010.

The Contract

Regardless of whether you go it alone or use an agent, you'll receive a publishing contract once you and your editor agree on the sale. Contracts vary in size and complexity, but all cover the main issues you will negotiate:

The advance: An advance is a loan against royalties. You will not earn any further income until after book sales reach the amount of the advance. Typically, advances for first-time authors range from $5,000 to $25,000. If you have worked on and developed your platform, the amount could be higher. You do not have to repay the advance to the publisher if the book fails to sell.

The royalties: Let's say you are offered a $10,000 advance, with the cover price of the book estimated at $20. Typically, royalties are 10 to 15 percent of the price of a hardcover, and 7.5 percent of the price of a paperback. At 7.5 percent, your take is $1.50 per book. Once the publisher has sold 6,667 books, equal to $10,000, you will begin receiving royalties if more books sell. Some publishers, particularly very small houses, pay royalties on a percentage of net sales rather than on retail price.

If the book will have color photographs, the royalty rates will be different. Sometimes publishers pay the photographer and sometimes you do. In that case, your advance should be larger to cover the cost.

Agents try for the biggest advance they can get because most books do not earn past their advance. Regardless of whether you use an agent, you may have to use the funds from your advance to pay for illustrations, travel, recipe ingredients, researchers, testers, and an index.

Timing: The time publishers give you to write your book varies, but usually they have a date in mind and work back from it to establish a deadline. It could be nine months or three years to publication, depending on the complexity of the book and whether it will have photographs. Most publishers release books twice a year, in spring and fall.

They choose the season based on when they think the book will do best. For example, it makes more sense to publish a cookbook of soups and stews in the fall—when readers are looking for hearty comfort foods—than it does in the spring. And most gift books come out in the fall, in time for the holidays.

"You want to fight for all the time you can get," advises cookbook author Janet Fletcher. "Take your time and do a good job." On the other hand, she has also written books quickly when the publisher has a launch date in mind. When I spoke to her she had recently begun writing a book with a chef due in six months.

The fine print: The publishing industry has its own private language of bonus clauses, subsidiary rights (the rights to use the material in abridged, adapted and condensed versions), options, and discounts you get for buying books. (To fully explain the various options and legalese would take pages, but since my expertise is in writing and not contracts, refer to Helpful Books on Getting Published, on page 275 to learn more.) If you have an agent you still have the final say on whether to accept the offer. Once you agree, it takes two to three months to get a signed contract and the first advance check.

If you've been doing the math as you've been reading, you'll see that writing a book is not much of a moneymaking proposition. If you spend one year writing a book for a $15,000 advance, it's not exactly a living wage. Now that you know you're not going to make much money, what's another 15 percent of "not much money" anyway? Agents are worth it. They want you to succeed, they'll work hard to get the best deal, and they'll help you move forward with your next book.

Agents want you as a long-term investment, not a one-shot deal. "Advice, recommendations, inspiration and consolation are also necessary components of a strong author-agent relationship," says Ekus. "I think of myself as a combination pitch woman, negotiator, and mother—which includes nurturing and nagging."

The Publishing Experience

Congratulations. You have a contract and you've started writing your book. The editor who purchased your book may be your editor, but not necessarily. You may work with someone new. The new editor could leave and you'll get another editor. Agent Coover says one of her authors was assigned to a new editor who had rejected her book idea earlier at another publishing house!

It's your job to establish a relationship with your editor and to meet your deadlines. You may have a few preliminary conversations about the book, but then you could be on your own. While every editor is different, it seems to me that most editors spend their time on the front end, acquiring books and dealing with contracts, and that they engage once you've turned in your manuscript, not before. Also, your editor may be editing between ten and twenty books simultaneously, so unless you're a big author, you're not going to get the most attention.

Don't let that stop you, however, if you have questions or concerns. Tell your editor if you're having problems with the deadline, have significant questions about the book's structure, or you're wondering whether to write a different book. Do so at the front end, not a week before the due date. "Editors are happy to hear from writers," says Fletcher. "They don't reach out but I think they'd love to help when a writer has questions. Publishing houses are so understaffed they don't have the time they'd like to shepherd manuscripts."

She recommends giving the editor a chunk of the manuscript early, perhaps the first third of it, and getting feedback. "They may have a different idea and good suggestions and you don't want to get to the end of it and then find out," she advises. That happened to a friend of mine. He turned in a book that had taken years to research and write, only to be given a few months to rewrite it according to the editor's instructions. In the end, he won a national award for the book, but it took him years to cool down.

Some publishers, such as Ten Speed Press, set up a schedule where it's part of the contract to produce a few chapters early on, for the reason Fletcher mentioned, and to drive sales. "Often editors will need a significant portion of a manuscript to circulate internally for sales purposes in advance of the due date," explains Wehner.

The art department will probably work on a book jacket early on as well, because the publisher needs a book cover image and title for the catalog. If your editor approves the cover design, he or she will be sent to you for your input. The author does not have final say over the design or the title. That's up to the publisher. Typically the contract will say only that you are to be consulted. If you have a disagreement, here's where an agent can be indispensable. The agent's job is to advocate for you, so he or she can speak to the editor on your behalf.

Even if you don't have an agent, speak up if you have specific issues. Janet Fletcher recalls when a publisher came to her with a cover almost identical to a book by another author. "It was so close in design, type and color, I thought this was totally dumb on their part because readers can be confused," she recalls. She contacted the author of the other book. "We both ganged up on the publisher and got them to change my cover," she says with satisfaction.

When it comes to writing the manuscript, unless you have deadlines for specific sections, it doesn't matter where you begin. Some authors start with the most difficult parts, as they take the longest. Some start at the beginning. Some write the easiest parts first, just to get going. As long as you make progress and gauge how you're doing in relation to your deadline, go in whichever order you like. Remember that you will have written a sample chapter or two for your proposal, and that should ease your mind, even if you have to revise them. Also be careful of getting waylaid by fascinating research. We food enthusiasts tend to be excited by everything we discover, and you will need discipline.

The most important thing is not to get overwhelmed by the idea of writing an entire book. Break it down into chapters, break it down into sections, and do a piece at a time, even if you tell yourself you're only going to write for 15 minutes per day. You'll get there.

As you complete your book, build in time to have others review your chapters. Line up at least one trusted advisor who will read your work as you complete it and give you constructive feedback. It's good to have a reality check before the editor sees it. Some people hire editors to review their work before sending their manuscript into the publisher, just to get an extra edge of professionalism.

The editor's job is to review your manuscript, edit it, and send it back for revision. You might not hear back for a week or more after turning in your magnum opus. Don't take it personally. Eventually, you'll get a call or an email. Your editor needs time to look at the big picture in what's called a developmental edit—whether material in one chapter would be better in another or combined with it, whether a section lacks focus or you've left things out, or whether you've written too much. He or she may query you on anything that seems confusing, tangential, incorrect, or poorly phrased. You may get this information in a phone call, a letter, or as questions in the text of the manuscript.

After you make the corrections and adjustments and turn in a second draft, your manuscript goes to a copy editor, who will edit it to fit the style of the publishing house and for punctuation and grammar. The copy editor will also question whatever appears to be unclear. Some of the comments might seem obtuse, such as "It seems if you want to keep the eggs, pork, etc. set off by em dashes, we should drop 'raised'—only 'produce' needs the verb." Sometimes they have opinions or questions, particularly on recipes. A good copy editor specializing in recipes is worth her weight in gold. She will question times, doneness, ingredients, pan sizes, what got left out, and perhaps suggest what you should add in. You may get these queries as tons of tiny yellow sticky notes on a printed manuscript, or—more commonly now—as electronic queries in a file.

If your book has photography, the process begins after you've turned in the manuscript. While you may suggest a photographer, again, the publisher has final say. Every publishing house works a little differently, but typically, your editor makes a preliminary list of which recipes will have photos. You'll also see a layout of the book, showing where photos will appear.

You probably will not be involved in the photo shoot, which takes place in a studio. Sometimes shoots take place elsewhere, such as in the countryside, at farms, or at famer's markets. (For more on photo shoots, see pages 197–200.) The photo shoot for the cookbook I wrote for Craig Priebe, *Grilled Pizzas & Piadinas*, took place at the New York home of the art director because he had a balcony, and we needed an outdoor location for grilling. On site were the editor, the art director, the photographer, the photographer's assistant, the prop stylist, the food stylist, and my co-author. He was there to make the pizza crusts.

The shoot took ten days and Craig saw each finished shot. I had to reconcile a few with their respective recipes. The worst offender was a salad. Salads are problematic because they wilt as soon as they are dressed, so the photographer has only a few moments to shoot. The food stylist placed eye dropper-size bits of creamy salad dressing on the greens, so small you couldn't see them. The cantaloupe was supposed to be chopped into the salad, but it was presented on the side, as slices. I asked Craig for a new vinaigrette to match the photo, and I rewrote the cantaloupe part to match the recipe.

Once the book gets laid out and the photographs inserted by the designer, you'll see page proofs that look just like the finished book. Take this opportunity to read every word and check every photo, caption, title, pull quote, etc. Even though your editor and copy editor have reviewed your manuscript, errors may remain, and you're the one with the most to lose if they go through. Look at each page as a whole, not just the text. I caught an error on a photo where the photographer had used a paper sheet for a plain background, and the edge of the sheet was visible. You never know what you'll find, and you want to find every possible error.

Often at this point the book is sent to the people who have agreed to give you an endorsement or blurb. It's your job to find the contact information and give it to the publisher. Your editor might have suggestions too on who would be best for your book.

From there it's on to production and printing. A print run of 5,000 to 10,000 books is considered typical for a first-time author, unless you're a big name. The number is based on pre-orders for the book. Publishers would rather print fewer books and reprint than keep thousands of books in their warehouse and pay storage charges. Most publishers depend on backlist books that continue selling long after publication. Some books stay in print decades after they were written, particularly if they don't include photos, which date the book.

You Could Also Self-Publish

While most of this chapter addresses traditional publishing, more and more people choose self-publishing. Whether it's right for you depends on your goal. If you're writing a cookbook or memoir for yourself or your family, and you have no intention of selling it, self-publishing is a great idea. It also depends what you mean by self-published. In the broadest sense, self-publishers are authors who pay the full cost of publishing their books. If you print your Word file out on 8 ½ x 11-inch paper, make twenty copies, and put each in a binder, that's self-published. If you want to produce a bound book, you have a few choices: Print on Demand, Print it yourself, or hire a custom cookbook publisher.

Print on Demand (POD): You write your book and submit the file to an electronic publisher. You either pay for a designer to lay it out first or pay the publisher to do so. Your book is stored in an electronic database. The company manufactures one book at a time when a sale comes in over the Internet.

Most POD books are trade paperback (5.5 x 5.8 inches) with a colored cover. A few publishers offer hardcover, full-color books with color photography, but they're expensive to produce. The publisher sets the price. At this stage, hardcover full-color books are still too expensive for you to resell them at a profit.

POD has advantages. The company mails the book and processes the funds. You don't store the books. POD companies give you royalties when copies are sold, often much higher than what traditional publishers pay. You can make revisions by submitting new copy and printing a new edition. On the other hand, most bookstores will not stock POD books, and book distributors will not sell them. So you do all the marketing. Many companies will arrange to put your book in online bookstores like Amazon, and some offer public relations and marketing services for additional fees.

Print it yourself: In this case you would hire all the same people a publisher works with to produce a book. You will:

- hire a copy editor
- find a graphic designer to design the book and create the cover
- choose the size and paper stock
- decide on whether to include color, photographs, or illustrations; and then work with a photographer or illustrator
- evaluate bids from printers
- take receipt of your published books and store them

In short, writing the book is just the first step. You make decisions on all aspects of design and production. This is a great way to go if you want to control every aspect of your book's production, down to the paper stock and typeface.

Hire a custom publisher that specializes in cookbooks: If you don't want to print it yourself, these publishers print customized high-quality cookbooks for food companies and non-profits such as Junior Leagues. Services include editing, marketing, and distributing your book. One of the websites offering that service is www.heritagecook book.com. (See Selected Resources for Self-Publishing on page 295.)

Several good reasons exist to self-publish. See if any of these are right for you:

- **Profits go directly to you.** You pay all the expenses up front, and profits go to you.
- **Get into print faster than traditional publishing.** Traditional publishing typically takes between eighteen months and two years from the time you submit your manuscript to the time you hold a finished book in your hands. Self-publishing is often a few months away.
- **Keep the copyrights and subsidiary rights to your work.** It is possible to keep the copyright with a traditional publisher, but difficult to keep the subsidiary rights, which include foreign rights and first and second serial, audio, and theatrical rights.
- **Establish a track record to sell to a traditional publisher, if you are a first-time author.** "If someone came to me with high sales, such as 10,000 copies in a year, and had a track record of public speaking and demonstrations, I would consider them," says agent Carole Bidnick. If you're committed enough to typeset, design, print and sell your book one copy at a time, you'll impress agents and editors as a go-getter.
- **Control every aspect of the entire process, from editorial to design to marketing.** If you are the type who doesn't want anyone telling you what to do, self-publishing is a better fit for you. You don't have to hire an editor to judge your

sentences, content, or structure, but I still recommend it. You design the cover, even if it's by using templates from the POD site. You decide on the book's size, paper quality, and typeface. Some people relish this new learning experience.

- **Print a small number of copies.** If you don't have much money, don't want stacks of books in your garage, and don't want to process and ship each order, POD makes sense.

JUDY KANCIGOR'S FAMILY COOKBOOK

"It all started because a favorite aunt was dying at the same time my daughter-in-law was expecting her first grandchild," says Judy Kancigor, author of *Melting Pot Memories: The Rabinowitz Family Cookbook and Nostalgic History.* "I wanted to preserve history of the family. I told everyone, 'If you're related by blood or marriage, you can be in the book.'"

She wrote a letter to all her relatives, suggesting the kinds of recipes she wanted. Some responded right away while others had to be nagged. "My cousin's husband copied my aunt's entire handwritten recipe book, because she was the primary cook in the family," she recalls. "She was close to ninety, she remembered everything. We went through her book page by page and she told me which recipes to put in."

At first, Kancigor became overwhelmed by the task, but eventually she worked on it full time. "If you can get people to help you, delegate," she advises. Three years later, she had a cookbook with 850 recipes about her family's Jewish heritage and foods. Working with a custom publisher of cookbooks, she sent in handwritten recipes on separate pages. A typist typed them into Microsoft Word files. Kancigor made "this huge leap" and ordered 500 copies, with 300 earmarked for friends and family. The other 200 sold. She made revisions and ordered more. "Another 500 were gone in six weeks," she says.

"My cookbook was very expensive," admits Kancigor. "I wanted the photos a certain way, and I wanted heavier stock and dividers." In total, she published 11,000 copies and sold them all. She did so by speaking to Jewish women's groups, putting a coupon in the back of the book for ordering, and getting the book into Judaica shops, cookbook stores, and temple gift shops. She put it on Amazon. Even so, her book was not much of a moneymaker. She jokes that her dad used to say, "You lose money on every sale but make it up in volume."

Kancigor writes terrific, funny recipes. Here's a sample: "If doubling the recipe, don't put it all in the food processor at the same time, because it overflows from the bottom. This I learned from personal experience. In my daughter-in-law's kitchen yet." "The writing is what I enjoy more than the cooking. I crack myself up. I sit there, enjoying me," she says.

"My kids are still scratching their heads and saying, 'How come people are reading about our family?'" she says. "People bought the book because they have photos like that, or they see their own family. The immigrant story is universal. People bought the book for a daughter-in-law who's not Jewish and coming into their family, or for bridal showers."

Kancigor promoted the book all over the country. At an International Association of Culinary Professionals annual conference, editors approached her when she spoke on a panel with Ruth Reichl. Later that year, she signed a contract. Workman Publishing published *Cooking Jewish* in 2007, with a printing of 35,000 books. She rewrote the book at her editor's urging. "They taught me how to write a recipe," she said. "I didn't have pan sizes, serving sizes, and Workman is very precise." They sent her on a twenty-four-city book tour, put her on TV, set up four radio tours where interviewers called her for four days by phone, plus she continued doing her own publicity.

Reasons to Hesitate

Before you get all excited and rush to self-publish, there are just as many reasons not to do it. If you plan to sell the book, you will have to promote it. Your chances of success are higher if you have a built-in marketing system or platform. You might already:

- teach cooking classes
- own a restaurant
- own a retail store
- have a television show
- have a heavily-trafficked Web site
- distribute a newsletter seen by hundreds of people

In each case, your book will appear in front of readers who could buy it. Carol Fenster self-published a book on dietary restrictions and sold it through the lecture circuit. "She had the numbers, database, touring, and platform within her area of expertise," says her agent, Lisa Ekus, who sold Fenster's self-published book to Putnam/Penguin in a two-book deal.

One of the writers I've worked with, Melissa Guerra, had a PBS television show called *The Texas Provincial Kitchen*. She self-published 5,000 professionally designed color paperback cookbooks and sold them at the end of each show for $19.95, then reprinted another 8,000 when those were gone. Her book sold around 12,000 copies before the show went off the air. She's still selling it on her Web site, www .melissaguerra.com.

While her cost per book was around $5, she says she broke even, and wouldn't have done so if she did not have free storage. (Do the math: 13,000 books at $5 each equals a $65,000 initial cash investment.) "The worst thing a novice writer can do is not listen when people tell you how the book industry functions," says Guerra. "Writing for a publishing house is definitely the way to go." Her query letter attracted the interest of eight agents. Wiley published her second book, *Dishes from the Wild Horse Desert*.

Here's my problem with self-publishing. When you publish traditionally, you receive a check. The publisher produces and distributes the book, and usually helps you market it. With self-publishing, *you* write the check, you figure out how to publish the book, and most often, you sell it yourself. It's almost impossible to get into bookstores and other retail stores with a self-published book.

Here's my list of reasons to hesitate:

- You believe your book will sell a million copies and you're going to get rich. This is not a good reason to publish anything, no matter how it's produced. It's too hard to write a book if money is your only motive.
- Your book will have less credibility than a traditionally published book. The stamp of a traditional publisher means that someone in the business thought your work was worthwhile. Otherwise, anyone can publish anything they want, regard-

less of quality. Granted, people start their own publishing companies to publish one book, and it's getting harder to tell whether a book is self-published.

- You might have to store several thousand books. "I didn't realize it," says Judy Kancigor, author of *Melting Pot Memories* (see page 292). "They come to your house. In your garage, you have to get them up on top of something in case your washing machine overflows." She stored her books in clear plastic cartons, raised off the floor.

- If you sell one at a time, it will take forever. Most stores buy from distributors, and most distributors don't take self-published books. Some self-publishing companies offer more distribution than others, but it's still limited compared to traditional publishers.

- If you don't like the idea of promoting yourself, it's going to be awfully hard to sell all those books.

- You have to become an expert on many aspects of publishing, including editing, design, paper stock, production, and printing. If you just want to write, these responsibilities can be overwhelming.

- Unless you choose POD, fulfillment is your responsibility. That's a fancy word for processing the order: cashing checks and taking credit cards, boxing up books and mailing them out, one by one.

- You want a full-color, hardcover coffee-table book. Forget it, unless you are very wealthy and want a book for yourself or a few copies for friends and family.

- Self-publishing can be astonishingly expensive. You pay all up-front costs, and you get stuck with the leftover inventory.

SELECTED RESOURCES FOR SELF-PUBLISHING

These Web and print sources provide lots more information, should you wish to pursue this type of publishing. The ultimate authority on self-publishing is Dan Poynter, at www.parapublishing.com, author of *The Self-Publishing Manual: How to Write, Print and Sell Your Own Book.*

Print-on-Demand publishers to explore:

- Authorhouse, www.authorhouse.com
- Create Space, owned by Amazon, www.createspace.com
- iUniverse, www.iuniverse.com
- Lulu, www.lulu.com
- Trafford On-Demand Publishing Services, www.trafford.com
- Xlibris, www.xlibris.com

Custom publishers specializing in cookbooks:

- Cookbook Publishers, www.cookbookpublishers.com, has a downloadable price sheet that calculates cost based on how many recipes you plan to print and how many books you want to publish. Minimum order is 100 books.
- Favorite Recipes Press, www.frpbooks.com. Custom cookbooks require a 4,000 minimum press run.
- Fundcraft, www.fundcraft.com, makes spiral-bound books with a minimum order of 200.
- Heritage Cookbooks, www.heritagecookbook.com, lets you print as few as four books. It operates on a monthly membership plan.
- Morris Press Cookbooks, www.morriscookbooks.com, lets you type your recipes into the company's own software program to save costs. Minimum order is 100 books. Books are spiral bound or binders.
- Wimmer Cookbook Distribution, www.wimmerco.com, requires a minimum 1,000-book order for its standard cookbook template, and a 3,000-minimum order for its custom cookbooks.

If you're not planning to sell your book to a traditional publisher, you might consider custom software programs, which let you store and organize recipes, then print them ready for binding. They include BigOven Deluxe Inspired Cooking, Living Cookbook, MasterCook, and Cook'n with Betty Crocker. Some generate grocery lists and nutritional analysis. But if you land a publishing deal, you'll end up doing lots of retyping and reformatting, because publishers want a standard Microsoft Word file.

In the End

You've made it to the end of this book. From *Will Write for Food*'s first chapter, my goal has been to help you write about food, whether for yourself or for publication. I hope you have the tools to express your ideas, thoughts, and opinions in words. Now it's up to you to believe you have something to say and a compelling way to say it. Believe in yourself and your ideas, and believe that you can move forward. Keep writing and rewriting, even if it's only for fifteen minutes per day.

At least half of the path to publication is about not giving up. Just remember that even Julia Child was rejected the first time an editor saw her manuscript. Imagine how much we would have lost if she gave up right then. As publishing veteran Harriett Bell told me, "Every successful cookbook author was once someone who just had an idea." Discovering a promising new writer is one of the things editors and agents love most about their jobs. Give them the opportunity to find you.

Acknowledgments

This book would not have been possible without the generous responses of the knowledgeable food writers, bloggers, editors, and agents I interviewed. Almost everyone, no matter how well known, gave me their time and came up with thoughtful responses. They read emails and took calls at the office, at home, on the road, on vacation, and after retirement. I am grateful for the time they spent educating me, sharing their sagacity, and giving advice so beneficial to my readers.

Several friends and colleagues gave me useful feedback, including David Lebovitz, Stephanie Stiavetti, Renee Schettler, Faith Kramer, Eva Heninwolff, Greg Patent, Laura Taxel, Greta Wu, Mary Margaret Pack, and Gary Allen. Kris Montgomery provided encouragement, brainstorming, and proofing. Josh Greenbaum came up with the witty title. Thanks to David Lebovitz, a veteran of blogging, cookbook writing, and freelance writing, for writing the foreword.

My husband, Owen Rubin, provided technical support. He also gave terrific neck and shoulder massages, and laughed with me over the funny parts.

Agent Carole Bidnick encouraged me from the first mention of this idea, and championed the second edition of this book.

My gratitude goes to all readers of my blog, also called Will Write for Food, who provided thoughtful comments relevant to the second edition of this book. I thank my clients and students, from whom I have learned so much. I am indebted to other authors of books and Web sites for resource material on good writing, blogging, freelancing, proposal writing, self-publishing, and finding agents.

Thanks to the team at Da Capo for skillfully handling the second edition: Renée Sedliar, senior editor; Alex Camlin, art director; Collin Tracy, project editor; Lara Simpson, publicist; Pam Getchell, copy editor; James Steinberg, indexer; and Merrill Gilfillan, proofreader.

Thanks to all those who've kept my skills sharp by hiring me to edit articles, proposals, manuscripts, and recipes; and to those who've taught me what it's like to be on the other side as a writer.

Appendix

Interview Subjects

- Allegra, Antonia, creator and director of the Symposium for Professional Food Writers at the Greenbrier
- Anderson, J. P., former restaurant editor, Chicago Citysearch
- Andrews, Colman, co-founder, *Saveur* magazine
- Baggett, Nancy, cookbook author
- Bauer, Michael, executive food and wine editor and restaurant critic for the *San Francisco Chronicle*
- Bell, Harriet, freelance book editor, former vice president and editorial director of William Morrow Cookbooks
- Bidnick, Carole, literary agent, Bidnick & Company
- Bittman, Mark, *New York Times* columnist and cookbook author
- Boorstin, Sharon, book author
- Bourdain, Anthony, TV chef and author of memoirs, novels, and cookbooks
- Byrn, Anne, cookbook author
- Caruso, Maren, food photographer
- Coover, Doe, literary agent, The Doe Coover Agency
- Doyle, Amanda, associate editor, *Where* magazine, St. Louis
- Dusolier, Clotilde, author and blogger
- Dystel, Jane, literary agent, Dystel and Goderich Literary Management
- Ekus, Lisa, literary agent, Lisa Ekus Public Relations Company
- Estabrook, Barry, freelance writer and blogger
- Fletcher, Janet, cookbook author and freelance writer
- Fluke, Joanne, author, culinary mysteries
- Furiya, Linda, memoirist and freelance writer

- Gage, Fran, cookbook author and essayist
- Goldstein, Darra, editor, *Gastronomica: The Journal of Food and Culture*
- Greenspan, Dorie, cookbook author and freelance writer
- Grimes, William, former restaurant reviewer, the *New York Times*
- Guarnaschelli, Maria, vice president, W. W. Norton & Company
- Guerra, Melissa, cookbook author
- Hesser, Amanda, author and co-founder, Food52 (Web site)
- Holmberg, Martha, former publisher, *Fine Cooking* magazine
- Jones, Judith, senior editor and vice president, Alfred A. Knopf
- Kancigor, Judy, cookbook author and columnist
- Kirchner, Bharti, cookbook author and novelist
- Knickerbocker, Peggy, freelance writer and cookbook author
- Laudan, Rachel, author and food historian
- LeBlond, Bill, editorial director of food and drink, Chronicle Books
- Lebovitz, David, blogger and author
- Leite, David, cookbook author and publisher of Leite's Culinaria (Web site)
- Madison, Deborah, cookbook author
- Mark, Rosemary, recipe developer
- Martin, Rux, executive editor, Houghton Mifflin Company
- McGee, Harold, author of *On Food and Cooking*
- McManus, Jeanne, former food editor, the *Washington Post*
- McPherson, Heather, food editor, the *Orlando Sentinel*
- Medrich, Alice, cookbook author
- Miner, Sydny, Crown Books executive editor
- Moskowitz, Dara, restaurant critic and senior editor, *Minnesota Monthly*
- Narayan, Shoba, author of *Monsoon Diary: A Memoir with Recipes*
- Nathan, Joan, cookbook author and freelance writer
- O'Neill, Molly, author, and freelance writer
- Oliver, Sandy, food historian
- Pack, Mary Margaret, food writer and restaurant reviewer, the *Austin Chronicle*
- Parsons, Russ, food section editor, the *Los Angeles Times*
- Patent, Greg, freelance writer and cookbook author
- Reichl, Ruth, memoirist and former editor of *Gourmet*
- Richman, Alan, *GQ* magazine contributing writer
- Richman, Phyllis, author of culinary mysteries and former restaurant reviewer for the *Washington Post*

- Ruhlman, Michael, author and blogger
- Sahni, Julie, cookbook author
- Severson, Kim, food reporter, the *New York Times*
- Shapiro, Laura, author and food historian
- Sheraton, Mimi, former *New York Times* restaurant reviewer
- Sietsema, Tom, food critic, the *Washington Post*
- Smith, Andrew F., author of food history and reference books
- Steingarten, Jeffrey, author and *Vogue* magazine columnist
- Sternman Rule, Cheryl, freelance writer and blogger
- Swanson, Heidi, author and blogger
- Taxel, Laura, freelance writer and guidebook author
- Trillin, Calvin, freelance writer and book author
- Unterman, Patricia, restaurant reviewer and guidebook author
- Werlin, Laura, cookbook author
- Wizenberg, Molly, author and blogger
- Wehner, Aaron, Publisher, Ten Speed Press
- Wood, Virginia, food editor, the *Austin Chronicle*
- Yan, Martin, cookbook author
- Zoloth, Joan, former restaurant reviewer, the *Oakland Tribune*

Bibliography

Ackerman, Diane. *A Natural History of the Senses.* New York, NY: Random House, 1990.

Alexander, Brian. *Atomic Kitchen: Gadgets and Inventions for Yesterday's Cook.* Portland, OR: Collector's Press, 2004.

Allen, Gary. *The Resource Guide for Food Writers.* Oxford, UK: Routledge, 1999.

Allen, Moira Anderson. *Starting Your Career as a Freelance Writer.* New York, NY: Allworth Press, 2003.

Allende, Isabel. *Aphrodite: A Memoir of the Senses.* New York, NY: Perennial, 1999.

Allison, Karen Hubert. *How I Gave My Heart to the Restaurant Business: A Novel.* New York, NY: Ecco, 1997.

Almond, Steve. *Candyfreak: A Journey Through the Chocolate Underbelly of America.* Chapel Hill, NC: Algonquin Books of Chapel Hill, 2004.

Avakian, Arlene Voski, editor. *Through the Kitchen Window: Women Writers Explore the Intimate Meanings of Food and Cooking.* Boston, MA: Beacon Press, 1997.

Baggett, Nancy. *The All-American Cookie Book.* Boston, MA: Houghton Mifflin, 2001.

Beard, James. *James Beard Delights and Prejudices.* Philadelphia, PA: Running Press, 2002.

Bellingham, Linda. *Food Styling for Photographers: A Guide to Creating Your Own Appetizing Art.* Burlington, MA: Focal Press, 2008.

Bemelmans, Ludwig. *Hotel Bemelmans.* New York, NY: Overlook Press, 2004.

Beranbaum, Rose Levy. *The Bread Bible.* New York, NY: W. W. Norton & Company, 2003.

Bittman, Mark. *How to Cook Everything: Simple Recipes for Great Food.* New York, NY: Wiley, 1998.

Boorstin, Sharon. *Cooking for Love: A Novel with Recipes.* Lincoln, NE: iUniverse, Inc., 2004.

Bourdain, Anthony. *A Cook's Tour: In Search of the Perfect Meal.* Waterville, ME: Thorndike Press, 2002.

———. *Bone in the Throat.* New York, NY: Bloomsbury USA, 2000.

———. *Gone Bamboo.* New York, NY: Bloomsbury USA, 2000.

———. *Kitchen Confidential: Adventures in the Culinary Underbelly.* New York, NY: Ecco, 2001.

Brenner, Joel Glenn. *The Emperors of Chocolate: Inside the Secret World of Hershey and Mars.* New York, NY: Broadway, 2000.

Brillat-Savarin, Jean-Anthelme, and M. F. K. Fisher (trans.) *The Physiology of Taste: Or Meditations on Transcendental Gastronomy.* New York, NY: North Point Press, 1986. Originally published in 1825.

Brite, Poppy Z. *Liquor: A Novel.* Three Rivers, MI: Three Rivers Press, 2004.

Brogan, Kathryn S., ed. *2005 Writer's Market.* Cincinnati, OH: Writer's Digest Books, 2004.

Brown, Alton. *I'm Just Here for the Food: Food + Heat = Cooking.* New York, NY: Stewart, Tabori & Chang, 2002.

Brown, Marcia. *Stone Soup.* New York, NY: Aladdin Picture Books, 1997.

Bruni, Frank. *Born Round: The Secret History of a Full-time Eater.* New York, NY: The Penguin Press, 2009.

Buford, Bill. *Heat: An Amateur Cook's Adventures as a Kitchen Slave, Line Cook, Pasta Maker, and Apprentice to a Dante-Quoting Butcher in Tuscany.* New York, NY: Random House, 2004.

Byrn, Anne. *The Cake Mix Doctor.* New York, NY: Workman, 1999.

———. *Chocolate from the Cake Mix Doctor.* New York, NY: Workman, 2001.

———. *The Dinner Doctor.* New York, NY: Workman, 2003.

Capalbo, Carla. *The Food and Wine Lover's Companion to Tuscany.* San Francisco, CA: Chronicle Books, 2002.

Capella, Anthony. *The Food of Love.* New York, NY: Viking Books, 2004.

Carl, Joanna. *The Chocolate Frog Frame-Up.* New York, NY: Signet, 2003.

Chalmers, Irena. *Food Jobs: 150 Great Jobs for Culinary Students, Career Changers and Food Lovers.* New York, NY: Beaufort Books, 2008.

Child, Julia. *Mastering the Art of French Cooking.* Reprint edition. New York, NY: Knopf, 2001.

Clark, Robert. *The Solace of Food: A Life of James Beard.* New York, NY: Steerforth, 1998.

Colwin, Laurie. *Home Cooking: A Writer in the Kitchen.* New York, NY: Perennial, 2000.

———. *More Home Cooking: A Writer Returns to the Kitchen.* New York, NY: Perennial, 2000.

Corpening, Sara, and Mary Corpening Barber. *Smoothies: 50 Recipes for High-Energy Refreshment.* San Francisco, CA: Chronicle Books, 1997.

Corriher, Shirley O. *Cookwise: The Hows and Whys of Successful Cooking.* New York, NY: Morrow Cookbooks, 1997.

Counihan, Carole, and Penny Van Esterik, eds. *Food and Culture: A Reader.* Oxford, UK: Routledge, 1997.

Coyle, Cleo. *On What Grounds,* a Coffeehouse Mystery. New York, NY: Berkley Publishing Group, 2003.

———. *Through the Grinder.* New York, NY: Prime Crime, 2004.

Crawford, Isis. *A Catered Murder.* New York, NY: Kensington Publishing, 2003.

Cunningham, Marion. *Lost Recipes: Meals to Share with Friends and Family.* New York, NY: Knopf, 2003.

Daheim, Mary. *Nutty as a Fruitcake,* a Bed and Breakfast Mystery. New York, NY: Avon, 1996.

———. *Just Desserts,* a Bed and Breakfast Mystery. Avon, 1999.

———. *Legs Benedict,* a Bed and Breakfast Mystery. Avon, 1999.

David, Elizabeth. *A Book of Mediterranean Food.* New York, NY: New York Review, 2002.

———. *An Omelet and a Glass of Wine.* Guilford, CT: The Lyons Press, 1997.

———. *South Wind Through the Kitchen: The Best of Elizabeth David.* New York, NY: North Point Press, 1999.

Davidson, Alan, editor. *The Wilder Shores of Gastronomy: Twenty Years of the Best Food Writing from the Journal Petits Propos Culinaires.* Berkeley, CA: Ten Speed Press, 2002.

———. *The Oxford Companion to Food.* New York, NY: Oxford University Press, 1999.

Davidson, Diane Mott. *Catering to Nobody,* a Culinary Mystery. New York, NY: Bantam, 2002.

———. *Dying for Chocolate,* a Culinary Mystery. New York, NY: Crimeline Books, 1993.

———. *Killer Pancake,* a Culinary Mystery. New York, NY: Crimeline Books, 1996.

———. *The Last Suppers,* a Culinary Mystery. New York, NY: Crimeline Books, 1995.

De Angeli, Marguerite. *Henner's Lydia.* Scotsdale, PA: Herald Press, 1998.

De Groot, Roy Andries. *Auberge of the Flowering Hearth.* New York, NY: Ecco Press, 1996.

————. *Feasts for All Seasons.* New York, NY: Random House, 2000.

————. *In Search of the Perfect Meal: A Collection of the Food Writing of Roy Andries de Groot.* New York, NY: St. Martin's Press, 1986.

Edge, John, T. *Southern Belly: The Ultimate Food Lover's Guide to the South.* Athens, GA: Hill Street Press, 2002.

Editor & Publisher. *Annual Directory of Syndicated Services.* New York, NY: New York Editor & Publisher Co., annual.

Egerton, March. *Since Eve Ate Apples: Quotations on Feasting, Fasting and Food from the Beginning.* Portland, OR: Tsunami Press, 1994.

Ehlert, Lois. *Eating the Alphabet.* New York, NY: Red Wagon Books, 1996.

Ephron, Nora. *Heartburn.* New York, NY: Vintage, 1996.

Escoffier, Auguste. *The Complete Guide to the Art of Modern Cooking.* New York, NY: Wiley, 1983.

Esquivel, Laura. *Like Water for Chocolate: A Novel in Monthly Installments with Recipes, Romances and Home Remedies.* New York, NY: Anchor, 1994.

Fenster, Carol. *Wheat-Free Recipes and Menus.* New York, NY: Avery Publishing, 1997.

Field, Carol. *In Nonna's Kitchen: Recipes and Traditions from Italy's Grandmothers.* New York, NY: HarperCollins, 1997.

Fielding, Henry. *The History of Tom Jones, A Foundling.* New York, NY: Oxford University Press, 1998. Originally published in 1749.

Fisher, M. F. K. *A Considerable Town.* New York, NY: Knopf, 1978.

————. *Among Friends.* New York, NY: Knopf, 1971.

————. *The Art of Eating.* New York, NY: Vintage Books, 1976.

————. *As They Were.* New York, NY: Knopf, 1982.

————. *Consider the Oyster.* New York, NY: Duell, Sloan & Pearce, Inc., 1941.

————. *The Gastronomical Me.* New York, NY: Duell, Sloan & Pearce, Inc., 1943.

————. *How to Cook A Wolf.* New York, NY: Duell, Sloan & Pearce, Inc., 1942.

————. *The Measure of Her Powers: An M. F. K. Fisher Reader.* New York, NY: Counterpoint Press, 1999.

————. *Sister Age.* New York, NY: Alfred A. Knopf, 1983.

Fitzgerald, F. Scott. *The Great Gatsby.* New York, NY: Scribner, 1995. Originally published in 1920.

Fluke, Joanne. *Blueberry Muffin Murder:* a Hannah Swensen Mystery, New York, NY: Kensington Publishing, 2003.

———. *Chocolate Chip Cookie Murder:* a Hannah Swensen Mystery. New York, NY: Kensington Publishing, 2001.

———. *Lemon Meringue Pie Murder:* a Hannah Swensen Mystery. New York, NY: Kensington Publishing, 2004.

———. *Strawberry Shortcake Murder:* a Hannah Swensen Mystery. New York, NY: Kensington Publishing, 2002.

———. *Sugar Cookie Murder:* a Hannah Swensen Mystery. New York, NY: Kensington Publishing, 2004.

Frey, James. *How to Write a Damn Good Novel: A Step-by-Step No Nonsense Guide to Dramatic Storytelling.* New York, NY: St. Martin's Press, 1987.

Gage, Fran. *Bread and Chocolate: My Food Life In and Around San Francisco.* Seattle, WA: Sasquatch Books, 1999.

Garten, Ina. *The Barefoot Contessa Cookbook.* New York, NY: Clarkson Potter, 1999.

Geffen, Alice, and Carole Berglie. *Food Festival: The Ultimate Guidebook to America's Best Regional Food Celebrations.* Woodstock, VT: Countryman Press, 1994.

George, Elizabeth. *Write Away: One Novelist's Approach to Fiction and the Writing Life.* New York, NY: HarperCollins, 2004.

Gold, Jonathan. *Counter Intelligence: Where to Eat in the Real Los Angeles.* Los Angeles, CA: L.A. Weekly Books, 2000.

Goldberg, Natalie. *Old Friend from Far Away: How to Write a Memoir.* Louisville, CO: Sounds True, 2002.

———. *Writing Down the Bones.* Boston, MA: Shambhala, 1986.

Gordon, Nadia. *Death by the Glass: A Sunny McCoskey Napa Valley Mystery.* San Francisco, CA: Chronicle Books, 2003.

Grimes, William. *Eating Your Words: 2000 Words to Tease Your Taste Buds.* New York, NY: Oxford University Press, 2004.

Grosset & Dunlap. *The Wiggles: Yummy, Yummy Fruit Salad.* Grosset & Dunlap, 2003.

Guerra, Melissa. *The Texas Provincial Kitchen Cookbook.* Linn, TX: The Provincial Texas Kitchen, Ltd., 1997.

———. *Dishes from the Wild Horse Desert.* Hoboken, NJ: Wiley, 2006.

H. W. Wilson Co. *Reader's Guide to Periodical Literature.* New York, NY: H.W. Wilson Co. annual.

Harris, Joanne. *Chocolat.* New York, NY: Penguin Books, 2000.

———. *Five Quarters of the Orange.* New York, NY: Perennial, 2002.

Hemingway, Ernest. *The Garden of Eden.* New York, NY: Scribner, 1995. Originally published in 1986.

Henderson, Fergus. *The Whole Beast: Nose to Tail Eating.* New York, NY: Ecco, 2004.

Herbst, Sharon Tyler. *The New Food Lover's Companion: Comprehensive Definitions of Nearly 6,000 Food, Drink, and Culinary Terms.* Hauppauge, NY: Barron's Educational Series, 2001.

Hesser, Amanda. *Cooking for Mr. Latte: A Food Lover's Courtship, with Recipes.* New York, NY: W. W. Norton & Company, 2003.

———. *The Cook and the Gardener: A Year of Recipes and Writings from the French Countryside.* New York, NY: W. W. Norton & Company, 2000.

Hoberman, Mary Ann. *The Seven Silly Eaters.* San Diego, CA: Voyager Books, 2000.

Holman, Sheri. *The Mammoth Cheese: A Novel.* New York, NY: Atlantic Monthly Press, 2003.

Huffington Post, Editors of the. *The Huffington Post Complete Guide to Blogging.* New York, NY: Simon & Schuster Paperbacks, 2008.

Hughes, Holly, editor. The Best Food Writing Anthologies. New York, NY: Marlowe & Company, annual.

Joachim, David. *A Man, a Can, a Plan: 50 Tasty Meals You Can Nuke in No Time.* Emmaus, PA: Rodale Books, 2002.

Jones, Evan. *Epicurean Delight: The Life and Times of James Beard.* New York, NY: Knopf, 1990.

Jones, Idwal. *High Bonnet: A Novel of Epicurean Adventures.* New York, NY: Modern Library, 2001.

Kancigor, Judy Bart. *Melting Pot Memories: The Rabinowitz Family Cookbook and Nostalgic History.* Fullerton, CA. Jan Bart Publications, 1999.

———. *Cooking Jewish: 532 Great Recipes from the Rabbinowitz Family.* New York, NY: Workman, 2007.

Kasper, Lynne Rossetto. *The Splendid Table: Recipes from Emilia-Romagna, the Heartland of Northern Italian Food.* New York, NY: Morrow Cookbooks, 1992.

Katz, Solomon H., and William Woys Weaver, eds. *Encyclopedia of Food and Culture.* New York, NY: Charles Scribner's Sons, 2002.

Kelly, Ian. *Cooking for Kings: The Life of Antonin Careme, the First Celebrity Chef.* New York, NY: Walker & Company, 2004.

Kiple, Kenneth, editor. *The Cambridge World History of Food.* New York, NY: Cambridge University Press, 2000.

Kirchner, Bharti. *Pastries: A Novel of Desserts and Discoveries.* New York, NY: St. Martin's Press, 2003.

Kurlansky, Mark. *Cod: A Biography of the Fish that Changed the World.* New York, NY: Penguin Books, 1998.

———. *Salt: A World History.* New York, NY: Penguin Books, 2003.

Lamott, Anne. *Bird by Bird: Some Instructions on Writing and Life.* New York, NY: Anchor, 1995.

Larsen, Michael. *How to Write a Book Proposal.* Cincinnati, OH: Writer's Digest Books, 2004.

———. *Literary Agents: What They Do, How They Do It, and How to Find and Work with the Right One for You.* New York, NY: Wiley, 1996.

Laudan, Rachel. *The Food of Paradise: Exploring Hawaii's Culinary Heritage.* Honolulu, HI: University of Hawaii Press, 1996.

Levin, Martin P. *Be Your Own Literary Agent: The Ultimate Insider's Guide to Getting Published.* Berkeley, CA: Ten Speed Press, 2002.

Levine, Ed. *New York Eats: The Food Shopper's Guide to the Freshest Ingredients, the Best Take Out and Baked Goods, & The Most Unusual Marketplaces in All of New York.* New York, NY: St. Martin's Griffin, 1997.

Levoy, Gregg. *This Business of Writing.* Cincinnati, OH: Writer's Digest Books, 1992.

Levy, Paul. *The Penguin Book of Food and Drink.* New York, NY: Penguin USA, 1998.

Lewis, Edna. *In Pursuit of Flavor.* Charlottesville, VA: University Press of Virginia, 2000.

———. *The Edna Lewis Cookbook.* New York, NY: Ecco Press, 1983.

———. *The Taste of Country Cooking.* New York, NY: Knopf, 1976.

Liebling, A. J. *Between Meals: An Appetite for Paris.* New York, NY: North Point Press, 2004.

Lin, Grace. *Dim Sum for Everyone.* New York, NY: Knopf Books for Young Readers, 2001.

Longbotham, Lori. *Luscious Lemon Desserts.* San Francisco, CA: Chronicle Books, 2001.

Lyon, Elizabeth. *Nonfiction Book Proposals Anyone Can Write: How to Get a Contract and Advance Before Writing Your Book.* New York, NY: Perigree Books, 2002.

Lyons, Nan. *Someone is Killing the Great Chefs of Europe.* New York, NY: Harcourt, 1990.

Madison, Deborah. *The Greens Cookbook: Extraordinary Vegetarian Cuisine from the Celebrated Restaurant.* New York, NY: Bantam, 1987.

———. *The Savory Way.* New York, NY: Broadway, 1998.

———. *Vegetarian Cooking for Everyone.* New York, NY: Broadway, 1997.

Malladi, Amulya. *Serving Crazy with Curry*. New York, NY: Ballantine Books, 2004.

Manna, Lou. *Digital Food Photography*. Florence, KY: Course Technology PTR, 2005.

Marken, Bill. *How to Fix (Just About) Everything: More than 550 Step-by-Step Instructions for Everything from Fixing a Faucet to Removing Mystery Stains to Curing a Hangover*. New York, NY: Free Press, 2002.

Marranca, Bonnie, ed. *A Slice of Life: Contemporary Writers on Food*. New York, NY: Overlook Press, 2003.

Mayes, Frances. *Under the Tuscan Sun*. New York, NY: Broadway, 1997.

McCloskey, Robert. *Blueberries for Sal*. New York, NY: Puffin Books, 1976.

McGee, Harold. *On Food and Cooking: The Science and Lore of the Kitchen*. New York, NY: Scribner, 2004.

McGrath, Mike. *Kitchen Garden A to Z: Growing, Harvest, Buying, Storing*. New York, NY: Harry N. Abrams, 2004.

McNair, James. *Cold Pasta*. San Francisco, CA: Chronicle Books, 1985.

Medrich, Alice. *Bittersweet: Recipes and Tales from a Life in Chocolate*. New York, NY: Artisan, 2003.

Melville, Herman. *Moby-Dick*. New York, NY: Bantam Classics, 1981. Originally published in 1851.

Mendelson, Anne. *Stand Facing the Stove: The Story of the Women Who Gave America the Joy of Cooking*. New York, NY: Henry Holt & Company, 1996.

Mesnier, Roland. *Dessert University: More than 300 Spectacular Recipes and Essential Lessons from White House Pastry Chef Roland Mesnier*. New York, NY: Simon & Schuster, 2004.

Mettee, Stephen Blake. *The Fast Track Course on How to Write a Nonfiction Book Proposal*. New York, NY: Quill Driver Books, 2001.

Murdock, Maureen. *Unreliable Truth*. Seattle, WA: Seal Press, 2003.

Myers, Tamar. *Eat, Drink and Be Wary*. New York, NY: Signet, 1998.

———. *Parsley, Sage, Rosemary and Crime*. New York, NY: Signet, 1997.

———. *Too Many Crooks Spoil the Broth: A Pennsylvania Dutch Mystery with Recipes*. New York, NY: Signet, 1995.

Narayan, Shoba. *Monsoon Diary: A Memoir with Recipes*. New York, NY: Villard, 2003.

Nathan, Joan. *Foods of Israel Today*. New York, NY: Knopf, 2001.

Nestle, Marion. *Food Politics: How the Food Industry Influences Nutrition and Health*. Berkeley, CA: University of California Press, 2003.

Orwell, George. *Down and Out in Paris and London*. New York, NY: Harvest/HBJ, 1972.

Ostmann, Barbara Gibbs, and Jane Baker. *The Recipe Writer's Handbook*. New York, NY: Wiley, 2001.

Ozeki, Ruth L. *My Year of Meats*. New York, NY: Penguin Books, 1999.

Page, Susan. *The Shortest Distance Between You and a Published Book: 20 Steps to Success*. New York, NY: Broadway, 1997.

Parson, Russ. *How to Read a French Fry, and Other Stories of Intriguing Kitchen Science*. Boston, MA: Houghton Mifflin, 2003.

Patent, Greg. *Baking in America: Contemporary and Traditional Favorites from the Past 200 Years*. Boston, MA: Houghton Mifflin, 2002.

Pellegrini, Angelo. *The Unprejudiced Palate: Classic Thoughts on Food and the Good Life*. Guilford, CT: The Lyons Press, 1992.

Pépin, Jacques. *The Apprentice: My Life in the Kitchen*. Boston, MA: Houghton Mifflin, 2003.

Peterson, Joan, and David Peterson. *Eat Smart in Poland: How to Decipher the Menu, Know the Market Foods & Embark on a Tasting Adventure*. Madison, WI: Gingko Press, 2000.

Pomaine, Edouard de. *Cooking with Pomaine*. Washington, DC: Serif, 1993.

Pottker, Janice. *Crisis in Candyland: Melting the Chocolate Shell of the Mars Family Empire*. Palo Alto, CA: National Press Books, 1995.

Prior, Lily. *La Cucina: A Novel of Rapture*. New York, NY: Ecco, 2001.

Proust, Marcel. *Swann's Way*. New York, NY: Viking Books, 2003. Originally published in French in 1913.

Rabiner, Susan, and Alfred Fortunato. *Thinking Like Your Editor—How to Write Great Serious Nonfiction and Get It Published*. New York, NY: W. W. Norton & Co., 2003.

Raichlen, Steven. *The Barbecue Bible*. New York, NY: Workman Publishing, 1998.

Rawles, Nancy. *Crawfish Dreams: A Novel*. New York, NY: Doubleday, 2003.

Rayner, Jay. *Eating Crow*. New York, NY: Simon & Schuster, 2004.

Reichl, Ruth, ed. *Endless Feasts: Sixty Years of Writing from Gourmet*. New York, NY: Modern Library, 2002.

———. *Comfort Me with Apples: More Adventures at the Table*. New York, NY: Random House Trade Paperbacks, 2002.

———. *Tender at the Bone: Growing Up at the Table*. New York, NY: Broadway, 1999.

———. *Garlic and Sapphires: the Secret Life of a Critic in Disguise*. New York, NY: The Penguin Press, 2005.

Riccardi, Victoria. *Untangling My Chopsticks: A Culinary Sojourn in Kyoto.* New York, NY: Broadway, 2003.

Richman, Alan. *Fork it Over: The Intrepid Adventures of a Professional Eater.* New York, NY: HarperCollins, 2004.

Richman, Phyllis. *Murder on the Gravy Train.* New York, NY: Avon, 2000.

———. *The Butter Did It: A Gastronomic Tale of Love and Murder.* New York, NY: HarperTorch, 1998.

———. *Who's Afraid of Virginia Ham?* New York, NY: Avon, 2002.

Robertson, Laurel. *Laurel's Kitchen.* Berkeley, CA: Ten Speed Press, 1993.

Roden, Claudia. *The Book of Jewish Food: An Odyssey from Samarkand to New York.* New York, NY: Knopf, 1996.

Rombauer, Irma S., and Marion Rombauer Becker. *The Joy of Cooking.* New York, NY: Scribner, 1985. Original version published in 1931.

Room, Adrian. *Dunces, Gourmands and Petticoats.* Chicago, IL: TC/Contemporary Publishing, 1998.

Roorbach, Bill. *Writing Life Stories.* Cincinnati, OH: Writer's Digest Books, 2000.

Root, Waverly, and Richard de Rochemont. *Eating In America: A History.* New York, NY: Ecco Press, 2004.

Rosenblum, Mort. *Olives: The Life and Lore of a Noble Fruit.* New York, NY: North Point Press, 1998.

Rosso, Julee, and Sheila Lukins. *The Silver Palate Cookbook.* New York, NY: Workman Publishing, 1982.

Ruhlman, Michael. *The Making of a Chef: Mastering Heat at the Culinary Institute.* New York, NY: Owl Books, 1999.

Sahni, Julie. *Classic Indian Cooking.* New York, NY: Morrow Cookbooks, 1980.

Sanger, Amy Wilson. *A Little Bit of Soul Food,* and other titles in the World Snacks series. Berkeley, CA: Tricycle Press, 2004.

Schlosser, Eric. *Fast Food Nation: The Dark Side of the All-American Meal.* New York, NY: Perennial, 2002.

Sendak, Maurice. *Chicken Soup with Rice: A Book of Months.* New York, NY: HarperTrophy, 1991.

———. *In the Night Kitchen.* New York, NY: HarperCollins, 1996.

Severson, Kim, and Cindy Burke. *The Trans Fat Solution: Cooking and Shopping to Eliminate the Deadliest Fats from Your Diet.* Berkeley, CA: Ten Speed Press, 2003.

Shapiro, Anna. *Feast of Words: For Lovers of Food and Fiction.* New York, NY: W. W. Norton & Company, 1996.

Shapiro, Laura. *Perfection Salad: Women and Cooking at the Turn of the Century.* New York, NY: Modern Library, 2001.

———. *Something from the Oven: Reinventing Dinner in 1950s America.* New York, NY: Viking Books, 2004.

Sheraton, Mimi. *Eating My Words: An Appetite for Life.* New York, NY: Morrow Cookbooks, 2004.

Silverman, Sharon Hernes. *Pennsylvania Snacks: A Guide to Food Factory Tours.* Mechanicsburg, PA: Stackpole Books, 2001.

Sinclair, Upton. *The Jungle.* New York, NY: Bantam, 1981. Originally published in 1906.

Slade, Sheryl. *A Lady at the Table: A Concise, Contemporary Guide to Table Manners.* Nashville, TN: Rutledge Hill Press, 2004.

Smalls, Alexander. *Grace the Table: Stories & Recipes From My Southern Revival.* New York, NY: Harlem Moon, 2004.

Smith, Andrew F. *Peanuts: The Illustrious History of the Goober Pea.* Champagne, IL: University of Illinois Press, 2002.

———. *Pure Ketchup: A History of America's National Condiment, with Recipes.* Washington, DC: Smithsonian Books, 2001.

———. *The Tomato in America: Early History, Culture, and Cookery.* Columbia, SC: University of South Carolina Press, 1994.

———. *The Oxford Encyclopedia of Food and Drink in America.* New York, NY: Oxford University Press, 2004.

Stein, Sol. *Stein on Writing: A Master Editor of Some of the Most Successful Writers of Our Century Shares His Craft Techniques and Strategies.* New York, NY: St. Martin's Press, 2000.

Steingarten, Jeffrey. *The Man Who Ate Everything.* New York, NY: Vintage, 1998.

Stern, Jane, and Michael Stern. *Roadfood: The Coast-to-Coast Guide to 500 of the Best Barbeque Joints, Lobster Shacks, Ice Cream Parlors, Highway Diners, and Much More.* New York, NY: Broadway, 2002.

Strunk, Jr., William and E.B. White. *Elements of Style,* 4th Ed. New York, NY: Longman, 2000.

Taxel, Laura. *Cleveland Ethnic Eats 2004: The Guide to Authentic Ethnic Eats in Northeastern Ohio.* Cleveland, OH: Gray & Company Publishers, 2003.

The Asia Society. *Asia in the San Francisco Bay Area: A Cultural Travel Guide.* New York, NY: Avalon Travel Publishing, 2004.

Theophano, Janet. *Eat My Words: Reading Women's Lives through the Cookbooks They Wrote.* New York, NY: Palgrave Macmillan, 2002.

Thorne, John. *Pot on the Fire: Further Confessions of a Renegade Cook.* New York, NY: North Point Press, 2001.

Todhunter, Andrew. *A Meal Observed.* New York, NY: Knopf, 2004.

Tolstoy, Leo. *Anna Karenina.* New York, NY: Modern Library, 2000. Originally published serially from 1875–77 in Russian.

Tower, Jeremiah. *California Dish: What I Saw and Cooked at the American Culinary Revolution.* New York, NY: Free Press, 2003.

Trillin, Calvin. *American Fried.* New York, NY: Vintage, 1979.

———. *The Tummy Trilogy.* New York, NY: Farrar, Straus & Giroux, 1994.

Unterman, Patricia. *Patricia Unterman's Food Lover's Guide to San Francisco.* Berkeley, CA: Ten Speed Press, 2003.

Various. Skinny series of cookbooks. Chicago, IL: Surrey, 1990s.

Various. Williams-Sonoma series of cookbooks. New York, NY: Time-Life, 2000.

Villas, James. *Between Bites: Memoirs of a Hungry Hedonist.* New York, NY: Wiley, 2002.

———. *Stalking the Green Fairy: And Other Fantastic Adventures in Food and Drink.* New York, NY: Wiley, 2004.

Visser, Margaret. *Much Depends on Dinner: The Extraordinary History and Mythology, Allure and Obsessions, Perils and Taboo, of an Ordinary Meal.* New York, NY: Grove Press, 1999.

Volland, Susan. *Love and Meatballs.* New York, NY: New American Library, 2004.

Walsh, Robb. *Are You Really Going to Eat That?* New York, NY: Counterpoint Press, 2003.

Wells, Patricia. *A Food Lover's Guide to Paris.* New York, NY: Workman Publishing, 1999.

Werlin, Laura. *New American Cheese.* New York, NY: Stewart, Tabori & Chang, 2000.

———. *The All American Cheese and Wine Book.* New York, NY: Stewart, Tabori & Chang, 2003.

Wexberg, Joseph. *Blue Trout and Black Truffles: The Peregrinations of an Epicure.* Chicago, IL: Academy Chicago Publishers, 1985.

Wharton, Edith. *The Age of Innocence,* New York, NY: Modern Library, 1999. Originally published in 1920.

Whitman, Joan, and Dolores Simon. *Recipes Into Type: A Handbook for Cookbook Writers and Editors.* Newton, MA: Biscuit Books, Inc., 1993.

Winston, Lolly. *Good Grief.* New York, NY: Warner Books, 2004.

Wolke, Robert. *What Einstein Told His Cook.* New York, NY: W.W. Norton & Company, 2002.

Wood, Monica. *Description* (the Elements of Fiction Writing series). Cincinnati, OH: Writer's Digest Books, 1999.

Wyler, Susan. *Great Books for Cooks.* New York, NY: Ballantine Books, 1999.

Young, Grace. *Wisdom of the Chinese Kitchen.* New York, NY: Simon & Schuster, 1999.

Zinsser, William. *Writing About Your Life: A Journey Into the Past.* New York, NY: Marlowe & Company, 2004.

———. *Inventing the Truth: The Art and Craft of Memoir.* Boston, MA: Mariner Books, 1998.

———. *On Writing Well: The Classic Guide to Writing Nonfiction.* New York, NY: HarperResource, 2001.

Selected Web Sites

Magazines That Take Freelance Writing

- *Bon Appétit*—www.bonappetit.com
- *Clean Eating*—www.cleaneatingmag.com/minisite/ce_index.htm
- *Conde Nast Traveler*—www.concierge.com/cntraveler
- *Cook's Illustrated.Com*—www.cooksillustrated.com
- *Cooking Light*—www.cookinglight.com
- *Eating Well*—www.eatingwell.com
- *Edible* magazines—www.ediblecommunities.com/content
- *Esquire*—www.esquire.com
- *Every Day with Rachael Ray*—www.rachaelraymag.com
- *Family Circle*—www.familycircle.com
- *Fine Cooking*—www.taunton.com/finecooking
- *Food Network*—www.foodnetwork.com/food-network-magazine/package/index.html
- *Food Arts*—www.foodarts.com/Foodarts/Home
- *Food & Wine*—www.foodandwine.com
- *Gastronomica*—www.gastronomica.org
- *GQ*—www.gq.com
- *Health*—www.health.com/health
- *Martha Stewart Living, Everyday Food*—www.marthastewart.com
- *Meatpaper*—www.meatpaper.com
- *National Geographic Traveler*—www.nationalgeographic.com/traveler
- *Natural Foods Merchandiser*—www.naturalfoodsmerchandiser.com
- *Oprah*—www.oprah.com
- *Plate*—www.plateonline.com

- *Prevention*—www.prevention.com/health
- *Real Simple*—www.realsimple.com
- *Relish*—www.relishmag.com
- *Restaurants and Institutions*—www.rimag.com
- *Sante*—www.santemagazine.com
- *Saveur*—www.saveur.com
- *Seafood Business*—www.seafoodbusiness.com
- *Southern Living*—www.southernliving.com
- *Sunset: Life in the West*—www.sunset.com
- *The New Yorker*—www.newyorker.com
- *Travel & Leisure*—www.travelandleisure.com
- *Vegetarian Times*—www.vegetariantimes.com
- *Vogue*—www.style.com/vogue
- *Where*—www.wheremagazine.com
- *Woman's Day*—www.womansday.com
- *Yoga Journal*—www.yogajournal.com

Web Sites That Take Freelance Writing

Check the websites of your city magazine, alternative weekly, television and radio stations, and other local media to see if they take freelance writing as well.

- AOL Food—http://food.aol.com/main?icid=navbar (recipe ideas, menus, drinks and entertaining)
- Culinate—www.culinate.com (sustainable eating)
- Delish—www.delish.com (recipes, party food, cooking guides, etc.)
- Fine Living—www.fineliving.com (cocktails, wine, recipes, party ideas)
- The FoodNetwork—www.foodnetwork.com (recipes and cooking)
- Forbes.com—www.forbes.com (has wine and spirit stories, and the occasional food story, such as "Who's Really Cooking Your Celebrity Chef Meal?")
- Grist—www.grist.org (environmental news and green living advice)
- iVillage—www.ivillage.com/food (recipes, bulletin boards)
- Leite's Culinaria—www.leitesculinaria.com/index.html (sometimes pays for essays)
- Nourish Network—http://nourishnetwork.com (articles and recipes)
- NPR's Kitchen Window—www.npr.org/templates/story/story.php?storyId =4578972 (a popular place for freelancers who write a personal essay followed by recipes)

- Sally's Place—www.sallys-place.com (online food and drink news, reviews, recipes, restaurants, and travel; accepts content but pays sporadically. "It depends on what content is offered to me and if the writer can fill a void. It also depends on the state of the economy," says Sally Bernstein)
- Salon—www.salon.com (Frances Lam, formerly of *Gourmet*, runs the food section, which features some freelance writing)
- Serious Eats—www.seriouseats.com (has a long list of contributors, many of whom are bloggers)
- Slate.com—www.slate.com (runs the odd food story, usually trend based opinion pieces)

Newspaper Food Section Aggregates

Keep up with what kinds of stories are getting published, to spur your own ideas for freelance writing:

- Food News Journal—www.foodnewsjournal.com (includes stories from blogs and food-based websites as well)
- Good Cooking Search—www.goodcooking.com/foodnews.asp
- Gourmet Spot—www.gourmetspot.com/newspapers.htm

More Websites for the Food Obsessed

- Chow—www.chow.com (recipes, cooking tips, resources and stories for people who love food)
- Chowhound.Com—http://chowhound.chow.com/boards (worldwide forum on restaurant, food, stores, and bars)
- Egullet Culinary Institute (eGullet)—www.egullet.com (discussion on cooking, dining and cookbooks)

Websites about Book Publishing

- Agent Query—http://agentquery.com, database of literary agents
- Literary Marketplace—www.literarymarketplace.com (lists literary agents alphabetically by name)
- Publishers Marketplace—www.publishersmarketplace.com (Web pages for writers and agents to promote themselves)

Food Writing, Classes and Conferences

- BlogHer and BlogHer Food—www.blogher.com (annual food blogger conference and annual blogging conference)

- Book Passage—www.bookpassage.com (I teach classes on general food writing and on cookbook writing at this San Francisco Bay Area bookstore)
- Camp Blogaway—campblogaway.com (3-day camp for food and recipe bloggers, launched in 2010)
- Club Med Food Blogger Camp—www.clubMed.us (first one was held in Ixtapa, Mexico in 2009. Check Web site for details)
- Gotham Writers' Workshop and Writing Classes.Com—www.writingclasses.com (New York-based and online classes in nonfiction writing, including food writing)
- The International Culinary Center—www.internationalculinarycenter .com/food-writing.htm (offers a six-week class on food writing taught by Alan Richman in New York)
- The International Culinary Institute—http://rec.iceculinary.com/Home/ FoodMedia (offers a variety of classes on food writing and blogging in New York)
- Leite's Culinaria—www.leitesculinaria.com/index.html (online classes on recipe writing, freelancing, cookbooks and proposals; I am one of the instructors)
- International Food Blogger Conference www.foodista.com/ifbc2010 (began in 2009, held in Seattle)
- Media Bistro—www.mediabistro.com/courses/cache/menu_1.asp (classes on food writing, freelance writing, proposal writing, etc.)
- The New School in New York—www.newschool.edu/generalstudies/food studies.aspx (Holds occasional classes on food writing)
- Okanagan Food and Wine Writers' Workshop—www.okanaganfoodand winewritersworkshop.com (held in British Columbia, Canada)
- Shaw Guides—www.shawguides.com (writing and cooking classes around the country)
- Symposium for Professional Food Writers at the Greenbrier—www.green brier.com/foodwriters (annual 3-day class at a luxury resort in W. Virginia)
- Writing Salon—www.writingsalons.com (I teach classes on food writing and proposal writing at this San Francisco and Berkeley school. You'll also find classes on freelancing and essay writing)
- Writer's Digest—www.writersdigest.com (online classes, conferences)
- Other food writers who teach food writing include Diane Morgan (Portland, OR), Kathleen Flinn (Seattle, WA), and Monica Bhide (online)

Associations and Non-Profits

- The American Culinary Federation, Inc.—www.acfchefs.org (promotes the culinary profession)
- American Institute of Wine & Food—www.aiwf.org (a nonprofit devoted to improving appreciation, understanding, and accessibility of food and drink)
- Association for the Study of Food and Society—www.food-culture.org (international organization dedicated to academic study of food, culture, and society)
- Association of Food Journalists—www.afjonline.com
- Les Dames d'Escoffier—www.ldei.org homeFrameset.asp (women's organization for food industry professionals, food writers and researchers)
- International Association of Culinary Professionals—www.iacp.com
- The Research Chefs Association—www.researchchef.org (professional group for food researchers)
- Slow Food—www.slowfood.com (studies effects of fast food on society and life)
- Women Chefs and Restaurateurs—www.womenchefs.org (promotes the education and advancement of women in the restaurant industry)

Food Studies

- New York University Graduate program in food studies and food management—http://education.nyu.edu/nutrition
- Boston University's Culinary Arts certificate and masters of liberal arts program—www.bu.edu/foodandwine/culinary
- Le Cordon Bleu Graduate Program in Gastronomy at the University of Adelaide, Australia—www.gastronomy.adelaide.edu.au

Cookbook Stores

For a comprehensive listing of cookbook stores from all over the world, see www.sallybernstein.com/food/chefs-corner/cookbook_stores.htm.

Index

Book of Jewish Food, The (Roden), 207
Book Passage bookstore, xvi
Book proposals, 266–275
Book recommendations, 52–53
Book reviews in blogs, 83
Book writing
    going from blog to, 59, 100, 102–105,
        189–190, 263, 264
    See also Cookbook writing; Fiction
        writing; Memoir book writing;
        Non-fiction food books
Boorstin, Sharon, 255
Born Round: The Secret History of a
    Full-time Eater (Bruni), 149, 151,
    168
Bourdain, Anthony, 15, 225, 227, 241, 256
    fearlessness of, 25–26
    mystery books by, 248
    and touch, 10
Braker, Flo, 222
Bread and Chocolate: My Food Life in and
    Around San Francisco (Gage),
    242–243
Brillat-Savarin, Jean-Anthelme, 9, 52,
    157
Britchky, Seymour, 173
Brite, Poppy Z., 255
Bruni, Frank, 149, 153, 168, 169
Buford, Bill, 240
Burggraaf, Charity Lynne, 72
Burton, Brooke, 151
Butcher and the Vegetarian, The: One
    Woman's Romp through the World of
    Men, Meat, and Moral Crisis
    (Weaver), 35
Butter Did It, The (Richman), 245–246,
    249
Byrn, Anne, 56, 57, 180–181, 183–184

Cake Mix Doctor, The (Byrn), 56,
    180–181, 183
California Culinary Academy, 56
Cambridge World History of Food, The, 236
Camp, David, 233
Canal House Cooking (Hamilton and
    Hirsheimer), 83–84
Candyfreak: A Journey Through the
    Chocolate Underbelly of America
    (Almond), 242

Capella, Anthony, 256
Carl, Joanna, 252
Caruso, Maren, 199–200
Casselman, Martha, 269
Catered Murder, A (Crawford), 253
Catering to Nobody (Davidson), 249–250
Chamberlain, Samuel, 53
Characteristics of food writers, 21–32
    storytelling, 28, 77, 159, 188, 225, 228
    See also Focus; Passion in food writing
Chez Panisse, 47
Chez Pim blog, 66
Chicago Tribune (newspaper), 54
Chicken Soup with Rice: A Book of Months
    (Sendak), 260
Child, Julia, 5, 6, 25, 214, 249
    biography , 238
    first manuscript rejected, 297
    hints in recipes, 210
    naming recipes, 207
    start as cookbook writer, 181
    substitution in recipes, 209
    on thorough recipes that work, 205
Children's books, 259–260
Chocolat (Harris), 256
Chocolate & Zucchini blog, 16, 64, 66,
    76, 106, 186
Chocolate Chip Cookie Murder (Fluke),
    250–251, 257
Chowhound Web site, 172
Christie, Agatha, 247–248
Claiborne, Craig, 154, 159, 165, 181, 222
Classic Indian Cooking (Sahni), 180, 192
Classic literature, 246–247, 258–259
Clementine in the Kitchen (Chamberlain),
    53
Cleveland Eats: The Guide to Authentic
    Eats in Northwestern Ohio (Taxel),
    37, 237–238
Cleveland Ethnic Eats blog, 38
Cookwise: The Secrets of Cooking Revealed
    (Corriher), 221, 240
Co-authoring, 194
Cod: A Biography of the Fish that Changed
    the World (Kurlansky), 223, 233
Cointreau, Edoard, 265
Cold Pasta (McNair), 187
Collaborating, 192–194
Colwin, Laurie, 7–8, 53, 208

327

Index